Great Plains Command

William B. Hazen
From Hazen, A Narrative of Military Service (1885)

GREAT PLAINS COMMAND
William B. Hazen in the Frontier West

by Marvin E. Kroeker

University of Oklahoma Press : Norman

Library of Congress Cataloging in Publication Data

Kroeker, Marvin E.   1928–
    Great Plains command.

    Bibliography: p.
    Includes index.
    1. Hazen, William Babcock, 1830–1887. 2. The West—History
—1848–1950. 3. Indians of North America—The West. I. Title.
F594.H422K76   355.3'31'0924 [B]   75-17709
ISBN 0–8061–1318–9

To Lily

Preface

The name William Babcock Hazen (1830–87) appears frequently in the annals of Western Americana. He spent more than two decades of his life as an army officer on the successive frontiers of the West. He was closely associated with many of the major events that high-lighted the great drama of the frontier advance beyond the Cross Timbers and the wide Missouri. Following his graduation from West Point, his tours of duty took him into the turbulent Oregon country, into sections of the Rocky Mountain region, and throughout the Great Plains from Texas to Dakota. He also served in the Civil War, rising from the rank of captain and brigade commander in 1861 to brevet brigadier general and corps commander by 1865. Hazen's extensive experiences in the West—scouting Indians and serving as inspector general, superintendent of Indian affairs, and commander of numerous army posts—gave him an understanding, surpassed by few of his contemporaries, of the lands along and beyond the ninety-eighth meridian. A man of scholarly interests, he wrote influential and controversial works reflecting his insights and candid views on Indian and land policies, manipulations of railroad interests, military administration, and the agricultural potential of the High Plains. Never one to pull his punches, Hazen became involved in a series of widely publicized controversies with George A. Custer, Philip H. Sheridan, Secretary of War William W. Belknap, and a number of other prominent officials. He had close connections with influential politicians and newspaper editors and was an intimate friend of James

A. Garfield. An 1885 edition of the *Nation* stated that "few officers were more generally known" by the American public than the controversial W. B. Hazen.

This work represents the first thorough study that has been made of the varied and controversial career of this once well-known army commander. Although frontier historians generally acknowledge Hazen's association with the implementation of military and Indian Bureau policies, the significant nature and scope of his activities in the West have not been clearly understood or adequately appreciated. The purpose of this book is to present a comprehensive account of Hazen's military career from 1855 to 1880, with an evaluation of his contributions and significance. It is hoped that this endeavor will bring proper recognition to a worthy frontier commander and add to our understanding of the history of the West.

MARVIN E. KROEKER

Ada, Oklahoma
August 15, 1974

Acknowledgments

I wish to acknowledge my indebtedness to a few of the many individuals who contributed in important ways to this book. Foremost among these is Professor Donald J. Berthrong who originally pointed me to Hazen's elusive trail and shared freely of his time and masterful knowledge of Western history. Gilbert C. Fite now of Eastern Illinois University and Arrell M. Gibson of the University of Oklahoma provided uplifting encouragement and helpful advice. Since no personal or family collection of "Hazen Papers" could be found, the competent and generous services of archivists and librarians were invaluable in my search for information relevant to the purposes of this study. I am particularly grateful to Milton K. Chamberlain of the National Archives, Jack D. Haley of the University of Oklahoma Western History Collections, and staff members of the Library of Congress who aided my research significantly. Alden Ewert meticulously perused several versions of the manuscript for errors and made numerous helpful suggestions. My wife, Lillian, contributed countless hours of time deciphering illegible copy and typing drafts. Without her unfailing patience and endurance this work could not have been accomplished. Josephine A. Gil and Phyllis Johnson typed the final copy with skill and efficiency. I sincerely thank them all.

Contents

Illustrations

Maps

Great Plains Command

I

A Shavetail in the Pacific Northwest

"The desire to attend West Point has been the height of my ambition for years," wrote William B. Hazen to Representative Thomas Corwin on March 13, 1851. In less than seven months he would be twenty-one years old and, therefore, automatically ineligible for admission to the military academy. The Hiram, Ohio, farm boy requested to be selected to replace a nominee from the Nineteenth Congressional District who had been disqualified. His earnest petition was rewarded. On August 15 Hazen's nomination was recommended to the Secretary of War, and six days later his appointment to West Point was confirmed.[1]

Cadet Hazen was described as physically short and stocky, independent-minded, frequently dogmatic, always outspoken, and possessed of an unfortunate faculty for getting himself into "hot water." His record shows that in his senior year alone he received over 150 demerits. Although academically far from outstanding—he graduated twenty-eighth in a class of thirty-four—Hazen was a serious student and considered his four years at the academy "rich in tangible advantages." Driving ambition, perfectionism, and a capacity for growth were characteristics that noticeably emerged in the years after West Point.[2]

On July 3, 1855, Brevet Second Lieutenant Hazen was assigned to Company D, Fourth Infantry, garrisoned at Fort Reading, California. He joined his unit at that remote northern California location on October 26. One week later, Company D was ordered to reinforce

Fort Lane, Oregon Territory, situated in a region seething with Indian unrest and violence.[3]

By 1850 Indians in southern Oregon began to disturb settlers to a degree which demanded military action. The increasing number of farmers disrupted the isolation and security of the primitive bands which inhabited this region. The Rogue Indians, numbering about 9,500, occupied valleys of several rivers north of the Siskiyou Range. Early-day French-Canadian trappers, familiar with their delinquent habits, thievery, and ferocity, may have given these Indians the name "Rogues." The river which flowed through their area was called "Rivière aux Coquins," the river of rogues. One pioneer claimed that "the only honest acquisition of the Rogue River Indians was their name."[4]

Location of the Rogue bands in southern Oregon was strategic, since the California Trail passed through this district. Because the traffic of miners and the "squatting" of settlers foreshadowed loss of hunting and fishing grounds, ancestral homes, and freedom, their reaction to the white influx was to attack immigrant trains and harass isolated valley settlements. The tendency of settlers, in turn, was to declare open warfare on all Indians, with the result that innocents often suffered with, and for the sins of, the guilty. Failure of the courts and police to punish offenses by both Indians and settlers made the situation worse. Hatred and race prejudice developed to an extreme as depredations and retributions increased. The result was a protracted period of hostility called the Rogue River wars, lasting from 1850 to 1856. This activity in southern Oregon was representative of the Indian-white culture clash then occurring simultaneously throughout the Pacific Northwest.

Legal efforts to secure title to the Indian lands through treaties were initiated in 1850 by Territorial Governor Joseph Lane. Many councils were held with Rogue River Indian leaders and other native chiefs to encourage peaceful relations between Indians and settlers. Eventually, several treaties were signed to relocate the Indians on lands removed from areas of white penetration.[5]

On September 14, 1851, an army garrison was established at Fort Orford on the southern Oregon coast to protect settlers coming into the gold district. Fort Jones was founded in the Scott Valley near

Yreka, California, for the same purpose on October 16, 1852, while on the northern frontier the force at Fort Vancouver was augmented in 1852 with 268 infantrymen under the command of Lieutenant Colonel Benjamin L. E. Bonneville. Military garrisons were also located at Astoria, Fort Steilacoom, and Fort Dalles; later, as the Indian wars spread, a number of one-company posts were set up throughout the Northwest. All these establishments were small. The total number of troops in Oregon and Washington territories between 1850 and 1855 averaged less than five hundred a year.[6]

Both the number and quality of troops were insufficient. George Crook was surprised at the amount of drunkenness, gambling, and carousing that prevailed at Benicia Barracks, California, when he arrived there in 1852. Major John Hatheway, commander of Fort Vancouver, attempted to slash his throat in fits of delirium tremens on several occasions and finally succeeded in 1853. Hazen found brawling and alcoholism a serious problem in the company he commanded in Oregon. Crook stated that most of the commanding officers in the Pacific Department were "petty tyrants" who had commanded small posts so long "that their habits and minds had narrowed down to their surroundings."[7]

In 1854, Governor George L. Curry complained that the entire army in Oregon was composed of men "unacquainted with equestrian exercises, altogether unsuited to the service in which they are engaged [and] unadapted to efficient operations against the Indians . . . ." Desertions, a common problem of the frontier army, were even more prevalent here because of the proximity to the gold fields. The Army Appropriations Act of 1851 provided extra pay to officers and enlisted men serving in Oregon and California. This did little to spur new enlistments or increase the fidelity of troops in the Far West. In his annual report for 1853, Secretary of War Jefferson Davis noted that desertions were "530 over the average of the three preceding years." Transportation problems, slow communication, and limited departmental budgets further hampered the military forces in 1855.[8]

Inadequate military protection against the truculent natives encouraged territorial governors to create volunteer regiments. Disagreement over authority, tactics, and policies caused considerable animosity between the regular army and the volunteer militia. The resulting confusion and bickering made a practical settlement of the Indian problem more difficult.

Rogue River hostilities intensified in 1852 and 1853. Widespread attacks on homes and some killings resulted in a major recruitment of volunteer patrols to counter the Indian threat. In September, 1853, a contingent of regular and volunteer troops, in a rare display of cooperation, forced a large body of Rogue River Indians to sue for peace near Table Rock. Joel Palmer, Superintendent of Indian Affairs for Oregon Territory, assisted by Joseph Lane, concluded the important Treaty of Table Rock on September 10. The Rogue River bands were represented by chiefs Jo, Sam, Jim, Limpy, and George. By this treaty the Indians agreed to give up claims to 2,180,000 acres of land for twenty annual payments totaling $55,000, plus additional considerations. A temporary reservation near Table Rock was set aside for the bands until a permanent reserve was selected. Other treaties with various small bands in the area were negotiated in the following months. By 1855 treaties negotiated by Palmer extinguished Indian title to all of Oregon Territory and led to the colonization and governmental administration of Indians on permanent reservations.[9]

The Treaty of Table Rock was ratified by the Senate in 1854. Indian agents were appointed for the Rogue River bands, and Fort Lane was built near the reservation eight miles north of Jacksonville to help enforce tranquillity of the tribe. This post, established September 28, 1853, by Captain Andrew J. Smith, was for three years the base of all regular army operations in southern Oregon.[10]

Some Indians and whites were displeased with the treaty, and outrages continued on both sides. Many of these clashes involved peaceful natives mistaken for renegades. When treaty Indians roamed off the reservations, nontreaty hostiles sought to punish them for consorting with the whites. Miners, militia, settlers, and regular troops were constantly at odds. The killings, burning of property, and acts of reprisal finally culminated in a general outbreak in the fall of 1855.

A major factor setting off hostilities was the "Lupton Affair." On the morning of October 8, a volunteer company led by "Major" J. A. Lupton attacked a camp of sleeping Indians near the confluence of Butte Creek and Rogue River, where twenty-three Indians were massacred and many more wounded. Daylight revealed that the encampment had consisted mainly of peaceful old men, women, and children. The more warlike bands of the area immediately went on a rampage of murder and destruction to avenge the outrage. As panic gripped the entire countryside, mines, farms, and homes were abandoned, and people sought refuge in larger settlements or forts. Fifteen companies of volunteers and regular army troops from Fort Lane were quickly in the field. When Hazen and his company arrived at Fort Lane on November 23, 1855, all of southern Oregon was threatened by the spreading conflagration.[11]

Severe winter weather in December brought army operations against the Indians to a standstill. Post records show that Captain Smith, who had spent much of the time since October out in the field with his dragoons, resumed command of Fort Lane on December 6. Reinforcements from Fort Reading were assigned to various post duties, and Hazen was appointed post adjutant. General Order No. 18, promoting Hazen from brevet rank to second lieutenant, Company F, Eighth Infantry, was received on December 13, but without instructions for him to join his new regiment.[12]

While the regulars waited for better weather, bands of volunteers and Indians continued to roam the Fort Lane area. On December 24, Captain Miles T. Alcorn attacked a camp of Indians on the north branch of Little Butte Creek, killing eight warriors. In another engagement Jake's band was surprised on the north bank of the Rogue River by a company under Captain E. A. Rice. Most of the Indian males were wiped out; the survivors, including women and children, were forcibly marched to Fort Lane. Many of the latter were barefooted and arrived with frozen feet. In reporting the incident, Captain Smith called the entire affair needless and barbaric, declaring the band peaceful.[13]

Early in January an attack was launched against a group of nontreaty Klamaths discovered on the headwaters of the south fork of Applegate Creek in the Siskiyou Mountains. The troops of the southern battalion of volunteers were led by Major James Bruce in their move against these Klamaths, presumably the culprits who had committed depredations in the Humbug Creek area. Noting that the Indians were well fortified, Bruce requested use of a mountain howitzer from Fort Lane. Thirty-five men of Company D, Fourth Infantry, including Lieutenant Hazen, were dispatched to participate in the engagement. They left the post with the howitzer on January 2 under command of Lieutenant Edmund Underwood and moved toward Star Gulch on Applegate Creek. This was Hazen's first expedition against hostile Indians after becoming an officer. He was to have many more confrontations with the red men during his thirty-two years in the military.[14]

Inclement weather and a foot of snow made the march very difficult. The venture had an inauspicious beginning when the mule packing the ammunition for the howitzer slipped off a mountain ledge. Not only was the clumsy beast killed, but the powder supply was also ruined, necessitating a detail back to camp for fresh powder. At mid-afternoon January 4 the men spotted the location of the tribesmen. Approximately thirty warriors plus some women and children made up the band. Several large volunteer companies surrounded the site, waiting anxiously for the howitzer to blast the cornered antagonists into the open. The armed Klamaths, however, used expert marksmanship to keep the whites from rushing their positions, killing one soldier and wounding three others at long range. The Indians occupied three "exceedingly well built" cabins, the smallest logs measuring a foot in diameter.

Hazen, who was in charge of the twelve-pounder howitzer, selected a suitable hillside position and began firing. The first shot penetrated the roof of one of the structures, and was followed by a second; these volleys killed two Indians and wounded three. The occupants immediately retaliated with such heavy sustained rifle fire that the exposed howitzer could no longer be utilized effectively. Since it was nearly dark, Underwood ordered the big gun withdrawn until fire could be resumed in the morning. The troops then encircled the area to prevent the enemy's leaving under cover of darkness. Despite these precautions, the Klamaths charged past the guards and, after a brief skirmish, made good their escape. The fact that several soldiers left their posts to warm themselves at a campfire contributed to the successful flight of the entire Indian camp.

Inspection of the deserted fortifications the next morning revealed that the Indians had built their defenses with considerable ingenuity.

They had dug tunnels from the log cabins to an outlet some distance away so that those not engaged in fighting could be completely safe. Deep pits were found in the corners of each building, with "loopholes" under the bottom logs through which rifle fire could be directed with comparative safety.

Underwood considered his force "too small and fatigued" to attempt a successful pursuit of the Indians. Wet and numb with cold, the command returned to Fort Lane on January 7. In his official report, Underwood severely criticized the two hundred volunteers, maintaining that they had rendered him "no assistance whatever." The volunteer commanders, on the other hand, accused the regulars of "botching" the entire venture. Both sides, embarrassed by the escape of the Indians, apparently needed a scapegoat.[15]

Formulation of military strategy was difficult because it was not known how many of the Indians in southern Oregon were on the warpath. Captain Smith made several futile attempts during the winter to ascertain the strength of the hostile forces in the area by sending out friendly Indian "runners"—an appropriate appellation, as they came back running for their lives each time, having been put to flight by enemy warriors. Trying a new tack, Smith on January 28 dispatched Hazen and an escort of twelve soldiers and two Indian auxiliaries to reconnoiter the region. Moving northwest from Fort Lane, the party came upon a large contingent of hostile Indians marching through the Grave Creek Hills. Keeping his men out of sight, Hazen directed his two friendly Indians to attempt to join the traveling caravan without arousing suspicion. The plan worked, with the two infiltraters accompanying the group to a place called the "Meadows," an encampment capable of accommodating about three hundred people. Sturdily-built log and stone defenses surrounded the well-established camp area at key points. The Indians were well armed and, with a few exceptions, anxious to carry on the war.

Through intelligence from the Indian collaborators and from reconnaissance reports, Hazen supplied the Fort Lane command with valuable information. The Indians were well supplied with ammunition, rifles, revolvers, and knives. Though the number of warriors did not appear to be overwhelming, terrain was a crucial factor favoring the hostiles. There was no evidence that the bands which had declared war in October were interested in "talking peace." Indeed, they attempted to augment their strength by luring coastal and other peaceful Indians into conflict with the whites. Indiscriminate killings by the white community aided them in this endeavor and kept their zeal for revenge burning white-hot. Chances for peace were poor as long as these acts continued. In sum, the situation in southwestern Oregon generally, and around Fort Lane particularly, appeared critical. Hatreds engendered on both sides made security of life and property highly uncertain. Based on Hazen's information, Captain Smith urgently requested additional forces for Fort Lane. "At least two or three more companies will be necessary to meet this threat," he informed General John E. Wool, who commanded the Department of the Pacific.[16]

Meanwhile, Superintendent Palmer and his agents sought to keep treaty Indians from joining the war parties. Immediately following the outbreak of war in October, 1855, Palmer issued regulations calling for the collection of Indians at safe places and compelling them to answer daily roll calls. Over three hundred members of a friendly Rogue River band headed by Chief Sam, or Ko-ko-kah-wah, after being menaced by Indians and whites alike, abandoned their reserve to claim protection at Fort Lane. Another sizable group sought protective custody in the Umpqua Valley.[17]

Under these circumstances the military felt obligated to protect the treaty Indians who refused to join the war parties. Volunteer forces, however, recognized no Indians as trustworthy and resented intervention in their behalf. In fact, during the fall of 1855 the cry for a war of extermination was often raised. The editor of the *Oregonian* declared that there was not one friendly Indian in the country. "These inhuman butchers and bloody fiends must be met and conquered, vanquished—yes, EXTERMINATED; or we can never hope for, or expect peace, prosperity or safety."[18]

Palmer, who had the welfare of the Indians at heart, held that the Rogue River wars were "wholly to be attributed to the acts of our own people." He wrote Wool that he considered it his duty "to adopt such measures as will tend to secure the lives of those Indians and maintain the guaranties secured to them by treaty stipulation." The Indians did not want war, Palmer said. They were "forced" into fighting by "reckless and lawless miscreants" whose actions were "sanctioned by a numerous population who regard the treasury of the United States a legitimate object of plunder." The whites, he maintained, had violated treaties and committed acts "that would disgrace the most barbarous nations of the earth."[19]

General Wool and other military commanders in the Pacific Northwest concurred in the views of the superintendent. Wool wrote army headquarters:

If there had been the same desire to do justice to the Indians and to maintain peace by the governors, as well as other persons holding prominent stations under the United States, as there was to make war and plunder the Indians of their lands, horses, cattle, we should have been relieved of all trouble, and the United States of a very large expenditure of money.[20]

This attitude earned Wool little popularity among the people of Oregon.

Convinced that the Oregonians were bent on a war of extermination, Palmer decided to protect friendly bands by immediately relocating them on a site removed from the conflict. As a result, the Grand Ronde reservation was created by Executive Order on November 9, 1855, on the western borders of Yamhill and Polk counties. Palmer envisioned eventual removal of all Indians west of the Cascade Range to reservations along the coast. He was convinced that, if left in their native habitats, the primitive aborigines could never be brought to peace and higher civilization. The topography of the area and the Indian style of warfare made it virtually impossible to subdue them, especially with the limited forces available. Palmer advocated peaceful negotiation, not indiscriminate warfare, as the more feasible solution. He believed that if the tribes could be persuaded to settle on reservations, with promises of government subsistence, peace could be secured and the Indian race preserved. This plan, an Indian policy new to Oregon, was adopted. Hazen was to have a role in its implementation, heading the first military command established on the closed Indian reservation.[21]

Measures to implement the removal program were initiated in late

1855. George H. Ambrose, Rogue River Indian agent, was directed to arrange the early transfer of Sam's band from Fort Lane to Grand Ronde. The Molala and some five hundred Umpquas and Calapooyas agreed to move to the same reservation.

Palmer's action met immediate opposition from settlers in the Willamette Valley who were aghast at the idea of moving savages so close to their homes. They failed to see how they would be safer from the tomahawk and scalping knife if the Indians were moved from their native haunts to a location more convenient to population centers. Some objected to the government's setting aside land that could be developed by whites. The general unfavorable reaction to the policy soon found vocal expression in the territorial legislature as some delegates suggested that the only removal necessary was that of Palmer from his office.[22]

So intense were the protests and so numerous the threats against agents and Indians that Palmer asked Wool to provide a military escort of twenty men for the removal of the Rogue River band. He also recommended establishment of a military post at Grand Ronde to insure "peace between our own citizens and these Indians." Captain Smith agreed that an escort should be furnished. "I have no doubt the whites will seek every opportunity to maltreat, if not massacre, the male portion of the little band," he informed his superiors. He considered twenty men adequate for the task, but added, "If there are many volunteers in the field I would recommend an escort of at least 100 men—regulars." Smith designated Lieutenant Hazen as commander of the escort, scheduled to leave the post in January, 1856.[23]

Bad weather and mounting threats against the safety of Sam's band forced a temporary delay in the removal program. A Polk County citizen wrote Ambrose that the state of excitement was such that he would "not be surprised if every Indian brought in by you is immediately killed." A group of settlers from the same area informed the agent, in a strongly worded petition, that "every Indian will be killed as soon as they cross the Calapoosi [sic] Mountains." The question of raising an armed force to prevent the Indians from being moved was considered in public meetings at several places.[24]

This public furor convinced Agent Ambrose that Hazen's detachment of twenty men was insufficient "to carry out the assignment in safety." He considered it an act of "injustice and bad faith" to take the Indians out under such threatening circumstances without positive protection. Departure was therefore postponed until additional troops were available.[25]

Since the troops stationed at Fort Lane in January, 1856, numbered only 183, Captain Smith was reluctant to detach any more men from his strategic outpost. He therefore asked the commander of Fort Jones, Captain Henry M. Judah, to send a detachment for escort duty. Forty-three men from Company E, Fourth Infantry, under command of Lieutenant George Crook, arrived at Fort Lane on February 18 in response to this call.[26]

Satisfied that the military escort was now adequate, the officers set February 25 as the date for the departure of the Rogue River band. Hazen's detachment was ordered to serve as a through-escort to Grand Ronde and then to police the reservation. The group, consisting of a sergeant, corporal, and eighteen privates, had supplies to last through April, and Hazen was authorized to make additional requisitions on the Vancouver post as necessary. Crook's detachment was to accompany the party only to Big Canyon, about fifty miles north of Fort Lane.[27]

Shortly before departure, rumors circulated that five hundred settlers were waiting along the route to annihilate the removal party. Indians hostile to Sam's people were also reported prowling in force near Canyonville. These disturbing reports made additional precautionary measures advisable. A second detail was therefore detached from Fort Lane to strengthen the escort as far as Big Canyon. This force of forty-three men under Lieutenant Underwood was to return to the post by March 13, as they were needed for a projected campaign against the Indians in the spring.

On February 22, 395 Indians left Fort Lane for nearby agency grounds to await removal. The entire operation was characterized by inadequate preparation on the part of Agent Wright. Many of the Indians were barefooted; few possessed blankets to protect themselves against the cold. The group's ill, aged, and infirm complicated matters. Too few wagons were available to haul all the Indians' goods and those unable to walk.[28]

The hazardous journey to the reservation began with "great weeping and wailing." Overloaded wagons, rugged terrain, fording of numerous streams, and the miserable physical condition of many of the Indians slowed the march to only eight miles per day. Fear of ambush by hostile whites or Indians added further discomfort.[29]

A military road extending from Fort Lane to the confluence of Myrtle Creek and the Umpqua River was the route of the removal party. Construction of this road had been authorized by Congress in January, 1853. Colonel Joseph K. F. Mansfield, inspecting the Department of the Pacific in 1854, had reported that portions of the road were "badly done" and in need of repair. Ambrose described that portion of the wagon road between Grave Creek and the south fork of the Umpqua as "horrible."[30]

Threat of attack became reality on the fourth day of the march. Early on February 28 an Indian retrieving his horse a short distance from camp was shot in the back and killed by a white sniper lurking in the bushes near the campsite. A group of men, presumably Oregon volunteers, fled the scene shortly thereafter. Lieutenant Crook and three Indians chased the suspects for several miles, but were unable to catch them.

Fear and excitement, which gripped the camp as a result of the unprovoked assault, was heightened by an unfounded rumor—readily believed by the Indians—that a volunteer company was planning an ambush farther down the Rogue River. Since a major attack appeared imminent, a messenger was dispatched to Fort Lane to report the murder and request more troops. Ambrose bitterly denounced the white snipers, calling the killing an act of "pure wantonness" committed by "men . . . who might properly be considered vagrants in any country in the world but this." Their objective, he believed, was to foil the removal policy by frightening the Indians into the mountains.

When news of the altercation reached Fort Lane, Smith took a force of forty men to investigate the situation, joining the escort party at Jump Off Jo Creek on February 29. Chief Sam, whose Indians were apprehensive about continuing the march, thought the troops were supposed to protect them from such attacks. To calm their fears, Smith authorized the arming of a portion of the band, ordering them to shoot the white murderers on sight.[31]

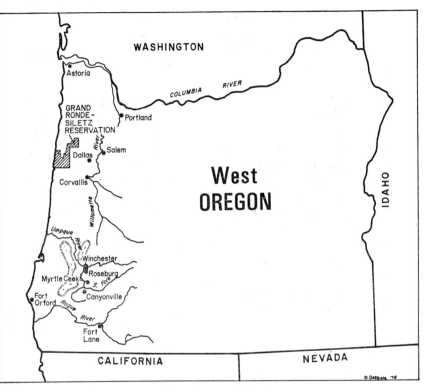

West Oregon, 1857

Under command of Captain Smith the escort conducted the Indians safely through the Grave Creek Hills in two days. This rugged area, between the Rogue and Umpqua rivers, was a favorite rendezvous of hostile bands led by chiefs George and Limpy. Hazen had reconnoitered this region in January and was aware of the danger spots. Signs indicated the presence of Indians, but the large escort apparently discouraged interference. The only troublemakers encountered were a small gang of whites who emerged from a cabin threatening to indulge in the popular frontier pastime of "gittin' themselves an Indian." The military personnel quickly cooled their ardor with a show of force. With the threat of danger apparently reduced, Smith returned to his post on March 2.[32]

Passage through the eleven-mile Big Canyon and across the south fork of the Umpqua River posed almost insurmountable difficulties. The canyon, through which Canyon Creek flows, was at many places completely obstructed by driftwood, mud, and rock slides. "God only knows when we will get through," Ambrose wrote dejectedly on March 3. Mansfield had in 1854 recommended spending $5,000 to improve the route through the canyon, but Indian hostilities had kept the work from getting under way. Hazen's detachment had the miserable assignment of clearing a roadway, a task accomplished in two days of backbreaking labor "in the worst mud ever seen."[33]

Crook and his men assisted the party through the canyon on March 6 and, their mission complete, returned to Fort Lane the next morning. Meanwhile, the caravan at Big Canyon met R. B. Metcalf, a subagent on the Grand Ronde reservation. He reported the tenor of the Willamette Valley population so antagonistic that "nothing short of the aid of a strong military force will enable us to reach the reserve . . . ." A through-escort of twenty men would be insufficient to deter opposition forces, he warned. Lieutenant Underwood thereupon delayed departure a few days to seek authorization from Fort Vancouver to continue the escort. The order was not granted because of intensified Indian hostilities, and Underwood's detachment left the party at Winchester.[34]

From Myrtle Creek, where the military road ended, the journey was along a less defined wagon trail to the Willamette River. The party moved along the Willamette valley to a point north of Corvallis and then turned northwestwardly to Dallas and Grand Ronde.

Hardship and danger continued to dog the weary sojourners. Wagons broke down in the mountains causing lengthy delays. Cattle, suffering from lack of forage, became hard to handle. Frequent sighting of hostile Indians necessitated forced marches to elude possible danger. Angry settlers along the way met them with threats, but the predicted violence did not materialize. Perhaps the greatest problems were travel weariness and sickness; many of the group were ill, and several died on this part of the journey. The wagons could not hold all those unfit to walk, despite the fact that several additional ones had been secured en route. Rain, which began to fall March 13 and continued for several days, made the road treacherous and the trek even more miserable. The destitute band and its escort finally reached the end of the trail the afternoon of March 25.

The march from Fort Lane covered 263 miles and took 30 days, an ordeal so difficult that eight Indians died on the journey. With an equal number of births on the trip, however, the number of Indians completing the removal was the same as at the start.[35]

The highly-publicized transfer of Rogue River Indians to the reservation was an event of considerable importance, paving the way for subsequent removals and helping to lay the foundations of the reservation system in Oregon.[36] Had public pressure and threats succeeded in halting this endeavor, the Indian Bureau's concentration policy in the territory would have been impeded and the period of Indian-white conflict prolonged. Neither the system nor its success was assured at this point, however, as other factors were to jeopardize the future of this policy.

Since most ranking officers in the Department of the Pacific were involved in Indian wars, Lieutenant Hazen was authorized to establish a command at Grand Ronde. Selecting a site in the northeastern section of the reservation, he ordered the erection of buildings to shelter his men. A blockhouse was also begun because, as Hazen put it, "cases are of frequent occurrence showing the treachery of Indian character and the necessity of such works of defense."[37]

Policing the many Indians who were brought to the reservation in the spring of 1856 was the responsibility of the military detachment. Many of these Indians, which included bands of Umpqua, Rogue, Shasta, Calapooya, and some Willamette valley tribes, were haughty and warlike and soon became disgruntled at conditions on the reserve. The Indian Bureau was unable to supply enough annuity goods to satisfy them. They also complained about inadequate shelter, wet climate, and an absence of game in the area. Some wandered off the reservation to nearby settlements, much to the consternation and fear of the residents. The Indian agents bickered among themselves, displaying notorious inability to administer reservation affairs. On April 10, Metcalf reported that the natives "are becoming very much dissatisfied" and that "everything is in confusion here. I run myself to death almost trying to attend a thousand things at once and consequently doing nothing right."[38]

The hostile white community made policing the Indians more difficult. Widespread publicity and dire predictions of danger had preceded the Indians; false and exaggerated reports continued after their arrival. In Dayton, Oregon, Superintendent Palmer complained that "almost every device imaginable is resorted to for the purpose of creating a panic and abusing the mind of the public against those instructed with the management of Indian affairs in the country."[39]

Hazen's limited force found it impossible to confine the Indians to the expansive reserve. Settlers complained that armed Rogues entered farm homes, frightened women, and generally threatened their safety. Twenty-seven citizens signed a petition demanding that the Indians be disarmed and kept on the reservation, threatening to "resort to such means as will render our houses safe from their intrusion." That members of the fierce Rogue River tribe had guns was understandably a disquieting revelation to area residents, but the Indians refused to relinquish them, saying they needed them for protection against irresponsible whites. Apparently Hazen and the agents decided not to force the issue.[40]

Friction between settlers and reservation Indians increased during the last half of April. A. D. Babcock, owner of the Union Farm near the reserve, was enraged when agency cattle destroyed some of his crops and repeatedly accused the Indians of malicious property destruction. Viciously assailing Grand Ronde authorities for not controlling the Indians, the irate farmer threatened to invade the reservation with a force strong enough to disarm and punish the guilty individuals unless remedial steps were taken at once.[41]

Aroused by the troublesome Babcock, the white neighborhood threatened a momentary expedition against the reservation Indians. Palmer had repeatedly asked for more troops to help establish order and discipline at Grand Ronde. In March, Hazen had urgently requested a larger force from Colonel George Wright at Fort Vancouver. Palmer informed Wool on April 14 that the future of his entire reservation program was in jeopardy. "Between disaffection among the Indians on the Reservation, and the alarm and excitement among the citizens, and backing out of agents ... I am likely to fail in the entire plan, unless I can obtain aid from the Military Department." He emphasized that over fifteen hundred Indians would soon be on the reservation, and that unless Hazen's force was enlarged immediately "everything may be lost."[42]

Palmer personally inspected the Grand Ronde situation on April 19 and in his report to Wool attributed much of the uneasiness to the machinations of "political demagogs" who sought to undermine the Indian service. He exonerated the Rogue River Indians from hostile intent against the settlers, but admitted that it was "highly impolitic" for them to retain guns. In pressing his case for more troops, he warned that it was too dangerous to disarm them without a larger force, and if the citizens tried to disarm the Indians it would "prove disastrous . . . and end in deluging the whole country in Blood."[43]

The military officers were also hindered by native beliefs. The superstitious Rogues attributed the high death rate on the reservation to the evil workings of medicine men who possessed power over life and death. They purportedly had the power to destroy an individual either instantly or by a lingering disease. So firm was this belief that when a death occurred the relatives of the deceased immediately wreaked vengeance on some medicine man, either of their own or another tribe. This caused frequent quarrels and nearly resulted in open warfare between the Rogues and Umpquas on numerous occasions.[44]

Seeking to curtail the roving of the Indians, Hazen established a line of sentinels along the eastern boundary of the reservation. Using Indian Bureau funds, he armed sixty citizens to help the troops man guard positions spaced to permit constant surveillance of all access routes. A sturdy boundary fence, eight to nine rails high, was also built, with a constantly guarded entrance gate near the blockhouse. Only authorized persons were allowed to enter or leave the reserve, and anyone attempting to slip past the sentinels was arrested. J. S. Rinearson, an officer in the volunteer corps, was appointed special agent in the Indian department to collaborate with Hazen in directing the work of the citizen force. Use of citizen guards did not contribute significantly to order or containment of the Indians, who neither respected nor feared a civilian force. Palmer noted that the experiment demonstrated that "there is a moral influence, depending upon the presence of Regular troops, not obtainable by Volunteers."

Hazen learned early in his career that only superior strength, based on large numbers of troops, cowed the Indian into a position of respect and submission.[45]

The frequent reports of trouble at Grand Ronde plus the threat that reservation Indians and hostiles might reunite forced General Wool to act. Lieutenant Philip H. Sheridan was ordered to proceed from Fort Vancouver with a detachment of dragoons on April 19, 1856, to reinforce Hazen's post. Simultaneously Wool announced that he would shortly send an entire company "and if necessary two, to protect both the inhabitants and Indians."[46]

Sheridan arrived at Grand Ronde on April 25. Strengthening of the garrison calmed the situation considerably; citizen guards were released by mid-May and reservation life gradually became more stable. Work on the post buildings, as laid out by Hazen, continued under command of Sheridan, who outranked the former by one grade.[47]

On July 4, 1856, Lieutenant Colonel R. C. Buchanan, commander of the Military District of Southern Oregon, announced the successful conclusion of the Rogue River wars. In the disposition of troops that followed, Captain De Lancey Floyd Jones, Fourth Infantry, assumed command of the Grand Ronde post, relieving Sheridan on July 23. The latter was detached to assist Captain Christopher C. Auger on the recently established Siletz reservation adjacent to Grand Ronde on the south. Hazen remained at Grand Ronde in command of Company F, Fourth Infantry, and performed the duties of commissary and quartermaster. Post returns show that seventy-five enlisted men and two officers were stationed there by the end of July.[48]

On August 30, Captain Smith of Fort Lane arrived with Company C, First Dragoons and assumed command. Since a garrison was needed on the reservation for some time, the veteran officer was instructed to establish a permanent post. Records in the Department of War credit Smith's dragoons and Company F, Fourth Infantry, with establishing the post—named Fort Yamhill—on August 30, 1856. Actually, Smith's only significant role in founding the fort was to select its name. Hazen had already laid out the site, built a blockhouse, and initiated other construction before Smith arrived.[49]

Fort Yamhill was situated three-fourths of a mile west of the south fork of Yamhill River, on the northeastern section of Grand Ronde reservation. It stood about twenty-five miles southwest of Dayton. Yamhill, a corrupt form of the Indian word "Che-am-ills," was the name of a tribe that had frequented the region.[50]

The building program at the fort made rapid progress under the more favorable conditions. Work on the storehouses, hospital, and soldiers' quarters was well advanced by mid-September, and the entire command of 154 men was in comfortable quarters by the first of November. Hazen's pioneering work at the coastal reserve drew high praise from both Captain Smith and General Wool, the latter specifically commending "the energy of Lieutenant Hazen" in performing the arduous duties associated with the early administration of affairs.[51]

Policing the reservation became the general routine of troops at Fort Yamhill. Several thousand Indians were brought to Grand Ronde and Siletz during this period, and they had to be convinced to stay. As long as there were Indian wars in the Northwest, a close surveillance over reservation bands was needed to insure their non-involvement. Two new posts to facilitate this task were established: Fort Hoskins near the Siletz reservation and Fort Umpqua near the mouth of the Umpqua River. Eventually the Indians ceased to be a military threat, becoming primarily an administrative problem for the Indian Bureau. Military garrisons were reduced or removed entirely, Fort Yamhill continuing to function until August, 1866.

Post returns and other scattered records indicate that life at Fort Yamhill after the summer of 1856 became routine and rather uneventful. Many of the Indians were moved to Siletz in 1857, making the military task easier. Virtually the only allurements at this isolated outpost were drinking parties and Indian maids, and a number of the soldiers at Forts Yamhill and Hoskins took Indian wives or mistresses.[52] During the fall and winter of 1856–1857 several men were killed in drunken brawls in the barracks at Fort Yamhill. Lieutenant Hazen developed a strong aversion to immoderate drinking during his early military career, a distaste which he retained throughout his life.[53]

Hazen remained at Fort Yamhill until April 20, 1857, when he was ordered to Fort Jones, California. On May 1 he was officially relieved from duty in the Department of the Pacific and ordered to "join his proper company" in the Eighth Infantry. Thus the veteran of nineteen months of service in the raw northwestern frontier was headed for the plains of Texas.

Like other young West Pointers Hazen was quickly initiated into Indian problems in the West. Just as quickly he was forced to face the hardships and privations typically associated with service on the rugged frontier. In successfully adapting to the varied and difficult circumstances, Hazen developed initiative, ingenuity, and personal confidence. His responsibilities as commander of a detachment of troops at the turbulent Grand Ronde reservation gave him, as a young "shavetail," the opportunity to display resourcefulness and leadership potential. Also, the practical knowledge he gained from his association with the reservation system proved beneficial in later years when he helped implement the reservation policy for the Plains Indians.

II

Scouting Indians on the Texas Frontier

Following a trip to the East Coast, and a leave of absence, Lieutenant Hazen joined the Eighth Infantry headquarters at Fort Davis, Texas, on February 13, 1858. The Eighth Infantry Regiment was significantly engaged in the military effort to subjugate the Indians of the southwestern plains. Since the end of the Mexican War, the wild Texas tribes had been challenging the advance of the white man with unprecedented intensity. Comanche, Kiowa, Kiowa-Apache, and other Southern Plains tribes saw their hunting lands appropriated, their game growing scarce, and a relentless stream of settlers and soldiers threatening to oust them from the country.

In anger and desperation they fought to preserve their way of life and, indeed, life itself in this vast western expanse. During the 1850's the entire Texas frontier seemed to be aflame with roving red men from Mexico, New Mexico Territory, and Indian Territory. Seeking food, plunder, and glory, they engaged in relentless and far-flung "hit and run" expeditions against the hated white intruders. The ferocity and ever-increasing boldness of the Indians indicated that they were committed to a valiant, albeit futile, stand against the further penetration of white civilization.

The federal government realized as early as 1848 that a vigorous policy of defense was required. In August of that year the military commanders in Texas and New Mexico Territory were directed to establish military posts and to station troops in a manner that would best facilitate the protection of the frontiers. More than fifteen hundred troops, commanded by Brevet General David E. Twiggs, were furnished the Texas Military Department, and special Indian agents were appointed to seek the good will of the natives. Funds were also appropriated to aid the Texas Rangers in a concerted effort to curb the growing Indian menace.[1]

As an integral part of the defensive policy an inner and outer chain of army posts was established. In 1853 the inner line of defense consisted of Fort Duncan on the Rio Grande, Fort Lincoln near D'Hanis, Fort Martin Scott near Fredericksburg, Fort Croghan fifty miles northwest of Austin, Fort Gates on the Leon River sixty-five miles northeast of Croghan, Fort Graham on the Colorado River in Hill County, and Fort Worth on the Trinity River.

Forming the outer chain were Fort Belknap on the Brazos River, Fort Phantom Hill on the Clear Fork of the Brazos, Fort Chadbourne on Oak Creek, Fort McKavett on the San Saba River, and Fort Clark about forty-five miles north of Eagle Pass. Additional military posts were established as settlement moved westward or as certain sectors of lines needed strengthening. One of these was Fort Davis, established on October 7, 1854, and situated at the foot of the Davis Mountains in the Big Bend country of West Texas.[2]

The elaborate defensive policy of the government failed to produce the desired effects. Swift-moving raiders managed to penetrate the lines and molest settlements almost at will.

Treaty agreements appeared to be equally ineffective in pacifying Indian-white relations. Comanche, Kiowa, and Kiowa-Apache representatives agreed to government peace terms at Camp Holmes in 1835 and 1837, and at Fort Atkinson in 1853. Many treaties were made with Texas tribes after that state entered the Union in 1846. Experience soon demonstrated that, although peace could be made for a season, violations on both sides would invariably occur.[3]

Major Robert S. Neighbors, federal Indian agent in Texas, sought a solution through the settlement of tribes on reservations. On February 6, 1854, Texas agreed to provide some of its public domain for reservations which the federal government might select. After a survey was made by Neighbors and Randolph B. Marcy, two reserves —one for the Comanche and one for more peaceful Indians—were established in the Fort Belknap area. By 1858 about eleven hundred

Anadarkoes, Caddoes, Delawares, Kichais, and Wacos had been located on their assigned site. Fewer than four hundred Comanches had consented to confinement on their reservation by that date. Hundreds of their kinsmen continued to wreak destruction throughout wide areas of Texas. Reservation Indians were often falsely accused of complicity in the raiding activities. Hazen found that in Texas, even more than in Oregon, public opinion overwhelmingly supported the view that the only good Indian was a dead Indian, reservation residents included. Opposition to the reservations became so great that Neighbors, in 1859, was forced to move his charges to the Wichita agency in Indian Territory.[4]

Thus the year 1858 witnessed a new peak in Indian raiding activity in Texas. The segregation policy, as well as all other state and federal efforts, had failed to solve the serious Indian problem. Walter Prescott Webb declared that there was more fighting on Texas soil in 1858 and 1859 than at any time since 1836. This alarming situation prompted the state legislature to appropriate $70,000 for frontier defense and to authorize a call for additional mounted volunteers. At the same time, Governor Hardin R. Runnels requested additional federal troops and urged increased military action against the Indians. General Twiggs agreed that the army's defensive policy was inadequate. Beginning in the spring of 1858 he ordered the troops at the frontier posts to take the offensive—to engage in active campaigns of pursuit and punishment until the Indians were thrashed into submission. "As long as there are wild Indians on the prairie," he stated, "Texas can not be free from depredations."[5]

Conforming to this new policy, both federal and state troops initiated military campaigns against the Indians. In May a force of Texas Rangers and reservation Indians, under the command of Captain John S. Ford, trailed a large band of Comanches into Indian Territory and defeated them on the banks of the Canadian. In September, Brevet Major General Earl Van Dorn led a cavalry force in an extensive campaign against the same tribe, successfully attacking them near the present site of Rush Springs, Oklahoma.[6]

Meanwhile, the troops stationed at Fort Davis were conducting military sorties on a lesser scale. Beginning in May, Hazen commanded a mounted detachment engaged in scouting Indians in the

Davis Mountains area. Near Fort Davis on May 31 a party of Mescalero Apaches stole some mules belonging to a government mail party. These raiders were identified as two bands under chiefs Marco and Gomez who resided in the Guadalupe Mountains east of El Paso. Ranging as far distant as Fort Davis, they frequently committed depredations along the San Antonio road. Lieutenant Colonel Washington Seawell, commanding Fort Davis, ordered a detachment under Hazen "to overtake and chasten" the Indians "and to recover the mules if possible." The full details of this punitive and recovery expedition are given in a lengthy report based on a daily journal kept by Hazen.[7]

According to Lieutenant Hazen's account, he left the fort on the morning of June 4 with eleven mounted men, nineteen infantrymen, and two Mexican guides. For four days he followed a northwest course, keeping close to the trail of the Indians. Then on June 8, finding no water in that barren wasteland, Hazen forsook the trail and headed for Buckskin Camp, about thirty miles to the west. The trek required a full day's forced march without any water under an "oppressively hot" sun. It was nightfall before the last of the parched and footsore infantrymen straggled into the camp.

The following morning Hazen resumed the march, pointing toward Guadalupe Peak. His course took him past a dry salt lake bed and a salt springs site and onto the Fredericksburg and El Paso road. There on the evening of June 10 the Indian trail was struck again. Following the trail up the eastern slope of the Guadalupe Mountains, Hazen's guides discovered the Indians camped in a canyon on the New Mexico side of the border. The encampment consisted of fifteen lodges and between 90 and 150 Indians. Hazen planned to surround the site during the night and launch a surprise attack at dawn. His scouts, however, apparently overestimated the distance separating the troops from the Indians. Marching forward, the command, to its great surprise, suddenly found itself on the edge of the encampment. Realizing that his presence would momentarily be discovered, Hazen ordered an immediate attack. Although surprised, the Indians had sufficient time to mount their horses and break for cover. They fled so rapidly up the canyon that the troops were unable to inflict any significant casualties. Only one Mescalero warrior was killed and one woman captured in the attack. After scouring the rugged mountains for a day and a half, Hazen decided that a further pursuit of the dispersed band was useless.

Although the Indians managed to escape, they were forced to abandon all of their possessions. Hazen captured twenty-nine horses and government mules and large quantities of arms and ammunition. The band's entire camp equipment—including lodge skins, peltries, furniture, and horse gear—was burned. Another damaging blow was the destruction of about one thousand pounds of prepared foods found in the village. The lodges also contained fifty scalps—evidence that the warriors of this band had perpetrated many acts of murder and rapine.

The return to Fort Davis along the edge of the hot and arid Pecos plains was an ordeal never to be forgotten by Hazen. Most of the men were "green" recruits from the East easily worn down by the vicissitudes of the plains environment. Furthermore, the grain-fed "American" horses were so broken down from the canyon operation and little nourishment that the entire command had to be dismounted. Hazen describes the difficult march from the Guadalupe Mountains to the "Salt Springs" as follows:

Our route lay across a level sand prairie, which with a verticle sun soon became scorching hot, so much so as to heat the soles of the shoes to a painful degree. The metal of the guns became so heated that it could not be touched by the hand.... The little water that was in the canteens became too hot to be drunk. The slight breezes that would occasionally pass over the plains, were nothing less than siroccos, it was necessary to hold one's breath til they subsided. Several of the men drank their urine, which only increased their terrible thirst.[8]

Arriving at the Salt Springs at sundown, the exhausted command made camp for the night. Despite its salty and sulfurous content, huge quantities of the cool spring water were consumed by both man and beast, producing some debilitating effects.

The night at the Salt Springs was marred by a weird and "melancholy occurrence" that resulted in the loss of two lives. At two o'clock in the morning as the third relief was posted, one of the sentinels,

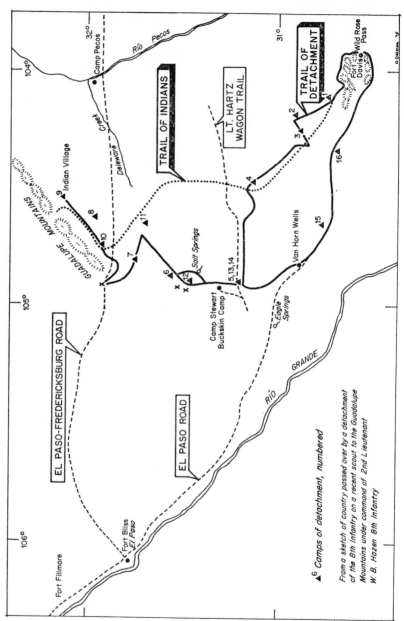

TRAIL OF INDIANS

LT. HARTZ
WAGON TRAIL

TRAIL OF
DETACHMENT

EL PASO-FREDERICKSBURG ROAD

EL PASO ROAD

GUADALUPE MOUNTAINS

Río Pecos

Camp Pecos

Deleware Creek

Indian Village

Salt Springs

Camp Stewart
Buckskin Camp

Van Horn Wells

O. Eagle Springs

RÍO GRANDE

Fort Bliss
El Paso

Fort Fillmore

Fort Davis
Wild Rose
Pass

106°   105°   104°

32°

31°

▲⁶ Camps of detachment, numbered

From a sketch of country passed over by a detachment
of the 8th Infantry on a recent scout to the Guadalupe
Mountains under command of 2nd Lieutenant
W. B. Hazen 8th Infantry

Guadalupe Mountains after Hazen's map of June 1858

Private Michael Kellett, Company D, was missed from his post. It was assumed by the new watch that he had gone to bed immediately upon seeing his relief approaching. In reality, the tired recruit had earlier wandered outside his post and fallen asleep in a patch of grass. After the new watch had been posted for an hour, one of the guards heard Kellett rustling in the grass and mistook him for an Indian. Without issuing a challenge, the startled guard fired, instantly killing Private Kellett. At the same time he frantically shouted, "Indians!" and thoroughly alarmed the camp. One of the other guards, Private Michael Hyers, Company C, panicked. He rushed into camp, firing his gun at random and screaming "more hideously than any Indian ever heard." Several soldiers, taking Hyers for a wild Comanche, leveled their guns on him and brought him down in his tracks, displaying a level of marksmanship heretofore not seen on the expedition. Some horses that had been hit by Hyer's stray bullets bounded through camp at breakneck speed, further giving the appearance of a real attack. As soon as Hazen realized that it was all a false alarm, he sought to restore some semblance of order. It took him several hours to piece together the chain of events that had produced this tragic debacle. At dawn Privates Kellett and Hyers were buried in the sand—mute testimony to the perils of army duty on the Texas frontier.

After retracing their trail to Buckskin Camp, the detachment followed a southward course until they struck the El Paso road at Van Horn's Wells. Then proceeding southeastward, Hazen and his group reached Fort Davis on June 20. An arduous march of approximately 450 miles had been completed.

In concluding his report of the expedition, Hazen, with characteristic frankness, both praised and damned the performance of his command. Three soldiers and the two scouts were singled out for special commendation; he obviously was not pleased with the other twenty-seven! "I never saw so worthless a set of men thrown together before in my life," he stated. "The recruits were of little service at any time, except to fill details, the duties of which they failed to execute. . . . While in the Indian country they were much frightened, ready to fire at any time, on anything, and it was with peril that I could visit the sentinels at night."

He also pronounced the large "American" grain-fed horses unserviceable in West Texas. Only three of the twelve horses taken out from Fort Davis survived the march. He recommended that mules and a breed of horses better acclimated to the semiarid plains be utilized by the military. The poorest mule, he observed, stood the trip much better than the best horse.

Hazen described the country he had traversed as "perfectly worthless for agricultural purposes." The only area possessing any value was around the Guadalupe Mountains where there existed "an abundance of the finest building stone of several varieties, lime, and salt." But even these resources, he assumed, "must remain valueless" because of their isolated location in a barren wasteland.[9]

For leading the scouting expedition against the Apache band and destroying their "entire possessions," Hazen was cited in General Orders by the Headquarters of the Army.[10]

On August 5, 1858, Hazen was transferred to Fort Inge, a subsidiary post supporting the outer chain of defense, located near Uvalde. An active force numbering between fifty and one hundred men was garrisoned there during 1858 and 1859. A major responsibility of the troops was to protect the road from San Antonio to Eagle Pass and to discourage raids into the northern Mexican states.[11]

The aggressive offensive operations initiated in 1858 by the army regulars and state rangers brought little relief to the settlements of southwest Texas. Indian depredations, kidnappings, and scattered killings continued to strike terror along the frontier line. Constant scouts, patrols, and recovery operations were undertaken by the troops at Fort Inge in an attempt to curtail the bold raiders. On February 13, 1859, a detachment of Company F fought a battle with a band of Indians near Uvalde. In May, when a party of Indians boldly pilfered a small herd of horses near the Nueces crossing, Captain R. P. Maclay, commanding Fort Inge, ordered Hazen to lead a detachment in pursuit. Numbering ten mounted men of Company F, one scout, and four citizen volunteers, the expedition rode out of the fort on May 16.

Picking up the raiding party's trail at the Nueces, Hazen's detachment proceeded northwestward for several days. On the evening of the nineteenth they sighted the bronzed bandits, numbering fewer than a dozen warriors, camped on the West Fork of the Nueces, approximately seventy-five miles from Fort Inge. After moving his men cautiously to the valley floor, Hazen gave the order to charge. The surprise was complete. Four Indians were killed in a brief fight, and none escaped without serious wounds. In addition, Hazen's unscathed command recovered seven horses and some other stolen property. "Safe conduct" certificates bearing the date 1845 identified the slain Indians as members of the Kickapoo tribe. Since the Indians possessed stolen goods, Hazen was of the opinion that either the certificates were no longer relevant or else his victims should have been more careful of the company they kept.[12]

For his "highly creditable" performance against the Kickapoo warriors, Hazen once again was cited in General Orders from the Headquarters of the Army. And, "for gallant conduct in two engagements with Indians in Texas," he was breveted a First Lieutenant.[13]

Mounting pressure on the outer perimeter of defense kept the troops at the frontier outposts fully occupied during the last half of 1859. In June, Hazen was sent to aid in the defense of settlements near Camp Verde; July found him engaged at Indianola; in August he temporarily bolstered the command at Camp Hudson. After returning to Fort Inge in September, Hazen engaged in far-ranging scouting operations against the increasing number of raiding parties molesting the area west of San Antonio. The energetic efforts of Lieutenant Hazen and other officers at Fort Inge to protect the frontier belies the charge made by the *Dallas Herald* in 1859 that the "three thousand regulars who live in comfortable quarters . . . are only serviceable in keeping up 'the pomp and circumstance of glorious war.'" The editor should have realized that the government had neither sufficient money nor troops to patrol and protect adequately the expansive plains of Texas against the hundreds of roving bands of Indians.[14]

In late September a Comanche raiding party stole a herd of two hundred saddle horses from a ranch on the Frio River and kidnapped two young Blacks who were tending them. The owner of the caballada, H. Ragsdale, requested the command at Fort Inge to undertake an expedition to recover his animals and slaves. Lieutenant Hazen, with two noncommissioned officers and eight privates of Company F, was ordered to scout the daring marauders. Three area civilians, including Ragsdale, volunteered to accompany the troops.

Leaving the post on the evening of September 29, Hazen picked up the trail where it crossed the Eagle Pass road not far southwest of the fort. Heading north and then west the Indians had crossed the El Paso road near its junction with the Nueces, and then pointed up that stream. Early on the third day en route, the detachment came upon one of the Blacks who only that morning had escaped from his captors. His companion, it was learned, had been killed by the Indians. Trailing close behind the Comanches, Hazen hoped to catch them before nightfall; however, after fifty miles of strenuous pursuit he had failed to gain any ground on the swift-moving raiders. Finally, at about ten o'clock on October 2 the Comanche party, consisting of seven men and one woman, was spotted near the headwaters of the Nueces River.

By careful stealth, Hazen was able to move his men within thirty yards of the Indians before being discovered. But the crafty warriors reacted quickly to the danger. Astride their fleet-footed ponies they headed for an open cedar brake. After a chase of about four hundred yards the soldiers succeeded in bringing two red men to bay, killing one and wounding the other. The remaining Comanches could not be pinned down. Pursued to the edge of a canyon, they bolted down the steep precipice and scrambled up the opposite side to safety. Hazen's men could only stand in helpless amazement before this demonstration of reckless horsemanship. Though the raiders escaped, 130 of Ragsdale's valuable ponies were rounded up and returned to his ranch. By his aggressive pursuit of this raiding party, Hazen not only recovered a kidnapped lad and valuable property, but also demonstrated that depredations around Fort Inge would not go unpunished.[15]

Unfortunately the Indians were not so easily convinced. During the latter part of October two settlers living along Sabinal Creek, east of Fort Inge, were murdered by a small Comanche war party. Citizens of Uvalde and Frio City, enraged by the massacre, immediately organized armed posses and took to the field. Captain Maclay of Fort Inge authorized Hazen, his most successful Indian fighter, to scout the murderers. The posse organizations thereupon agreed to join Hazen's regulars in a combined punitive expedition.

Numbering thirty civilians and nine soldiers, Hazen's force left the post on October 30. Trailing the fleeing Comanches, the command traveled north to a point approximately twenty-five miles northwest of Camp Verde. There the trail veered northwest toward the Llano River. After several more days of tracking, on the morning of November 3, the elusive raiders were discovered breaking camp near the headwaters of the Llano.

Utilizing superiority of numbers Hazen ordered a massed charge against the party of eight Comanches. The surprised warriors fought desperately to save their lives, or failing in this, at least to extract a heavy toll before they died. Fully armed with rifles, revolvers, and bows, they gave and received no quarter. In a fierce melee that lasted less than five minutes four Indians were killed and three others mortally wounded. Hazen was struck in the hand and side by a bullet as he led the charge into the camp, and at the same time his horse was shot from under him. Three volunteer citizens—Samuel Everett, a Mr. Pallium, and a Mr. Williams—were also wounded by bullets or arrows in the close-range combat. Apparently only one Comanche survived the fight, but not without suffering injury. After the battle the troops captured thirty horses and seized eight guns, including two Lancaster rifles.

Critically disabled by his wounds, Hazen dispatched five men to Fort Clark, eighty-five miles away, to secure medical aid. For three days he lay in agony waiting anxiously for the arrival of a relief party. On the morning of the sixth, with still no sign of help and his water and rations almost exhausted, Hazen decided to start back to Fort Inge.[16] With Hazen so weak from the loss of blood that he had to be supported on his horse, the command slowly made its way southeastward across rough gully-washed country. After two days of torturous travel the troops reached an old mission station on the headwaters of the Nueces. From there an express was dispatched to Fort Inge requesting medical supplies and a conveyance for the wounded. On November 10, a week after having exercised vengeance on the Comanches, the weary detachment was escorted into Fort Inge.[17]

Lieutenant Hazen was in dire need of medical care. The wound in his side was infected, putting his life in peril. The post surgeon's examination revealed that the bullet had penetrated his hand, breaking and crushing several bones, and then had entered the right side of his chest between the sixth and seventh ribs. On December 5, because of his critical condition, Hazen was transferred to the hospital in San Antonio. A special order was issued by the Headquarters of the Department of Texas assigning Assistant Surgeon R. L. Brodie to attend and "remain with that officer until his condition is such as to justify his being left alone." Brodie's medical treatment was effective; however, he did not attempt to remove the bullet. By Christmas Hazen's recovery—although destined to be slow—was assured.[18]

Hazen's virtual annihilation of a Comanche war party did not go unnoticed in high military circles. In the report of his inspection of the Department of Texas, Lieutenant Colonel Joseph E. Johnston, who later gained fame leading Confederate forces, gave Hazen recognition for his "third successful pursuit of Indians in which he had exhibited activity, perseverance, and courage."[19] Colonel Robert E. Lee, who assumed command of the Department of Texas on February 20, 1860, also cited Hazen for his operations against the Comanches. And for the third time in eighteen months the Headquarters of the Army cited the promising young officer for "gallant acts and patient endurance under great and varied hardships."[20]

The most gratifying—and unexpected—expression of praise and appreciation came from the frontier settlers around Fort Inge. In a public meeting held in San Antonio in December, 1859, the grateful citizens adopted the following resolutions:

Whereas, *Lieutenant W. B. Hazen, of the United States Army, in his services for the protection and defence of our Western frontier from the ravages of hostile Indians; by his uniformly prompt, timely and determined action in their pursuit; by his deeds of marked daring and bravery in their encounter, of which he bears the unmistakable evidence in a dangerous wound received in his last Indian engagement, which for a time threatened to prove fatal, and has disabled him for life; and by his repeated success in the recovery and restoration to our suffering frontier settlers of their stolen property, has deservedly won the confidence, high esteem, and admiration of the people of Texas, and especially of those upon our extreme frontier and of this community, and alike distinguished himself as a true and gallant officer, winning a high position in the army;*

Resolved, *That the thanks of this community and entire frontier are hereby tendered him.*

Resolved, *That as an evidence of our appreciation of his distinguished services, as a token of our sympathy for his sufferings and wounds, and as an acknowledgment of his noble gallantry, a sword be presented him.*

Resolved, *That Colonel John A. Wilcox, Hon. Thomas H. Stribling, H. Wechsler, and C. Upson be appointed a committee to raise funds for the purchase of a sword to be presented to Lieutenant W. B. Hazen.*

Resolved, *That a copy of this preamble and resolutions be forwarded to Lieutenant Hazen, and also to the Secretary of War.*

Jno. A. Wilcox, President
C. Upson, Secretary[21]

On January 28, 1860, Hazen was granted an extended leave from the army "for the benefit of his health." Dr. Brodie, in recommending the leave, stated that the nature of Hazen's wounds precluded his fitness for duty "for a period of at least twelve months." This sick leave terminated Lieutenant Hazen's brief but action-packed military career in Texas.[22]

During his two years with the Eighth Infantry, Hazen played an active part in a major effort to bring security to the highly exposed frontier settlements. Before the wounded lieutenant left Texas, it was obvious that the military was not achieving its objective. During the closing months of 1859 almost every frontier county reported acts of plunder. In November, General Twiggs, admitting the collapse of the offensive policy, wrote the Adjutant General that he was ordering the troops "to resort to the defensive system again."[23] Serious Indian hostilities were to continue in Texas for another fifteen years. Nevertheless, as a result of the zealous service of responsible officers like Hazen a number of settlements were provided a measure of protection sufficient to assure their survival.

In his period of service in Texas, Hazen gained valuable leadership experience, practical military knowledge, and considerable confidence in his own abilities. This prepared him for military leadership in the Civil War and for noteworthy service in the West after 1865. On the other hand, the lingering effects of his wounds were to cause him frequent misery; and the Comanche bullet which he carried in his body ultimately contributed to his death.

III

The Civil War Years

Following a twelve months' period of convalescence, William B. Hazen, on January 28, 1861, was nominated assistant instructor of military tactics at West Point. Assuming his new position the following month, he was promoted to first lieutenant on April 1 and captain on May 14. He soon earned the reputation of a strict disciplinarian, on one occasion placing Cadet George A. Custer under arrest for violation of regulations. It was while teaching at the military academy that Hazen developed a lasting and scholarly interest in military science.[1]

When the Civil War began on April 12, 1861, Hazen sought immediate active assignment in the field. Through the influence of James A. Garfield, a boyhood friend from Hiram, Ohio, he was appointed colonel in command of the newly organized Forty-first Ohio Volunteer Regiment. Garfield, originally designated to command the regiment, accepted instead a commission in the Forty-second Ohio unit.[2]

A talented organizer, Hazen began assiduously training his young volunteers. With firm discipline, unflagging instruction and drill, he quickly transformed the green civilians into a model regiment and reported the Forty-first Ohio ready for duty at Gallipolis, Ohio, November 16, 1861.[3]

In late November his regiment joined the Army of the Ohio organizing at Louisville, Kentucky, under General Don Carlos Buell. Hazen was appointed commander of the Nineteenth Brigade in General William Nelson's division on January 7, 1862, his brigade consisting of four volunteer infantry regiments—the Forty-first Ohio, Sixth Kentucky, Forty-sixth Indiana, and Forty-seventh Indiana. Before seeing any action the latter two units were replaced by the Ninth Indiana and the Sixth Ohio regiments.[4]

Buell's army left Louisville in February to participate in the major operations opening in the West. Forts Henry and Donelson had fallen into Union hands, and the Confederate forces were in full retreat by the time he reached Paducah. The Army of the Ohio occupied rebel-evacuated Nashville on February 25.[5]

With the collapse of the Kentucky front and the loss of Nashville, the Confederates formed a new defense line farther south. General Albert Sidney Johnston, commander in the West, designated Corinth, Mississippi, as the concentration point for the scattered Southern troops, and by the end of March had laid the ground for a powerful effort to regain everything that had been lost. The result of this effort was Shiloh, one of the most bitterly contested battles of the war.[6]

Seeking to consolidate his victories at Forts Henry and Donelson, Ulysses S. Grant moved the Army of the Tennessee to Pittsburg Landing on the Tennessee River's west bank and awaited the arrival of Buell's army from Nashville. The two armies were to move in concert against Corinth under the supreme command of General Henry W. Halleck.

Johnston, realizing that he must act quickly and strike Grant's army before Buell's large force arrived, started his Confederate army north from Corinth on April 3 and encamped only two miles from the unsuspecting Union troops the night of the fifth. Neither Grant nor his trusted divisional commander, William T. Sherman, anticipated an attack. They saw no reason for Buell to hasten his movement to the Tennessee, advising him on April 3 to "come on by easy marches."[7]

Colonel Hazen's brigade was in the vanguard division of the Army of the Ohio as it proceeded from Nashville. General Nelson pushed the division forward steadily, disregarding Grant's dispatch, and about noon on April 5 encamped one mile from Grant's Savannah headquarters nine miles below Pittsburg Landing. The advance command, assuming "no need of haste," did not report to Grant until

seven o'clock the following morning—several hours after Johnston
had launched his surprise attack.

The Confederate assault caught Grant completely off guard. Although encamped at Pittsburg Landing for three weeks, he had arranged "no line or order of battle, no defensive works of any sort, no
outposts, properly speaking, to give warning, or check the advance of
an enemy, and no recognized head during the absence of the regular
commander."[8] By day's end the Union forces, fighting in hapless
confusion, were close to defeat. In late afternoon Nelson's troops
crossed the Tennessee River, bringing desperately needed reinforcements, but a shortage of boats prevented Hazen's brigade from ferry-
ing the river until sundown. They formed in line of battle just as the
day's fighting halted.[9]

The night of April 6–7 saw three divisions of Buell's army, some
twenty thousand men, cross the river. Arrival of Lew Wallace's "missing" division increased the fresh troops to twenty-five thousand, and
Grant was able to take the initiative on the morning of the seventh
with overwhelming superiority of forces. The Confederates were
further handicapped by the loss of Johnston, who was killed the afternoon of the sixth.

In the second day's battle, Hazen's brigade formed the right wing
of Nelson's division. In his first action, Hazen made a diagonal
charge to the right, across the front, driving the Rebels in his front
back beyond their second battery, but in the process his brigade sustained heavy losses. Hazen's force was suddenly attacked in flank
and lost its formation while advancing into a thickly wooded area.
Under relentless shrapnel fire, his decimated brigade broke into dis-
orderly retreat. In the confusion of the tangled underbrush, Hazen
lost contact with his men and for several hours "went in circles"
searching for his "lost" brigade; he was reunited with his command
only after the enemy had been driven from the field.[10]

The roles of prominent officers on both sides of the slaughter at
Shiloh[11] have caused endless controversy and acrimonious debate;
Hazen's conduct did not escape these post bellum analyses. David S.
Stanley later accused him of cowardice, of deserting his men under
fire, and of issuing reports deliberately distorting his role in the Battle
of Shiloh.[12] In the manner of Hazen's retreat, the official records

reveal nothing necessarily impeaching his courage. He may have erred in allowing his men to make a long, rapid charge through dense woods without occasional halts to regroup; disordered and far ahead of the other troops, they apparently came upon a large force and were easily routed. His separation from his men, though embarrassing, was not judged an act of desertion or cowardice. On the contrary, official reports of his superiors have nothing but praise for Hazen's conduct at Shiloh. Reporting that more than half of his division's losses occurred in the Nineteenth Brigade, Nelson said of Hazen: "The gallantry with which he led his troops to the attack was most conspicuous, and he handled them ably."[13] Buell considered Hazen's contribution to the Union victory worthy of special recognition and recommended him for promotion to brigadier general of volunteers.

Hazen was well satisfied with his command's performance in its "baptism of fire." "They went into the fight with an impetuousness I never saw equaled afterward," he later observed. However, his brigade sustained heavy losses—one-third of its members killed or wounded—and as a memorial to his dead, Hazen erected a monument near the site on the Shiloh battlefield where they fell.[14]

Following the capture of Corinth in late May, the Army of the Ohio was entrusted with operations in central and eastern Tennessee. Inactive because of malaria from May 25 to July 4, Hazen rejoined the army at Athens, Alabama, and participated in the movements against Braxton Bragg at Murfreesboro, Louisville, and Perryville. In October, when Buell abandoned his pursuit of Bragg, Hazen retired with the army to Nashville. William S. Rosecrans succeeded Buell as commander of the Army of the Ohio.[15]

As 1862 drew to a close, Rosecrans moved his troops, now called the Army of the Cumberland, southward to attack Bragg below Nashville. On the night of December 30 the opposing armies bivouacked within cannon shot of each other in a three-mile line on opposite sides of Stone's River near Murfreesboro. Rosecrans positioned Thomas L. Crittenden on the left, resting on Stone's River, George H. Thomas in the center, and A. McD. McCook on the right. The Union had about forty-one thousand effectives, the Confederates, about thirty-four thousand. Hazen's brigade, now formed in John M. Palmer's division and Crittenden's corps, was posted in a cotton field with his left resting on the Nashville Pike. His command, numbering thirteen hundred men, was consolidated into four regiments: the Sixth Kentucky, Forty-first Ohio, Ninth Indiana, and One Hundred Tenth Illinois.[16]

Striking first on the morning of the thirty-first, four Confederate brigades under Patrick R. Cleburne surprised McCook's extreme right with a furious charge, while divisions of Benjamin F. Cheatham and John McCown struck near the center. The Union skirmishers were driven back upon their lines at both points. McCown, swinging right, overcame two brigades holding the first line, captured most of their artillery, and swept them from the field. With equal vigor the Confederates struck McCook's left flank, composed of the divisions of Philip H. Sheridan and J. C. Davis, and after a sustained, bloody struggle these divisions were forced back upon James Negley and Lovell Rousseau of Thomas' command on the left of the Wilkinson Pike. Every brigade commander in Sheridan's command was killed or wounded in the desperate effort to stem the Confederate offensive.[17]

At 8:30 A.M., meanwhile, Palmer had made his move, ordering Hazen to seize the commanding positions in his front. His troops had advanced only about twenty yards when Palmer realized that the right side of the Union line was being forced to the rear of his own division. He then ordered his men to face the rear and prepare for the Confederate onslaught. As two lines of gray-clad troops charged them, Hazen's right regiments moved into a nearby skirt of woods. His two left regiments seized the crest of a low-wooded hill in front of a little-timbered area known as Round Forest, a protective eminence abandoned by Thomas J. Wood's division earlier when ordered to support the Union's collapsing right line. Hazen's brigade was then the extreme left of Rosecrans' army.[18]

As action in this section intensified, Negley gave way, and Palmer was exposed and fiercely assailed on his front and right flank. His right brigade was forced back, exposing Hazen's flank; the latter at first had only one regiment to protect the area, but two reserve battalions soon came to his assistance. Crittenden saw that Hazen's position must be held at all costs, as it was the only section of the line not yet weakened. Rosecrans' entire right and center line had been driven back to the Nashville Pike by noon, with nearly one-third of his army broken up and with heavy losses in captured guns, wagons, and ammunition.

Rosecrans sought frantically to rally his troops and form a new line just west of the Nashville Pike. To gain the time needed to accomplish this formation, it was essential that Colonel Hazen's grip on Round Forest be maintained. Sensing a tremendous victory, the Confederates attacked Hazen in double lines—in front, in rear, on flanks—attempting desperately to demolish his force. At the cost of one-third of his brigade, he beat back the foe time after time, receiving valuable assistance from the rest of Palmer's division in late afternoon. In the furious struggle, one Confederate regiment, urged on by the bishop-general, Leonidas Polk, lost 207 of 402 men; surpassing even this rate of carnage, another regiment persisted till it had lost 306 of its men. Despite these odds, the outnumbered Union troops held, giving Rosecrans sufficient time to rally his reeling army.[19]

The Comte de Paris in his history of the Civil War stated: "Fortunately for the Federals, this important point was confided to one of those indomitable, strong-minded men who can conquer adverse fortune by their courage. The Union army, once saved by Sheridan, was saved a second time by General Hazen." Benson J. Lossing declared:

To Hazen's brigade is freely given the honor of saving the day, and perhaps the Army of Cumberland. Thirteen hundred men, skillfully handled, had kept thousands at bay, by repelling them time after time, and stayed the tide of victory for the Confederates, which had been rolling steadily for hours.[20]

The Battle of Stone's River, ending January 3, 1863, produced on neither side a result commensurate with the cost. During the four-day engagement Bragg lost 1,294 killed and 7,945 wounded; Rosecrans 1,677 killed and 7,543 wounded. Since the battle resulted in Bragg's evacuation of Murfreesboro and his retirement from middle Tennessee, it has been claimed as a Union victory.[21]

For his part in this action, Hazen was promoted to the rank of brigadier general of volunteers. His valiant stand also brought him wide national recognition, for the early published accounts of the battle mentioned his name prominently.[22]

At the site where his thin brigade so doggedly held the Confederates at bay, Hazen staked out a cemetery lot for the graves of sixtynine men of his command who died in the engagement. At its center, enclosed by a stone wall, he erected a limestone monument to the "sacrifice and glory" of his men. Ten feet square at its base and about ten feet tall, the monument bore the inscription, "Hazen's Brigade. To the memory of its soldiers who fell at Stone River, December 31st, 1862. Their faces toward Heaven, their feet to the foe."[23] An unusual procedure, this elaborate landmark was regarded by some as an inappropriate arrogation of the honors of the battle. Both its location and its claims to special distinction were subsequently criticized by Hazen's detractors.

In June, 1863, Rosecrans pointed his army toward Chattanooga, gateway to the East. The maneuver against Chattanooga called for the major part of the army to cross the Tennessee River below Bridgeport. As a decoy, four brigades numbering between six and seven thousand men were to be detached about ten miles north of Chattanooga to convince Bragg that the crossing would be attempted there.[24] Brigades headed by Hazen, George Wagner, John Wilder, and Robert Minty were selected for this operation, with Hazen in command.[25]

By late August Hazen had strategically positioned his men along the Tennessee River to carry out their assignment. According to his account "troops were made to appear simultaneously at three or four different crossings; and by ingeniously arranging campfires and beating calls, and by the dexterous use of artillery, they contrived to represent a division of troops at each place." The ruse proved highly successful. Bragg's system of scouts was inefficient; he was perplexed by the appearance of Rosecrans' various units in different places and bewildered by "the popping out of the rats from so many holes." By September 9, Bragg had been maneuvered out of Chattanooga, and Rosecrans crossed the river at Bridgeport to occupy the town without a battle.[26]

Hazen rejoined Palmer's division northeast of Chattanooga, and on September 19–20 fought in the Battle of Chickamauga. During the first day's clash, he was sent to take charge of four Confederate batteries, containing twenty guns, left on the Rossville road without guards. As he reached the position, enemy forces threatened to drive the Union divisions on the left back beyond the road. Quickly putting the guns into position, and with available infantry support, Hazen bombarded the Grays at short range as they dashed into the road in pursuit of the reeling Union troops. That slaughterhouse technique caused them to recoil in disorder, momentarily saving the day on the left.[27]

Hazen's troops suffered five hundred casualties in that bloody encounter. In the end the sacrifice was to no avail. On the twentieth, James Longstreet, coming from the East to reinforce Bragg, broke through Rosecrans' weak right and drove the corps of Crittenden and McCook off the field. A large part of Rosecrans' army was swept into the retreating current and ordered to Chattanooga. George H. Thomas, outnumbered and unaware of the debacle on the Union right, stood firm against severe assaults. Hazen, asking and receiving Palmer's permission to aid Thomas, formed his brigade in a corn field and helped the "Rock of Chickamauga" repel the Confederate attack and save the Army of the Cumberland from complete disaster. Nevertheless, the entire army, amid loud Confederate cheers, was forced to withdraw to Chattanooga.[28]

According to Hazen, the Union reversal at Chickamauga resulted primarily from "the lack of steady and systematic direction in placing and maneuvering the different parts of the army." That there were "grave errors" by Rosecrans and his subordinates seemed to him "almost beyond question." It was only due to "equally great mistakes" by Bragg that the Union forces escaped total destruction.[29] As it was, the Federals lost 1,600 killed and about 15,000 more in wounded or missing. The victory cost the Confederates 2,300 in deaths and nearly 18,000 total casualties. For "gallant and meritorious service in the Battle of Chickamauga, Georgia," Hazen on September 20, 1863, was breveted major in the regular army.[30]

The Army of the Cumberland was virtually besieged in Chattanooga. Rosecrans, appearing unable to shake the traumatic effects of Chickamauga, was superseded in command by George H. Thomas; Crittenden, McCook, Negley, and Horatio Van Cleve were likewise relieved, and Grant was given supreme command of operations in the West. The changes in military command caused Hazen's morale to rise "with a great bound," although he had high personal regard for his corps commander, Crittenden. The "interests of the service," he wrote, "and the welfare of the country imperatively demanded the removals that were made . . . for the disaster at Chickamauga, added to previous ill fortune, had destroyed necessary confidence."[31]

Grant's first concern was to relieve the army at Chattanooga of its beleaguered condition and open up a supply line. Bragg had the great advantage of commanding the railroads, of occupying the main heights facing the city—Missionary Ridge and Lookout Mountain— and of holding extended positions blocking Union navigation of the Tennessee. In lieu of opened supply lines, Thomas faced the momentary choice of evacuation or starvation; an ingenious plan, however, soon unfolded and solved the problem.

General William Farrar Smith, chief engineer of the Army of the Cumberland, contrived a plan for opening the supply line via Bridgeport by laying a pontoon bridge at Brown's Ferry. His scheme entailed building pontoons in Chattanooga, floating them downstream to the ferry, and getting a force past the Confederate pickets to construct and hold the bridge. After elaborate preparations, the operation commenced at three in the morning of October 27 under the general command of Smith. Thirteen hundred men commanded by Hazen embarked in fifty boats and headed down the Tennessee, past Lookout Mountain, and on to Brown's Ferry, a distance of about nine miles. At the same time, a force of 3,700 men, with three batteries of artillery, marched overland to cover the landing of the boats.[32]

The darkness of the night and a slight fog hid the boats from the pickets positioned along the river. The oars were used only to maintain proper position in the current, and great care was taken to move silently. Landing successfully on the south bank at Brown's Ferry, Hazen's troops completely overwhelmed the enemy's surprised picket. The columns sent by land quickly ferried the river in the same boats used by Hazen and took up positions covering the ferry. Joseph Hooker moved up with his two corps to assure control of the location. The carefully executed plan was a complete success; the army subsistence problem had been solved.[33]

Thomas declared that "the seizure of Brown's Ferry and the splendid defense of Lookout Valley by General Hooker's command decided the question of our ability to hold Chattanooga." The entire venture, he reported, "reflected great credit on all concerned."[34] As a result of his part in the operation, Hazen was breveted a lieutenant colonel.

With the supply problem solved, Grant moved to consolidate his forces for a new campaign against Bragg. The clash came in the three-day battle of Lookout Mountain–Missionary Ridge, November 23–25, 1863. The left side of the Union line, under Sherman, attacked the Confederates at the north end of Missionary Ridge east of Chattanooga. Hooker, formed on the extreme right near Lookout Mountain, overcame great resistance in the "battle above the clouds" and carried that mountain position. Hazen, as part of Thomas' army in the center, engaged the enemy's picket reserves at Orchard Knob. In a furious encounter, in which 125 of his brigade were killed or wounded, Hazen captured nearly the entire Twenty-eighth Alabama Infantry with their colors.[35]

Despite Sherman's persistent efforts, Bragg still held firm control of Missionary Ridge at midafternoon of November 25. Seeking to relieve pressure on Sherman, Thomas ordered the divisions of Wood and Sheridan to take the enemy's rifle pits at the foot of the ridge. Hazen's brigade, as they led the charge in the vanguard of Thomas Wood's division, felt the brunt of an "appalling fire" of some fifty pieces of Confederate artillery. The works were successfully carried by the two divisions, but instead of taking cover behind them as the orders stipulated, the men pushed on up the ridge. This spontaneous and impulsive action is described as follows by Hazen:

. . . receiving the order to move forward and take the enemy's line of works at the foot of Mission Ridge we did so. . . . The ridge was so high as to render their [the Confederates'] artillery comparatively harmless, but gave deadly effect to their musketry upon our men seeking shelter behind their works at the foot of the ridge. Many of the men sought protection in the curvature of the hill, and so many went forward for this purpose, that I gave the command to my whole line to move forward. General Willich's troops, the only ones as far

advanced as mine, moved forward at the same time. The necessity
of taking advantage of ravines, cuts, and depressions in the ground for
cover, made it out of the question to keep up lines. But the men moved
forward always preceded by their colors, in large groups. These colors
were frequently shot down, that of the First Ohio, five times, but the
men never stopped, and soon reached the top of the ridge, capturing
about 200 prisoners behind the works, the remainder fleeing.[36]

Hazen states that after reaching the crest he took command of about
four hundred men and cleared the front of Sheridan, who was still
"not more than half-way up the hill." In the action on the ridge his
troops captured eighteen pieces of artillery, two of which were later
relinquished to August Willich's command. The brigade's casualties
in the three-day operation, dramatically terminating atop Missionary
Ridge, totaled 529, including 93 killed.[37]

After the battle of Missionary Ridge, a lively controversy was
initiated over the question of whether Hazen's brigade in Wood's
division or members of Sheridan's division had reached the crest of
the hill first. Sheridan alleged in his report that his men deserved the
honor. Furthermore he charged that "General Hazen and his brigade
employed themselves in collecting the artillery from which my men
had driven the enemy, and have claimed it their capture." He asserted that eleven cannons rightfully prizes of his division had been
"gleaned" by Hazen's men in rear of his advance.[38] Sheridan's charge
was based on information received from his subordinates; however,
official evidence seems to refute his claims to priority. Hazen certainly presents a strong array of evidence supporting the assertion that
his brigade reached the summit some minutes in advance of Sheridan's vanguard troops.[39]

On learning of the "misunderstanding" that had developed over the
captured artillery, Hazen wrote Sheridan, inviting him to produce
"any facts you may have in the matter, so that in case you are correct
it can be rectified." In response, Sheridan came to Hazen's quarters
"and insisted rather imperiously upon an unquestioning giving up of
the guns." Hazen refused.[40]

Sheridan's side of the argument is stated in his memoirs:

*... at the time the occurrance took place, I made the charge in a plain
official report, which was accepted as correct by the corps and army
commanders, from General Granger up to General Grant. General
Hazen took no notice of this report then, though well aware of its
existence. . . . He endeavored to justify his retention of the guns by
trying to show that his brigade was the first to reach the crest of
Missionary Ridge, and that he was therefore entitled to them. This
claim . . . is made by other brigades than Hazen's, with equal if not
greater force, so the absurdity of his deduction is apparent.*[41]

Less apparent to Sheridan, noted one of his biographers, was the
fact that "if all the artillery claimed by his brigade and regimental
commanders had actually been captured, the enemy armies would
hardly have been able to raise a battery for the balance of the war."[42]
This unfortunate incident led to lasting animosity between the two
men and had some interesting overtones in Hazen's subsequent
career.

On November 28 the Fourth Corps left Chattanooga for east Tennessee to engage in the campaign against the able Confederate commander James Longstreet. Supply problems, generally futile ma-
neuvers, and a run-in with General Gordon Granger made the winter
of 1863–64 a frustrating period for Hazen.

The altercation with his corps commander occurred in a staff meeting at Dandridge in January, 1864. Granger, possibly suffering from
fatigue and tension, impetuously called on Hazen for a report of conditions on his front. Irritated by his tone of voice—addressing him
"as a pedagogue might do with a class of derelict children"—Hazen
declined to report until due courtesy was extended him. Apparently
encouraged by Sheridan, Granger placed Hazen under temporary
arrest. Fortunately tempers cooled almost as rapidly as they had
flared; aided by the mediation of a mutual friend, General Jacob D.
Cox, the misunderstanding was amicably settled.[43]

On May 3, Hazen's troops joined Sherman's army as it launched
the important campaign resulting in the capture of Atlanta on September 2. Defending the gateway to the lower South was the outstanding southern general, Joseph E. Johnston. The road to Atlanta was
marked by a series of severe battles. At Resacca, on May 16, Hazen

lost about one hundred men as part of an untimely postmidnight venture against an enemy line. His command also engaged in sharp skirmishes at Adairsville and Cassville on the seventeenth and nineteenth respectively. At Pickett's Mills on May 27, the brigade experienced its worst defeat of the war, suffering over five hundred casualties in an unsuccessful advance against the right flank of Patrick Cleburne's division. Hazen was also engaged at Kenesaw Mountain (June 27), Chattahoochee (July 17), and Peach Tree Creek (July 20). J. B. Hood, having superseded Johnston on July 17, suffered the loss at Peach Tree Creek and withdrew to the defensive line outside Atlanta.[44]

On August 17, as Sherman was closing the ring around Atlanta, Hazen was named commander of the Second Division in the Fifteenth Corps of the Army of the Tennessee. This promotion resulted from the consistent courage and leadership the young officer displayed while a brigade leader in a long list of severe battles. This appointment made Hazen one of the youngest top commanders in the Army of the Tennessee.

Nevertheless, it was with mixed feelings that he left the brigade he had trained and led the previous thirty-two months. Commencing with Shiloh, 2,763 men of his command had been killed or wounded in action, signifying a bloody history of involvement; this represented about 200 per cent of his brigade's average strength, an exceptionally high figure. Hazen had nothing but praise for the Nineteenth Brigade, stating later in retrospect: "They were magnificent material . . . no troops ever behaved better. Those Western boys preferred to stay in the army rather than go home."[45]

Upon assuming command of the Second Division, Hazen discovered a "deplorable" lack of discipline and organization. A series of orders realigning administrative procedures and strict enforcement of neglected military regulations was needed to bring the units up to his high standards. Especially irritating was the "vicious and almost mutinous habit, if rations were late, of calling out 'hard-tack' and 'sow-belly' to general officers—or making other disrespectful demonstrations." Hazen moved effectively and with dispatch to end this type of behavior.[46]

Hazen led his division into action on August 27, skirmishing with the Confederate cavalry at Jonesboro near Atlanta. He seized a strategic height overlooking the Macon Railroad outside Jonesboro on the thirtieth and, formed in line at this position, helped repulse the futile efforts of two enemy corps to dislodge Sherman's divisions. Fourteen hundred Confederates were killed and wounded in the Jonesboro battle, most of the casualties occurring in S. D. Lee's corps. Hazen lost fourteen killed and sixty-eight wounded in dueling Lee, but his division had displayed great valor under severe assault. Inside its picket lines lay 211 Rebel bodies; 178 prisoners and over 1,000 stands of small arms were captured as well.[47]

This victory did much to establish Hazen's reputation in the Army of the Tennessee. "Nothing could have been more admirable than the marching and fighting of the Second Division," he wrote. "The whole Army of the Tennessee recognized it, and warmed toward me; and I found myself, from Jonesboro on, standing solidly in my shoes."[48]

Atlanta was evacuated by Hood's tired and demoralized army on September 1 and occupied by Sherman the following day. Although this key city had been taken, Hood's army of about forty thousand was still basically intact and thus posed a serious threat to Sherman's plans to move farther south. Hood hoped to draw Sherman away from Atlanta, succeeding for a time. Beginning in late September, Sherman pursued Hood through northern Georgia and Alabama for a month without catching him. The Army of the Tennessee, including Hazen's division, marched several hundred miles in this futile operation without fighting a major engagement. At the end of October, Sherman assigned Thomas the task of watching Hood and assembled the rest of his command at Atlanta preparatory to the "march to the sea." General O. O. Howard, commander of the Army of the Tennessee, directed the right wing of these troops, General H. W. Slocum, the left. Hazen's division, numbering an effective strength of 4,426 officers and men, was posted on the extreme right flank of Howard's wing. Each wing had approximately twenty-seven thousand men, and the cavalry brought the total force to about sixty thousand.[49]

The famous march began on November 15, the army advancing by four parallel roads. Meeting little or no opposition the uninhibited

Union troops cut a wide swath of destruction across central Georgia. Factories, cotton gins, warehouses, railroads, bridges, and any other materials susceptible to warlike use were systematically destroyed. Sherman ordered his soldiers to "forage liberally on the country," but abusive conduct and trespassing were to be avoided. Once out of Atlanta, however, wild looting and wanton destruction occurred.

William Hazen had no use for ruthless plundering and did his best to prevent the worst abuses in his division. On December 3, 1864, at Lot's Creek, Georgia, he issued the following order:

The foraging parties will be sent to these headquarters for inspection this evening, and receive tickets from the provost-marshal. Any person hereafter foraging without these tickets will be punished.

The attention of the entire command is called to the fact that all property taken in an enemy's country belongs to the Government; and any appropriation of it except by prescribed methods, or by trading and receiving pecuniary consideration for it, is an act of felony, and shall be punished as such.[50]

The efforts of Hazen and other officers did not control the excesses of the men, however.

Not until Sherman neared Savannah were the Confederates able to offer opposition "worth speaking of." Swamps and marshes about Savannah enabled William J. Hardee's comparatively small army to control all access routes. Rather than "assault an enemy of unknown strength at such a disadvantage," Sherman decided to cut off its supply lines and thereby "surely attain the same result by the operations of time." Meanwhile he tried to communicate with Union supply ships scheduled to meet him somewhere on the Georgia coast. Failure to contact the fleet would have made his supply problem in the marshy barrens critical. On December 9, three men from General Howard's command were sent to contact the fleet by way of the Ogeechee River, which enters the Atlantic some distance below Savannah. They discovered the fleet waiting off the coast and informed the naval officers of Sherman's location.

With Savannah still in Confederate hands, the only way supplies could be transported to the army was via the Ogeechee. The mouth of that river was well guarded by Fort McAllister, situated on the right bank where the stream entered Ossabaw Sound fifteen miles below Savannah. Capturing the fort was thus the first requirement. Upon General Howard's recommendation, Sherman designated Hazen's Second Division "to proceed against Fort McAllister and take it." Sherman told Hazen to "go about taking the fort in his own way," jokingly warning him not to "get behind any creek you can't get across," a standard excuse for failures on a mission.[51]

Hazen's operation began early December 13. A strong enclosed redoubt, Fort McAllister was manned by about two hundred men and mounted 23 guns and a mortar. The Confederates had planted land mines and had covered the surrounding area with ditches, abatis, palisades, and other defensive works, making Hazen's approach hazardous. A captured picket was forced to point out the torpedoes so that Hazen could safely deploy his troops. His main force formed an arc just beyond musket range of the fort, his left flank resting on the Ogeechee. Two regiments of sharpshooters were in the woods close enough to drive the fort's defenders into their "bomb proofs." At 5:00 P.M. Hazen's careful preparations were complete, and the attack was launched.[52] Sherman and his aide-de-camp, Brevet Major George Ward Nichols, watched the exciting assault from an excellent observation point on a rice mill. Nichols described the scene in his diary:

The sun was now fast going down behind a grove of water-oaks and as his last rays gilded the earth, all eyes once more turned toward the Rebel fort. Suddenly white puffs of smoke shot out from the thick woods surrounding the line of works. Hazen was closing in, ready for the final rush of his column directly upon the fort. A warning answer came from the enemy in the roar of heavy artillery—and so the battle opened. General Sherman walked nervously to and fro, turning quickly now and then from viewing the scene of conflict to observe the sun sinking slowly behind the tree-tops. No longer willing to bear the suspense, he said: "Signal General Hazen that he must carry the fort by assault, tonight if possible."

The little flag waved and fluttered in the evening air, and the answer came:

"I am ready, and will assault at once!"

The words had hardly passed when from out the encircling woods there came a long line of blue coats and bright bayonets, and the dear old flag was there, waving proudly in the breeze. Then the fort seemed alive with flame; quick, thick jets of fire shooting out from all its sides, while the white smoke first covered the place and then rolled away over the glacis. The line of blue moved steadily on; too slowly, as it seemed to us, for we exclaimed, "Why don't they dash forward?" but their measured step was unfaltering. Now the flag goes down, but the line does not halt. A moment longer and the banner gleams again in the front. We, the lookers-on, clutched one another's arms convulsively, and scarcely breathed in eager intensity of our gaze. Sherman stood watching with anxious air, awaiting the decisive moment. Then the enemy's fire redoubled in rapidity and violence. The darting streams of fire alone told the position of the fort. The line of blue entered the enshrouding folds of smoke. The flag was at last dimly seen, and then it went out of sight altogether.

"They have been repulsed!" said one of the group of officers who watched the fight.

"No, by Heaven!" said another; "there is not a man in retreat— not a straggler in all the glorious line!"

The firing ceased. The wind lifted the smoke. Crowds of men were visible on the parapets, fiercely fighting—but our flag was planted there. There were a few scattering musketshots, and then the sounds of battle ceased. Then the bomb-proofs and parapets were alive with crowding swarms of our gallant men, who fired their pieces in the air as a feu de joie. Victory! The fort was won. Then all of us who had witnessed the strife and exulted in the triumph, grasped each the other's hand, embraced, and were glad, and some of us found the water in our eyes.[53]

A few hours after the victory, Sherman had dinner with Hazen and congratulated him on the "handsome manner" in which he had accomplished his assignment. Hazen obviously had made his mark with Sherman; a lasting friendly relationship was the result. The Second Division's losses were about 24 killed and 110 wounded, buried torpedoes being responsible for nearly all casualties.[54]

Storming Fort McAllister was the only engagement of the war commanded exclusively by Hazen. From a tactical military standpoint, his services in a subordinate role at Stone's River overshadowed it, but his capture of the fort was of immediate importance, as supply ships could enter the river and deliver needed provisions and clothing to Sherman's large army. These enabled Sherman to occupy Savannah without a shot December 21 and offer President Lincoln the city as a Christmas present. The dramatic seizure of Fort McAllister and the occupation of Savannah capped Sherman's triumphant Georgia invasion. In the words of Nichols, "The victory of Fort McAllister, and the way it was done, is a grand ending to this most adventurous campaign. . . . Our soldiers are electrified by the brilliant episode just enacted, and are eager to go wherever the General [Sherman] directs."[55]

On December 13, 1864, in recognition of "long and faithful service of the highest character, and for gallant service in the capture of Fort McAllister," Hazen was appointed a major general of volunteers. Secretary of War Edwin Stanton personally presented the commission to him on his visit to Savannah. Nichols characterized the qualities that distinguished the thirty-four-year-old Hazen in 1864 and won for him this latest military recognition:

. . . he has a fine, open, manly face; resolute withal, but that kind of resolution which does not seem to need constant assertion. You are impressed with it at the first glance, and rest there, always after with confidence. His manner is that of an accomplished and refined gentleman. On the field of battle he is alert, self-assured, concentrated, brave, and capable. . . . He will never fail when the honor of the nation demands his presence in the front of the battle.[56]

After a month in Savannah, Sherman's corps fanned northward through South Carolina, wreaking even greater destruction than in Georgia.

. . . no sooner had we passed Pocotaligo [wrote Hazen] than the demon of destruction seized possession of everybody. South Carolina

had fired the first gun, and even the smallest drummerboy seemed determined to get even. . . . Here began a carnival of destruction that ended with the burning of Columbia, in which the frenzy seemed to exhaust itself. There was scarcely a building far or near on the line of that march that was not burned. Often have I seen this work going on in the presence of the highest officers, with no word of disapproval.[57]

Hazen did not approve such destruction, but his most diligent efforts to control it proved hopeless. He tried his best to preserve the beautiful home of a relative of Dr. R. L. Brodie, the physician who had attended him in Texas after his nearly fatal encounter with the Indians, but to no avail.[58]

The worst destruction of the Carolina campaign was by the disastrous fire which swept a large part of Columbia. The Army of the Tennessee entered the capital city February 17, and the Confederates under General Wade Hampton beat a hasty retreat. Upon arrival, Hazen noticed considerable cotton scattered in the streets and hanging from fences and trees; some of it was burning, but not extensively enough to create a major hazard. Soon, many of the soldiers detailed to occupy Columbia were helping themselves to "bucketfuls" of liquor from various sources. Unbounded revelry and pillage followed despite attempts of some officers to control the situation. During the afternoon a high wind sprang up, and by nightfall fires broke out in several buildings.

Hazen dined in Sherman's quarters the night of the great fire. After dinner the two went outdoors and noticed the "lurid hue of a conflagration" reflected on the night sky. With a tone of regret Sherman remarked, "They have brought it on themselves." Hazen did not believe this comment implied that Sherman had either plotted or necessarily condoned Columbia's destruction, and his statements on this tragedy do not support the accusations by some that Sherman ordered the city burned. But Hazen did disagree with Sherman's later assertion in his memoirs that the fire was accidental, begun by Confederates setting cotton on fire before leaving the city.[59] Based on personal surveillance in the afternoon and night of February 17, Hazen explained the burning thus:

I have never doubted that Columbia was deliberately set on fire [by Union soldiers] in more than a hundred places. No one ordered it, and no one could stop it. The officers of high rank would have saved the city if possible; but the army was deeply imbued with the feeling that as South Carolina had begun the war she must suffer a stern retribution.[60]

From Columbia, Howard's right wing marched northward to Winnsboro, and then turned eastward across the rain swollen Catawba, Lynch, and Pee Dee rivers, arriving in Fayetteville, North Carolina, by March 10. Sherman planned to take Goldsboro and there join forces with General John M. Schofield, advancing inland from New Bern.

Robert E. Lee had meanwhile reinstated Joseph E. Johnston, assigning him the task of stopping Sherman's advance through the Carolinas. The Confederate commander assembled some thirty to forty thousand men and on March 19 attacked Henry Slocum's isolated left wing at Bentonville. Slocum was in serious trouble until right wing reinforcements turned the tide. A part of Hazen's division made an all-night march to Bentonville, becoming engaged at dawn on the twentieth. The smaller Confederate force was driven back, permitting Sherman on March 21 to take Goldsboro with its important railroad connections. The Battle of Bentonville was the last major engagement of the war for Sherman's army and for Hazen.[61]

The war's end was imminent. News of the fall of Richmond arrived April 6, and four days later the army moved to avert a union of Lee and Johnston forces. On April 12, news of Lee's surrender reached Hazen's division as it approached Raleigh, and within a week Johnston and Sherman were negotiating surrender terms.[62]

The Army of the Tennessee left for Washington on April 28, 1865, to participate in the grand review of the triumphant Union armies. Some important changes in command occurred en route. Howard, selected to head the Freedmen's Bureau, was succeeded as commander of the Army of the Tennessee by John A. Logan. Hazen replaced Logan as commander of the Fifteenth Corps on May 19, and thus, five days later, marched at the head of a corps in the famed Army of the Tennessee as it tramped in review along Pennsylvania Avenue.

Disbandment of the military forces proceeded rapidly after that display. Hazen's corps was sent to Louisville, Kentucky, and mustered out in July of 1865. He assumed command of the District of Middle Tennessee after a welcome thirty-day leave and remained in that duty until reorganization of the regular army resulted in his reassignment to the West.[63]

At the beginning of the Civil War Hazen was an experienced but comparatively unknown Indian fighter with the rank of lieutenant; at its close he was a major general in command of an army corps. The official record of his career from Shiloh to Bentonville abundantly reveals intelligence, zeal, and courage. General Oliver O. Howard judged Hazen "one of the best and most efficient officers I have ever known," and Sherman considered him "an officer of the highest professional attainments."[64] His most significant contribution and greatest demonstration of valor undoubtedly occurred at Stone's River. As late as 1885 the renowned General Joseph E. Johnston maintained that, except for Hazen, the Confederates clearly would have won that battle.[65] He also rendered solid service at Shiloh, Chickamauga, Atlanta, Jonesboro, and Savannah. According to Hazen's reports, casualties in his commands totaled approximately 170 per cent of their average strength. This high rate of carnage attests to the fact that Hazen's men were in the forefront of many bloody engagements.[66]

Fighting for the Union implied more to Hazen than mere fulfillment of duty as a professional soldier. He abhorred slavery—calling it "an inherent poison"—and considered the South's die-hard adherence to the institution the basic cause of the Civil War. "The egg [of the Rebellion] was laid by the importation of slavery. The incubation had been going on ever since. The age doomed slavery, and war was inevitable."[67]

As Hazen advanced in rank and responsibility during the war, he exhibited some negative personal characteristics. Jacob D. Cox noted that his fellow Ohioan was prone to find fault with the performance of other officers "and apt to dilate upon them in his official reports when such officers were wholly independent of him." His criticism, at times through innuendo, often sought—justifiably or not—to rationalize some failure on the part of his command. His official records and correspondence also revealed an occasional tendency to overstate his claims to fame, a practice, however, not uncommon among Civil War officers. A virtual perfectionist, Hazen became greatly irritated if military matters of even a minute character did not proceed systematically and effectively. Failure and ineffectiveness, he felt, could be generally attributed to negligence or lack of intelligence. When he presumed to see—or actually witnessed—such manifestations, he unhesitatingly pointed the finger of guilt. No doubt the energetic officer frequently pointed in the right direction, but his traits, said Cox, made him "a good many enemies notwithstanding his noble qualities . . . and real ability as an officer." His aggressiveness and outspoken manner, combined with a stubborn adherence to personal convictions, held significant implications for his postwar career.[68]

Hazen's illustrious Civil War record gave him a solid reputation in professional military circles and wide prominence, especially in his home state of Ohio. Thus, when he returned to the West in 1866, he was an officer with considerable stature, and one whose career held promise for further noteworthy achievement.

IV

Inspector General, Department of the Platte

In the summer of 1866, Brevet Major General William B. Hazen returned to the West as acting assistant inspector general of the Department of the Platte. Congress and the military command were at that time reorganizing the army, and Hazen hoped to retain the grade of general officer. Future opportunities for the experienced Indian fighter, including appointment to a command, obviously lay on the Trans-Mississippi West Indian frontier; Hazen thus welcomed the application of General Philip St. George Cooke to have him detailed to his department.[1]

Arriving at Omaha in July, Hazen sought to acquaint himself thoroughly with the country west of the Missouri River. Official information on the region he was to inspect, the "Mountain District" of the Department of the Platte, was sparse. The few available maps revealed little about the territory, and there were no guide books. The vast military department embraced Iowa and Minnesota and the territories of Nebraska, Montana, and portions of Dakota. The newly created "Mountain District" encompassed the Powder River country and was commanded by Colonel Henry B. Carrington.[2] Before 1850, Northern Plains Indian tribes had permitted settlers and gold seekers to cross their lands with only occasional interference, but when the government erected forts and built roads for overland stage routes, the Indians began to retaliate in earnest. Pressures on these Indian lands increased during and after the Civil War. In 1862 the Sioux in western Minnesota went on the warpath against the settlers, inaugurating a new turbulent period in the Indian country to the west. Seeking to intimidate the restive bands, a large military expedition was sent into the Powder River region in 1865 under General Patrick Edward Connor, a show of force which failed to subdue the Indians. Nor was peaceful persuasion more effective; over a fifteen-year period, beginning in 1850, treaties had been made and broken. The most recent, the "lasting peace" of Fort Laramie, had been negotiated in 1866 only a few days prior to Hazen's arrival in Omaha, but few westerners held any hope for its success.[3]

Active campaigns against the Sioux following the Minnesota uprising ushered in military occupation of the upper Missouri area. Fort Sully was established near present-day Pierre, South Dakota, in 1863, and the following year Fort Rice was built about forty miles south of present Bismarck, North Dakota. Troops were likewise garrisoned at the fur trading posts at Fort Union and Fort Berthold, and a number of posts were simultaneously established in eastern Dakota Territory.

Discovery of gold in Montana in the early 1860's, with the stampede into the district, demanded additional movements of troops. To keep the routes to the mining country open, new forts were needed. Approaches to the Montana mines were from the east along the Lewis and Clark Trail up the Missouri and from the south along the Bozeman Trail. The latter left the Overland Trail west of Fort Laramie and angled northwestward into Montana Territory east of the Big Horn Mountains. As it ran directly through their best hunting grounds, the Sioux naturally resented white intrusion. The federal government undertook to protect the miners by constructing a string of military posts north from Fort Laramie. Fort Connor was built on the Powder River 180 miles northwest of Fort Laramie in 1865, but was abandoned during the summer of 1866 in favor of Fort Reno, a new post constructed by Colonel Carrington about a mile farther up the river. Carrington's orders called for erection of two additional forts farther north along the Bozeman route.[4]

General Cooke, the veteran dragoon commander, doubted the necessity of more forts along the Bozeman Trail, claiming that westerners tended to exaggerate threats of Indian hostility. One objective of Hazen's inspection tour was, therefore, to assess accurately the temper of the Indians in the "Mountain District." He was also to ascertain whether the existing military force was adequate to protect the emigrant routes, and whether established forts were properly distributed and functioning effectively.

With preparations completed at Omaha, Hazen left for the troubled land west of the Missouri. He was accompanied by a small detachment of soldiers and a civilian topographer, Ambrose G. Bierce. Bierce, destined to literary fame, had been a topographical officer in Hazen's brigade during the Civil War. He agreed to join the expedition after military authorities rejected Hazen's request for the services of an army topographical engineer. The maps drawn by Bierce of the trip route were included in the final inspection report. Following the Platte Valley, the inspector general proceeded without major incident to Fort Laramie, stopping en route at Forts Kearney, McPherson, and Sedgwick.[5]

North of Laramie lay the "Mountain District" of the Department of the Platte. Near Fort Laramie the Bozeman Trail branched off from the Overland or California Trail, moving northwesterly toward the Montana mines. Though purportedly three hundred to four hundred miles shorter than the Salt Lake and Fort Hall route, this road was made decidedly hazardous by Red Cloud's "folk." Reports circulated at Laramie that emigrant trains moving north were frequently attacked despite the travel-protection clause in the Treaty of Fort Laramie. Freighters and other interests were skeptical of a small military force's ability to protect the road adequately against the many belligerent bands.[6]

Traveling uptrail about 180 miles, Hazen arrived at Fort Reno on August 10. Commanded by Captain Joshua L. Proctor, the post had been occupied since the Laramie council by Companies B and F of Colonel Carrington's Second Battalion of the Eighteenth Infantry.[7]

The visiting inspector soon had occasion to judge the temper of the Indians firsthand. On August 12 a band attacked a civilian train camped near the post, capturing cattle and horses. On the fourteenth two emigrants were killed within four miles of Fort Reno. In other action at the post on the Powder River, Indians stole a herd of mules from the fort's corral. A detachment sent in pursuit of the bold raiders recovered only one broken-down animal and found, to its chagrin,

that it was packed with goods received from treaty commissioners at
Laramie. The wide-scale depredations convinced Hazen that additional troops were needed to protect the trail, and he undoubtedly
influenced the transfer of cavalry units from Fort Laramie to the
Powder River region at this time.[8]

Reporting on conditions at Fort Reno, the meticulous investigator
described the aging Proctor's administration of post affairs as highly
inefficient and strongly berated the post quartermaster for gross neglect of duty.[9]

Preparing to resume his inspection trip, Hazen dispatched the following letter to the commander of Fort Phil Kearny:

August 20, 1866

Col. H. B. Carrington,
  Commanding Mountain District:
*Dear Colonel: I am on my way through the district as assistant in-
spector-general of the department, and will be at your post as soon
as cavalry escort ordered to join me reaches here in about one week.*

  *The mail going up will carry from General Cooke authority for
you to suspend establishing the extreme west post (C. F. Smith) if
you think from the condition of Indian affairs it is expedient. He
telegraphed me at Laramie to consult with you about it, and since
coming within the theater of Indian troubles I am of the opinion that
there is no sufficient reason for longer delaying the establishment of
that post, but, on the contrary, it should be established without further
delay.*

  *I think there is no danger on the route to parties well organized and
that do not straggle, but that the greatest caution will be necessary
both on the route and at the posts till the Indians are thrashed.*

W. B. Hazen
Bvt. Brig. General,
Asst. Inspector,
Dept. of the Platte[10]

Hazen's references to Fort C. F. Smith indicate that he had discre-
tionary power to determine its fate. Washington military officials had
short-sightedly suggested that the fort be abandoned, despite Car-

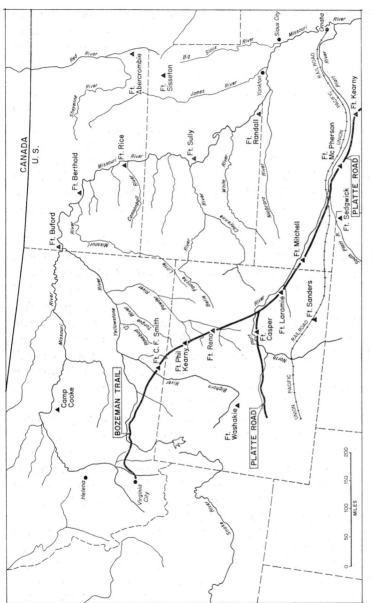

Northern Plains, 1866

rington's advice to the contrary. Hazen realized that abandoning the post would leave the most dangerous part of the trail, the region beyond Phil Kearny, without protection. His strong feelings on the necessity of the fort, seen in his letter to Carrington, seems to have ended the foolish talk of suspending its establishment.

When the cavalry expected from Laramie failed to arrive on schedule, Hazen pushed on to Carrington's headquarters with a mounted escort provided by Proctor. Fort Phil Kearny, about sixty-seven miles northwest of Fort Reno, was situated on the Little Piney fork of the Powder River. Arriving on the twenty-seventh, Hazen spent three days inspecting the partially completed establishment and found that the post was garrisoned by only four companies. He expressed satisfaction with Carrington's progress in erecting what was intended to be a substantial permanent post.[11]

On August 30 Hazen left for Fort C. F. Smith, about ninety miles northwest on the Big Horn River, escorted by a mounted detachment of twenty-six infantrymen under command of Lieutenant James Bradley. This detachment was to accompany Hazen until it reached Fort Benton, with Scout James J. Brannan guiding the party. Fort C. F. Smith, the newly authorized two-company post, was commanded by Lieutenant Colonel Nathaniel C. Kenney; Jim Bridger, who had helped open the fort August 12, served as post scout until recalled to Fort Phil Kearny in November. Although the garrison was under almost constant attacks, Inspector Hazen found it fulfilling its duties with "ability and activity."[12]

From Fort C. F. Smith, Hazen's tour took him about 185 miles northwest to Camp Cooke, at the confluence of the Judith and Missouri rivers; west to Fort Benton, an American Fur Company post forty miles below the Great Falls of the Missouri; south to Virginia City, Montana Territory, at the terminus of the Bozeman Road; and finally to Camp Douglas, Utah Territory, at the base of the Wasatch Range, about three miles east of Salt Lake City.

Having completed his inspection of the "Mountain District and other points," the acting inspector general on October 16 set about summarizing the findings in a formal report. He described the Platte River valley between Omaha and Fort Kearney, a distance of about two hundred miles, as possessing an abundance of "highly productive" farm land. The region west of Fort Kearney, however, he considered almost totally devoid of agricultural potential. "Of this entire country one-half may be considered of no value, the other half, for pastoral purposes, of about one-tenth the value of good grazing land in the northern States." Narrow bands of fertile soil in the valleys of the Sun, Jefferson, Madison, and Gallatin rivers could, he said, be made productive by irrigation, as demonstrated by the Mormon success in the Great Salt Lake basin. But lands susceptible of cultivation by this means were limited. Even in the "better half" of the vast expanse, only "an average of about one acre in one thousand can be made abundantly productive by irrigation and in no other way." Hazen's evaluation of the area supported the "Great American Desert" theme introduced by the explorers Zebulon Pike and Stephen H. Long. These barren lands would never be of much use, Hazen declared, "and can never be sold by government at more than nominal rates. It will in time be settled by a scanty pastoral population. No amount of railroads, schemes of colonization or government encouragement can ever make more of it." He deplored misleading information being circulated about the High Plains region, stating that "every one interested in this country systematically deceives everybody else with regard to it."[13] In the next fifteen years he persistently propagated the theme that the High Plains were unfit for agricultural purposes.

As to posts and the distribution of troops, Hazen recommended establishment of two additional forts in the department—one to be located on the Bozeman Trail near the Big Bend of the Yellowstone; the second on the Sun River, garrisoned by cavalry to protect the road from the mines to Fort Benton. He further recommended that several temporary blockhouses be constructed in the Powder River country to buttress the defense between existing forts. With these additional installations, he wrote, "the route will have all the posts it will be advantageous to establish." No troops were needed in the mining towns, he advised, because "miners are better Indian fighters than soldiers, are numerous and always armed, and organized for defense."

He felt that troops should be distributed on the basis of two companies for each fort and blockhouse, an arrangement "sufficient . . . and in case of active operations the posts could be reduced to thirty men without risk." This seems an overly optimistic outlook in view of the hostilities General Carrington had experienced all summer and was destined to encounter the remainder of the year. Apparently Hazen's recommendation assumed a continuation of the army's defensive policy along lines of communication, and certainly did not anticipate reckless operations such as the one undertaken later in the year by William J. Fetterman.

Hazen believed that the posts on the Upper Missouri served no military purpose and should be abandoned. They were not situated on any roads, gave little protection to river navigation, and "can never become nuclei of colonization from the utter poverty of the country." Location of Camp Cooke, he stated, "is the subject of ridicule with every man I have met in the Territories." It was situated at the mouth of the Judith "at a point where neither white nor red men ever go." He recommended transfer of troops in these posts to areas where they could be utilized more effectively for "vigorous field service." A garrison near the Musselshell River and one "up the river" for part of the year would offer more protection, in his estimation, than the existing deployment.

To provide an alternate route to the Montana mines from the east, Hazen recommended establishing a wagon road from a point on the Missouri near the mouth of the Musselshell to the Powder River Road near Fort C. F. Smith. He proposed that a branch of the road proceed up the north bank of the Yellowstone to the Big Bend, where a new fort and ferry should be established. This route toward the Gallatin valley, he argued, would circumvent the dangerous rapids of the Missouri route below Fort Benton, and also serve as a boon to the settlers of Montana. In the interest of economy, the road should be opened by troops rather than by civilian government employees. "The immense appropriations of money by Congress for these western roads shows no fruits," the outspoken officer wrote. "It is all dissipated in salaries and pay of men who travel across the country, but never stop to do any labor."[14]

A large share of the inspection report was devoted to analyzing the Indian problem. Undoubtedly conditioned by his grim encounters with the Comanches in western Texas before the Civil War, Hazen offered the following candid observations:

The ideal Indian of the popular mind is found only in poetry and Cooper's novels. The Indian who now inhabits the plains is a dirty begger and thief, who murders the weak and unprotected . . . keeps no promises, and makes them only the more easy to carry on his murder and pillage. He knows no sentiment but revenge and fear, and cares only to live in his vagrancy. All efforts to better his condition have and will but add to his debt of ingratitude, and prove unproductive of any good. The fact that one in a thousand have been civilized proves nothing, neither does it that our people can sometimes become so low and deceitful and murderous as the Indian. The white man owes the Indian nothing. He is in the way of the evolutions of progress, and when the government pays . . . for his title to the territory, or for privileges in it, the debt is as perfectly cancelled as when a corporation pays the assessed value of the site of a public school.[15]

His policy recommendation was stated precisely: Allot each tribe its prescribed territory or reservation, give them food and clothing but definitely no instruments of war, and make "vigorous, unceasing war on all that do not obey and remain upon their grounds." Impracticable? Not at all, he argued. The troops in the department, if placed under command of "determined men," could visit the haunts of the Indian each season and, applying the red man's own tactics, destroy all villages found off the reservation. Based on his own wide-ranging operations against the Indians in 1858–59, he understood the futility of using conventional methods to fight a foe whose techniques and aims were unconventional. In this respect he possessed a degree of insight not found among most of his contemporaries. Elaborating on the "proper methods" of plains warfare he recommended that the army "should take no lumbering wagon trains nor artillery, but move with pack mules, say one for each four men, to carry blankets and food for infantry. . . ." If the cavalry was utilized, which he indirectly discouraged, only "half-breed" horses should be taken. Expeditions must be prepared to make forced marches, and should not be held back by jaded horses. "It will be of no use," he wrote, "to send these expeditions under men who are not willing to carry them out under circumstances the most discouraging and laborious, without tents, with a single blanket, and often on insufficient food, and who will fight on every occasion and attack at the instant."[16]

If adopted, this general policy would in a few years solve the Indian troubles. "When once thoroughly whipped there will afterwards be no trouble with them." Indian affairs would merely become an administrative problem. ". . . we would only have him on our hands as a peaceable pauper, in place of a thieving, murdering one, and at half the cost." The Indian Bureau's practice of pampering, equipping, and yielding to the demands of "these rascals" was playing with crime, Hazen grumbled. Noting that about forty people had been slain the past season in the "Mountain District," he concluded that it was high time "that murder of innocent people for a false sentiment should cease." Later experiences and closer contact with Indians would broaden Hazen's perception of the causes of the "Indian Problem."[17]

Depredations on the Bozeman Trail continued even as Hazen completed his report to General Cooke. The almost incessant harassment culminated on December 21, 1866, in the "massacre" of eighty-one men of William J. Fetterman's command near Fort Phil Kearny. Captain Fetterman impetuously attempted an offensive foray against a contingent of Sioux warriors who cleverly lured him into a fatal ambush. Both Colonel Carrington and General Cooke were relieved of command in the tragedy's aftermath, and a court of inquiry was set up to investigate the cause of the disaster. Hazen's October inspection report was part of the record examined by the investigative group. The government simultaneously launched a new and concerted effort to bring peace to the troubled West. On July 20, 1867, a commission was authorized to negotiate still another treaty with the Indians of the former "Mountain District." That development set the stage for abandonment in 1868 of Forts Reno, Phil Kearny, and C. F. Smith, and surrender of the Bozeman Trail to the Sioux. Because of the changed military situation and the re-evaluation of policy after 1866, Hazen's inspection report resulted in no immediate action but it provided a pertinent source of information on conditions in the Northern Plains and Rocky Mountains region.[18]

Meanwhile, at Camp Douglas, Utah Territory, Hazen in mid-October received notification that he had been commissioned a colonel in the reorganized army and named in command of the

INSPECTOR GENERAL, DEPARTMENT OF THE PLATTE 69

Thirty-eighth Infantry. Prior to moving to his new assignment, he was granted permission to spend the winter of 1866–67 visiting Europe.[19]

The Thirty-eighth Infantry was one of six Negro regiments authorized by Congress in 1866. Following its formation at Jefferson Barracks, Missouri, the regiment was sent to New Mexico Territory to bolster the military strength in the southwestern section of the Department of the Missouri. Colonel Hazen received his commission in March, 1867, and thereupon assumed the functions of his command. Special assignments soon limited his active service with the regiment. General Sherman, commander of the Division of the Missouri, planned more important duties for his subordinate—duties that would place him in the heartland of the country occupied by the restive Southern Plains tribes.

V

Sherman's Agent on the Washita

The Southern Plains Indians, like their racial brothers to the north, were markedly affected by the advance of the western frontier. The migrations of miners and settlers into their homeland inaugurated over a decade of almost constant Indian warfare in the Great West. The Colorado gold rush of 1859 provided a foretaste of the movement into this area. Few of the fifty thousand gold seekers struck it rich; many wanderers spilled across the Cheyenne and Arapaho lands after 1859 and established permanent residences. The government officials in 1861 sought to avert a general uprising in Colorado by removing the Indians to a reservation situated primarily between the Arkansas River and Sand Creek in eastern Colorado. Since many of the warriors resented this decision, Indian depredations in the following years increased in number as well as in intensity. Isolated settlements were attacked, horses stolen, immigrants harassed, and overland trade and mail routes generally disrupted.[1]

In 1864, Governor John Evans and the Colorado officials decided to take things into their own hands in an effort to squelch the Indian resistance. Their efforts culminated in the "Chivington Massacre" on the morning of November 29, 1864. Black Kettle, who claimed to be resting under the protection of the military, was among those who luckily escaped annihilation in this surprise attack on the sleeping Cheyenne village. The Sand Creek disaster solved nothing. Indeed, it only served to intensify the bloody fighting which came to be called the Cheyenne-Arapaho War.[2]

In an effort to pacify the hostiles, the federal government in October, 1865, met for peace talks with representatives of various plains tribes. The negotiations were conducted six miles above the confluence of the Big and Little Arkansas rivers, in the northwestern section of present-day Wichita, Kansas. The Cheyennes and Arapahoes agreed to make peace with the United States and accept a more out-of-the-way reservation, located partly in Kansas and partly in Indian Territory. The Kiowa, Comanche, and Kiowa-Apache tribes gave up claims to central Texas, western Kansas, and eastern New Mexico, receiving in exchange hunting rights to areas of what is now the Texas Panhandle, and that part of southwestern Oklahoma south of the Canadian.[3]

Misunderstandings, dissatisfaction, and delays in congressional ratification made adherence to the Treaty of the Little Arkansas an impossibility. The government, in making treaties, acted upon a legal fiction that the Indian signatories had binding authority; yet the various chiefs often had little control over their people. After nearly every treaty there were bands or chiefs who maintained that they had not been included. Nevertheless, the government took the position that all terms should be faithfully kept by all members of a given tribe once a supposed leader of such tribe had affixed his mark. It also proceeded immediately to use its specified rights to open roads or lands to white settlers.[4]

Following the Sand Creek massacre pressure mounted on Congress to re-evaluate the philosophy and conduct of the existing Indian policy. On March 3, 1865, Congress appointed a commission composed of seven of its own members "to inquire into the condition of the Indian tribes, and their treatment by the civil and military authorities." The committee's report issued in 1867 presented evidence that "much inefficiency and corrupt practice were to be found in almost every branch of the Indian service." Also much of the blame for the hostilities of the past and present was placed on the "fire and sword" policy of the military.[5]

The committee's report was widely publicized in the East and led to strong demands for a new and more humanitarian approach to the Indian problem. Congress reacted to this pressure by passing an act on July 20, 1867, which created the Indian Peace Commission. The commission was to remove the causes of Indian wars, provide just settlement of grievances, and induce the Indians to settle down on restricted reservations. The accomplishment of these goals, it was hoped, would bring permanent peace to the frontier, acculturate the Indian, and permit the unimpeded development of the West. If the Indians accepted neither the reservation system nor peace offered by the commissioners, then the act authorized the Secretary of War, under the direction of the President, to take military steps to suppress hostilities.[6]

In August, 1867, the peace commission journeyed to the West, olive branch in hand, to carry out its lofty assignment. Two large reservations were envisioned for the Indians: one in the Dakota country, for the Sioux and other bands; the other in Indian Territory, which was proposed as a home for the Southern Plains tribes.[7]

By October the commissioners had arranged for a great Indian peace council to be held on Medicine Lodge Creek in present Barber County, Kansas. After much ceremony, dissension, and consumption of government food, treaties were signed with representatives of the major tribes south of the Arkansas. On October 21 the Kiowas, Comanches, and Kiowa-Apaches agreed to relinquish the whole of their ranges in the panhandles of Texas and Indian Territory and accept a reservation in southwestern Indian Territory between the Red and Washita rivers. A week later the Cheyennes and Arapahoes agreed to move to a reservation largely in the Cherokee Outlet, between the Arkansas and Cimarron rivers. All five tribes swore to give up their nomadic ways, and in general seek to "walk the white man's road." The government in turn promised to provide agents, schools, churches, farms, clothing, and food, until the Indians would at last be adjusted to a sedentary life. The Cheyenne and Arapaho desire for unlimited hunting ranges was not met, but the government did give permission to hunt as far north as the Arkansas River. The tribes pledged to refrain from making forays against any travelers or settlements, and to "never kill or scalp white men, nor attempt to do them any harm."[8]

The treaties of Medicine Lodge Creek were not ratified by the Senate until July, 1868, and not proclaimed until August of that year. The delay in the appropriation of funds to put the treaties into effect caused destitution among the Indians and retarded the work of the Indian agents. Also, during the interim, whites entered parts of the old reservations and began to make settlements. No effort was made to check this trespass. The Indians were pushed out of their ranges before any provisions were made to care for them on their new reservations. Suspicion, anger, and a return to violence was the result. Thus, less than a year after the treaties of Medicine Lodge, war parties were out in force once again.[9]

When Congress failed to act promptly on the Medicine Lodge treaties, the commissioner of Indian affairs repeatedly requested appropriations to provide for the Indians in the interim period. The Radical Republicans were too preoccupied with efforts to "lift the scalp" of President Andrew Johnson through impeachment proceedings to worry about averting scalpings out West. Some of the Indians wandered to their newly assigned reservations but, finding no agents present, migrated back to the Arkansas River area. Distributions of annuities were made from time to time at forts Larned and Zarah. Commissioner of Indian Affairs Nathaniel G. Taylor's third appeal for money was finally met, in part, on July 27, 1868. By an act of Congress, a sum of $500,000 was appropriated for the following purposes:

> ... carrying out the treaty stipulations, making and preparing homes, furnishing provisions, tools and farming utensils, and furnishing food for such bands of Indians with which treaties have been made by the Indian peace commissioners and not yet ratified, and defraying the expenses of the commission in making such treaties, and carrying their provisions into effect.[10]

This money was appropriated to the Department of the Interior, but General William T. Sherman, in command of the Division of the Missouri, was designated to expend the funds.

Sherman, when informed of the act of July 27, telegraphed the Secretary of the Interior, O. H. Browning, for a clarification of the new duties thrust upon him. He was concerned that the law would lead to conflicts with the Indian Bureau which was already performing similar duties through its agents. Browning informed Sherman that the intent of the law was to provide for special agents who would assist in the big task of getting the Indians moved onto their reservations and started along the road to civilization. Sherman was at liberty to select either civilians or soldiers as the agents. He was, furthermore, empowered to assign the agents their specific duties. Browning stated that the regular Indian agents would continue their work as heretofore, "but without, in any manner, interfering with you in the performance of your duties." They would be instructed to cooperate fully "to such extent as you may desire and ask their cooperation."[11]

On August 10, 1868, Sherman issued General Order No. 4 to implement the act of July 27. Two large Indian military districts were designated and special "commanders" were appointed to administer them. The Northern District, embracing the Sioux reservation authorized by treaty in April, 1868, was put under the command of Brevet Major General William S. Harney. The Southern Indian Military District comprised an area "bounded on the east by the state of Arkansas, south by Texas, north by Kansas, and west by the 100th meridian." Sherman selected William B. Hazen, whose views on Indian affairs coincided with his own, to head this district and "have the supervision and control of all issues and disbursement to the Cheyennes, Arapahoes, Kiowas, and Comanches, and such other bands as are now or may hereafter be therein located by proper authority." Fifty thousand dollars was set aside for his use in providing for the Indians. The order made Hazen responsible only to General Sherman except in matters "affecting the troops stationed in said district" wherein he would be subject to the commander of the Department of the Missouri, Major General Philip H. Sheridan.[12]

The officers assigned by Sherman were to serve until June 30, 1869, after which they would return to their regular army duties. Sherman's decision to appoint army officers as his special agents, rather than experienced civilian agents already in the Indian service, was based on two considerations. In the first place, he was more familiar with the army form of accounts; secondly, as he frankly stated, he had "more faith in their manner of business."[13]

Hazen received official notification of his appointment on September 2, 1868. Subsequently he learned that Sherman and Sheridan had agreed on an extensive punitive winter campaign to drive the Southern Plains Indians to the reservations assigned at Medicine Lodge. As early as August 21, 1868, Sherman informed the War and Interior departments that he had authorized Sheridan to use military force to move the Indians south, killing if necessary. The Indian Bureau immediately demanded assurances that peaceful tribes would be granted protection. The Kiowas, Comanches, and Kiowa-Apaches, according to Central Superintendent Thomas Murphy, "have committed no depredations since they signed their treaty at Medicine Lodge creek, except for a few raids into Texas." These tribes, it was contended, should not be made to suffer at the hands of the military just because of the war activities of the Cheyennes and Arapahoes. Sherman was willing to concede that the peaceful tribes deserved safety and fair treatment. But as for the Cheyennes and Arapahoes, he believed that "no better time could possibly be chosen than the present for destroying or humbling those bands that have so outrageously violated their treaties and begun a desolating war without one particle of provocation." With this Hazen agreed. He only wished that he had been chosen to fight rather than feed the Indians.[14]

Hazen's first assignment in his role as special agent was to assist in separating the peaceful tribes from the declared hostiles. In early September he was sent by Sherman to assemble the Kiowa and Comanche bands at Fort Larned, Kansas. Portions of these tribes, in June, 1868, had left their reservation south of the Washita River in Indian Territory because there were no government officials present to implement the arrangements made at Medicine Lodge. Since then they had been camped along the Arkansas in the Big Bend country. Together with some Kiowa-Apaches there were approximately 1,900 Indians in the vicinity of Fort Larned who claimed to be friendly.[15]

On September 18, Hazen and Sheridan conferred at Fort Larned on means to isolate the friendly Indians in order that the unfriendly could be dealt with in the proposed frontier army manner. It was agreed that a council with the peaceful tribes should be held to warn them that unless they moved to their reservation, they, too, would be attacked by the troops. Sheridan promised to furnish rations for their journey to Indian Territory and Hazen agreed to accompany them. Old Fort Cobb, near the confluence of Pond Creek (later called Cobb Creek) and the Washita River, was designated as the site for Hazen's headquarters and the rendezvous for the peaceful Indians. September

19 and 20 were spent in council with all the principal Kiowa chiefs and with Ten Bears of the Comanches. Hazen assured them that their only possibility of safety was to accompany him to Fort Cobb and remain there under his protection. The chiefs at first balked but finally consented to go. Sheridan later maintained that the chiefs accepted the proposition "only as a decoy to get their families out of the proximity of the post."[16]

Since it required about ten days to get the rations ready for the long journey, the Indians were told to hunt buffalo during that time. After ten days they were to return for their rations and then proceed to Fort Cobb. Shortly after their departure a flurry of Indian raids occurred along the Smoky Hill and elsewhere. When the Kiowas and Comanches failed to return at the stipulated time, Sheridan assumed they had joined the raiding Cheyennes and Arapahoes, but Hazen found "no evidence of that fact." He reasoned that the Indians, knowing they were under suspicion, would proceed directly to the reservation on their own. Thomas Murphy agreed with this latter view. Waiting until October 11 for the return of his Indians, Hazen then decided to set out for Fort Cobb, on the assumption that the tribes would meet him there. Since there were not enough troops available to provide him with an escort, he decided to skirt the Indian country by proceeding via Forts Smith, Gibson, and Arbuckle. Prior to his departure, he instructed Major James Roy at Fort Arbuckle to assign an officer to supervise affairs at Fort Cobb until he could arrive. Captain Henry E. Alvord, Tenth Cavalry, was dispatched to the fort in response to this request. He was accompanied by two companies of troops from the Tenth Cavalry commanded by Lieutenant Philip L. Lee.[17]

Also in October, Commissioner Taylor ordered agents A. G. Boone and Edward W. Wynkoop "to repair without delay" to Fort Cobb to assist Hazen in caring for the Indians who might choose to gather there. Wynkoop, the Cheyenne and Arapaho agent, did not trust Sheridan or his troops. He feared that he was being used as "a decoy to lure Indians into a trap at or near Fort Cobb." Rather than becoming an "accessory" to such a "crime," he resigned as agent.[18]

While Hazen was on his roundabout journey to Fort Cobb, Captain Alvord, his "stand-in," was busily occupied. Several hundred

Indians were already in the vicinity when Alvord arrived at the fort. Before the end of October, the chiefs Hazen had met at Fort Larned reported to the post, thus fulfilling his trust in them. The Indians told Alvord they had not returned to Fort Larned because they feared some trick and because they did not care to travel with soldiers. Since neither Hazen nor the promised supplies had arrived, the chiefs decided to hunt on the Canadian in the region of the Antelope Hills. They promised to return as soon as Hazen made his appearance but, wary of the white man's promises, gave the opinion that they did not really expect him to arrive. On October 31, Alvord held council with representatives of the Caddoes, Anadarkoes, Wichitas, Wacos, Keechies, Tawakonies, and three Comanche bands. He sought to assure these Indians that Hazen and their promised food supplies would arrive shortly. The Comanche bands were especially restless. They threatened daily to break camp and return to their old ranges unless their needs were supplied.[19]

Captain Alvord had few subsistence stores at his disposal. It had been assumed that Hazen would arrive much sooner than he did, and so adequate provisions were not available. As early as September 25 the commanding officers at Fort Arbuckle reported that they "were expecting Hazen daily." S. T. Walkley, acting agent of the Kiowas and Comanches, had used this "information" for nearly a month in an effort to induce his Indians to remain near the agency. Henry Shanklin, the harassed agent of the Wichita and affiliated tribes, also anxiously looked for the officer's arrival. Shanklin finally left the agency on October 11 because he thought Hazen would soon be there and could take care of his disgruntled charges for him. On November 5, Alvord reported that the situation at Fort Cobb was precarious. He could no longer placate the Indians with only beef, and his supplies of flour, sugar, and coffee were nearly exhausted. He had on hand only one-half a barrel of coffee and 170 barrels of flour to be distributed among some 1,700 Indians. The troubled officer was convinced that without additional stores he would be unable to keep the Comanches at the fort. Two days after this gloomy report Hazen finally arrived via Fort Arbuckle, accompanied by a squadron of cavalry and a company of infantry.[20]

Colonel Hazen immediately launched into his work. In a briefing

session with Alvord he learned that there were around seven hundred
Comanches near the fort and approximately a thousand Caddoes,
Wichitas, and affiliated Indians. Alvord, through diligent effort, had
been able to ascertain the locations and note the movements of the
various bands throughout the entire area. Hazen was pleased that
the Kiowa and Comanche bands with whom he had held council at
Fort Larned had reported to the post. These bands were still camped
in the Antelope Hills region. He, therefore, on the first day of his
arrival dispatched scouts to notify them of his presence and to tell
them to proceed to the fort. He feared that Sheridan's forces might
encounter and attack the bands since he knew that the general was
under the impression that they had broken faith. Reports were also
sent to Sheridan informing him of the status of those bands. One day
spent examining the situation at Fort Cobb was sufficient to impress
upon Hazen the magnitude of the task which lay before him. Thousands of Indians surrounded the fort looking to him for subsistence
and direction. No Indian Bureau agents were present to lend him
assistance. Instead of having only Kiowas and Comanches as his
charges, as he originally anticipated, he had bands of many other
tribes on his hands. This heavy responsibility, as well as the challenge
of the assignment, prompted him to inform General Sherman on
November 7 that duties would now "preclude . . . taking an active
command, as before requested."[21]

News of the military agent's arrival spread rapidly to the various
encampments along the Washita and Canadian rivers. Delegations
from many different bands came in to see what arrangements were
to be made for them. However, the Kiowas and the Yamparika
Comanches, camped on the upper Washita and on the Canadian near
the hundredth meridian, were more hesitant. They had been warned
by a trusted interpreter, John Smith, not to fall into the trap set for
them at Fort Cobb. The scouts sent out to warn the Kiowas and Ten
Bears' band of Comanches had not reported back by November 10.
This caused Hazen again to express his concern that Sheridan might
attack these bands before he could collect them. A report a few days
later indicated that a major portion of the Kiowas were moving down
the Washita. By November 20 the principal chiefs, including Lone
Wolf, Satanta, and Satank, had come to confer with Sherman's agent.

Acting under Sherman's instructions of October 13 to "make provision for all the Indians who come to keep out of war," Hazen issued rations to the Kiowas, Comanches, and Apaches with the understanding that they were to camp peacefully near the agency.[22]

Hazen considered the Cheyenne and Arapaho tribes beyond his sphere of authority since they had officially been declared hostile by Sherman and Sheridan. Thus when Black Kettle and Big Mouth, representing several Cheyenne and Arapaho bands, sued for peace on November 20, he turned them away despite the fact that they had come in of their own accord and seemed sincerely desirous of settling down near the agency. The officer reasoned that he could not shelter Indians against whom war was then being waged. He told Black Kettle that only Sheridan could make peace with him because he represented a portion of the tribe that had started the war in Kansas. Black Kettle was urged to return to his camps on the upper Washita, then contact Sheridan and express his desire for peace. If peace were made from that quarter, then Hazen said he would be happy to provide for his band at Fort Cobb, but they were not to come in unless they heard from him. Disappointed in their quest for protection and supplies, Black Kettle and Big Mouth prepared to return to their people. Before leaving they secured some food and other goods from a trader at the fort named "Dutch" Bill Griffenstein.[23] As the Cheyenne and Arapaho delegation departed the agency, some of the young warriors were heard to express pleasure that the peace talks had failed. They boasted that they would now be able to continue their raids, and that in the following spring they planned to join other bands to "clear out this entire country."[24]

Colonel Hazen's conference with Black Kettle and Big Mouth was fully discussed in his lengthy November twenty-second report. He expressed fear that if he made peace with the chiefs Sheridan "might follow them in afterwards and a second Chivington affair might occur." Such an assumption was plausible because Sherman had written that it might be necessary for General Sheridan "to invade the reservation in pursuit of hostile Indians."[25] Hazen suggested that it might be advantageous for Sheridan to make peace with the "distinct bands" of Black Kettle and Big Mouth, even though they apparently did not represent or control a majority of their tribes. Their submission, he reasoned, would weaken the enemy forces out in the field. Colonel Hazen believed he had dealt with the chiefs according to military policy and the general instructions given him previously. Nevertheless, he requested Sherman to give him "definite instructions in this and like cases."[26] But this "case" was closed five days later when Custer wiped out Black Kettle and many of his band.

Black Kettle's death at the Battle of the Washita on November 27, 1868, led to a new wave of criticism against the military handling of the Plains Indians. Representatives of the Indian Bureau, former agent Wynkoop, and many others decried a policy that led to the slaughter of a prominent chief who they claimed was earnestly striving for peace. Sherman sought to defend the army's role by proving that Black Kettle's camp was not friendly and that Custer was not another Chivington. Chivington had attacked Black Kettle when the latter was under the protection of the commanding officer at Fort Lyon. Sherman had documentation to show that in the Washita battle the chief had explicitly been refused protection until he made peace with Sheridan.[27] Hazen was quick to defend himself and his fellow army officers. In a letter to Sherman dated December 31, 1868, the special agent said he wished to refute the statements "that Black Kettle's camp, destroyed by Custer, were peaceable Indians on their way to their Reservation. In his talk with me . . . before he was killed, Black Kettle stated that many of his men were then on the war path, and that their people did not want peace with the people above the Arkansas."[28] The emphasis in this letter was in contrast to the report of November 22, in which he professed belief that Black Kettle was sincere for "peace" and even suggested that Sheridan make peace with his "distinct" band. To Congressman James A. Garfield of Ohio he wrote that the Cheyenne chief had not been tricked into a false sense of security. He specifically had told Black Kettle that troops were approaching the Washita and that "they were liable to attack him at any time." Charging Wynkoop with irresponsibility, Hazen stated that if the Indian Bureau official had been at his post of duty, "probably Black Kettle whose death he so loudly mourns, would now be living."[29]

The procurement and distribution of food was one of the major duties incident to the work in the Southern Indian District. The

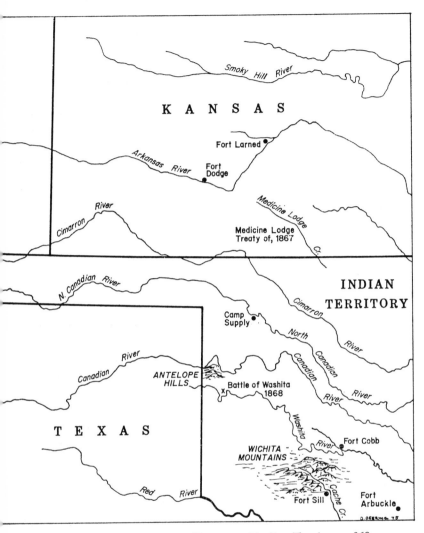

Military Posts in Southwest Kansas and Indian Territory, 1868

$50,000 allotted for Indian services in the area was not originally intended for Indian subsistence. The failure of Congress to appropriate sufficient funds for that purpose forced Hazen to spend most of his money on food. Furthermore, he had been informed that regular agency personnel would be available to assist him in caring for the Indians. But Jesse Henry Leavenworth, Kiowa-Comanche agent, and his temporary successor, S. T. Walkley, had left Fort Cobb prior to Hazen's arrival. Henry Shanklin never returned from his sudden "leave of absence"; instead, on January 9, 1869, he resigned as agent of the Wichita and affiliated tribes because of a "severe affliction of rheumatism contracted in Indian Territory."[30] Probably a more accurate diagnosis would have shown that he had been scared stiff by the thousands of Indians that suddenly appeared at his isolated agency. The only agent to show up at Fort Cobb during Colonel Hazen's tenure was Albert G. Boone, grandson of Daniel Boone, who assumed duties as the Kiowa-Comanche agent in December, 1868. Despite repeated requests for more funds, Hazen was unable to get any additional aid from either Congress, the Indian Bureau, or the army.

Hazen estimated that he would need to provide six months rations for approximately eight thousand Indians at a total cost of $115,220. In addition his itemized budget called for the hiring of two clerks, a storekeeper, an interpreter, four scouts, a butcher, a teamster, roofing an old storehouse, and other miscellaneous expenses. His total budget, as submitted on November 10, amounted to $127,700.[31]

Through a process of programmed experimentation a standard fixed ration system was gradually instituted. Arrangements were made to secure beef in the area at three cents per pound net. This was about one-half the price agents Leavenworth and Walkley had paid for beef.[32] The ration system was based on the following formula for each 100 rations: 150 pounds of beef, 75 pounds of corn meal, 25 pounds of flour, 4 pounds of sugar, 2 pounds of coffee, 1 pound of soap, and 1 pound of salt. In midwinter the beef allowance was increased to 250 pounds per 100 rations. Rations were issued on a weekly or ten-day basis. They were distributed to the chiefs of each band according to the actual number of their followers present at the place of disbursement. Previously, by exaggerating their numbers, the chiefs had been able to secure much more liberal food allowances. The practice of issuing rations based on actual count did not set well with the chiefs. Hazen reported that they were "always disappointed, usually angry, and always giving annoyance, which had to be endured at the risk of revolt." Through careful checking and observation Hazen concluded that the population of Indians at the time of his arrival had been rated "at fully double their real numbers." Hazen's own estimate, which he admitted was subject to error, placed the number of Indians in the area on June 30, 1869, at about seven thousand. This figure included the following tribes, both on and off the reservation: Comanche, Kiowa, Apache, Caddo, Wichita and affiliated bands, Arapaho, and Cheyenne.[33] Sugar and coffee, according to official instructions, were to be issued only occasionally and sparingly. But because of pressure and agitation previous agents had diverted much of the ration money into those two commodities. Hazen found it "almost impossible to correct the abuse."[34] He ultimately capitulated and agreed that they should form a part of the regular allowance. General Sherman, noticing that the costs of subsisting the tribes under Hazen's administration were "one-tenth of what they were under Indian agents," suggested to the Secretary of War that he use Hazen's reports as "ammunition" before Congress to get the management of Indian affairs transferred to the army.[35]

A food distribution program was fraught with many perils. The tribesmen, used to an ample supply of buffalo meat, complained bitterly about the scanty portions of beef they received, and universally detested corn meal. The dissatisfaction over the food situation became so intense that Hazen, on November 26, requested that additional troops be sent from Fort Arbuckle. He also asked that two howitzers with one hundred rounds of ammunition be forwarded to him. This call for reinforcement was prompted by the surly attitude of a group of Kiowas and Apaches who, upon receiving their rations, grumbled menacingly because "they could not have everything there is at the Post."[36] Satanta was one of the complaining Kiowas. He and others moved among the various camps threatening serious trouble before going on to their own lodges, thirty miles up the Washita. Reinforcements temporarily strengthened the garrison, and the approach of Sheridan's forces helped pacify the Indians. Otherwise, Hazen said he would not have remained at Fort Cobb. By June 30, 1869, Hazen had spent $41,250 for food out of his funds. In addition he had purchased, apparently on his own authority, $56,106.86 worth of commodities for the government on credit. The Secretary of the Interior agreed in May, 1869, to honor the bill.[37]

The extensive military operations in western Indian Territory through the winter of 1868–69 kept the Indians near Fort Cobb in a constant state of restlessness and anxiety. When reports of the Battle of the Washita were first received, it was feared that the Cheyennes and Arapahoes might seek revenge and attack the fort. On December 16, Hazen learned that Sheridan, with the Seventh Cavalry under Custer and the Nineteenth Kansas Volunteer regiment, was moving down the Washita. He was immediately concerned about the safety of the Kiowa and Comanche camps situated along the valley of the river. Already on December 14 Hazen had taken the precaution to write to Sherman: "General Sheridan should understand that my camps extend up and down the Washita for about thirty miles, and some miles south."[38] Fearing that Sheridan might attack the camps resting under his promise of security, Hazen promptly dispatched two runners with the following note:

HEADQUARTERS SOUTHERN INDIAN DISTRICT
FORT COBB, 9 P.M., DEC. 16, 1868

To the Officer commanding troops in the field:
Indians have just brought in word that our troops today reached the Washita some twenty miles above here. I send this to say that all camps this side of the point reported to have been reached are friendly, and have not been on the warpath this season. If this reaches you, it would be well to communicate at once with Satanta or Black Eagle, chiefs of the Kiowas, near where you now are, who will readily inform you of the position of the Cheyennes and Arapahoes, also of my camp.

Respectfully,
(Signed) W. B. Hazen,
Bvt. Major General[39]

A group of Kiowas intercepted the messengers and kept one as a hostage. The second was escorted onward until they made contact with Sheridan and Custer on December 17 near the present site of Cloud Chief.[40] The officers were obviously provoked by the letter from the commander of the Southern Indian Military District. An all-out attack on a Kiowa village was to have commenced momentarily. Custer claimed the Kiowas had been vitally involved in the Battle of the Washita and therefore did not deserve protection. In his reports and later accounts he frankly charged Hazen had been "completely deceived" and "misled" by the Indians and had seriously erred in preventing the attack on the seventeenth. Sheridan regretted losing an opportunity to fight Indians but did not feel he could ignore Hazen's letter. He believed that labeling the Kiowas friendly was ridiculous, and subsequently said that if Hazen had not interfered "the Indian problem on the Texas frontier" would have been solved at that time. Hazen was convinced that the Kiowas and Comanches did not participate in the Battle of the Washita as a group and had not been on the warpath since his agreement with them at Fort Larned. In this view he was supported by Alvord, who had remained at Fort Cobb under special assignment to supply Sherman with data on Indian movements, and interpreters H. P. Jones and Philip Mc-Cusker.[41]

Hazen admitted that undoubtedly some individual Indians from those bands had been with the Cheyennes and Arapahoes from time to time. He was likewise cognizant of the fact that some individuals had raided into Texas. But it had been consistently established and reported by the officers at Fort Cobb that the bands with whom agreements had been made in Kansas had not engaged in any hostilities since. Hazen was only fulfilling a trust and his assigned duty when he sought to assure the safety of the bands under his charge. Sherman himself virtually dictated the course of procedure Hazen followed on December 16 when he sent him the following instructions:

Every appearance about Fort Cobb should be suggestive of an earnest desire to afford a place of refuge where the peaceable Indians may receive food and be safe against the troops. . . . If you have not already notified General Sheridan of the fact that some of the Kiowas are peaceful, get word to him in some way, lest he pursue them and stampede your whole family.[42]

After reluctantly agreeing to honor Hazen's letter, Custer seized Satanta and Lone Wolf to be held as hostages until all the Kiowas would report to Fort Cobb. Many of the camps, thoroughly suspicious of the huge army before them, scattered in panic. Some of these came in to Fort Cobb promptly; others did not arrive until weeks later. Sheridan's army arrived at the post on December 18. Negotiations were undertaken with the Cheyenne and Arapaho chiefs on the basis of unconditional surrender. After considerable coaxing, threats, and troop movements, an increasing number of these Indians began to find their way to the place of surrender. This "gathering" process extended well into the month of April, 1869. The Cheyennes and Arapahoes were then moved north to their own reservation.[43]

Sheridan had been at Fort Cobb only about a week when he decided to abandon the site for a more favorable location. A reconnaissance party composed of Colonel Benjamin Grierson, Hazen, and Major George A. Forsyth left that post on December 27 to investigate other possible locations. The group found what they considered an ideal site near the junction of Medicine Bluff and Cache creeks, approximately thirty-six miles south of the Washita. In 1852 the explorer Randolph B. Marcy had recommended this locality for a fort. Here was plenty of water, grass, and building material. Grierson and Hazen both agreed the place had definite advantages over Fort Cobb. Sheridan accepted their recommendation and by January 10 all the troops had been transferred to the new post, first called Camp Wichita but later named Fort Sill. Sheridan strongly advised Hazen to move his Indians to Camp Wichita also; therefore, as soon as the troops were established in their new camp, this was done. At the new post the Indian goods were placed in a huge tent, strategically located for safekeeping near General Sheridan's closely guarded headquarters. Some of the Kiowas and Comanches camped along Cache and Chandler creeks while others located near Mount Scott. On the east bank of Cache Creek, Hazen built an adobe house which served as his winter residence. In the spring he moved into a large tent. Contracts were let for the construction of two agency warehouses, and

by the spring of 1869 they were ready for use. The only other buildings constructed under the supervision of Hazen were two houses
for Indian chiefs.[44]

After the arrival of Sheridan, Hazen devoted more time to the
long-range goal of adjusting the Indian to a sedentary life. Since most
of his $50,000 was necessarily diverted for food purchases, the scope
of all other activities was severely limited. Nevertheless, considerable
efforts were made to introduce farming among the Indians. Agricultural implements, seeds, and other farming supplies were ordered
from Leavenworth, Kansas, in mid-December, through the Indian
Bureau. These were to be delivered on or before February 1 in time
for spring planting. A. G. Boone was delegated to hire competent
farmers to assist on the agencies as provided in the Treaty of Medicine Lodge. During the spring months, twelve hundred acres of sod
were plowed, many fields were fenced, three hundred acres of corn
were planted, and numerous gardens were started by the Indians with
the help of the agency farmers. Fortunately for the success of the
work, adequate spring rains resulted in good crops. Some of the Indians raised enough corn, watermelons, and vegetables to be able to
market a surplus at the trading post. Hazen boasted that the garden
plots were "as cleanly kept as the best gardens in Ohio."[45] Amazingly
enough, even some of the Comanche chiefs were stimulated to help
hoe the corn and vegetables. Generally, however, it was left to the
women to do the hard labor. As a result, only seventy-two acres were
put in cultivation by the Comanches in 1869.

It was difficult to make farmers out of Kiowas. The few fields of
corn started for them were used to pasture their ponies as soon as a
good stand was evident. The Wichita and affiliated tribes, traditionally agriculturists, were provided assistance to re-establish farming
activities. The Wichitas were a peaceful and docile people who had
been forced out of the Washita valley during the Civil War. When
they returned after the war they found their homes and farms destroyed and their lands assigned to other tribes by the Medicine Lodge
treaties. Hazen found them occupying both sides of the Washita near
Fort Cobb in very "destitute condition" and decided to include them
in the food distribution program. He was impressed with the desire
of these neglected people for their own plots of ground, as well as

with their cooperative spirit. On January 20 he appointed Philip
McCusker as acting agent of the Wichita and affiliated tribes. Mc-
Cusker was instructed to take necessary measures to assure farm
plots for all the Indians of the Wichita tribe.[46]

Ground was broken for these Indians in the Eureka valley bottom
lands immediately to the east of Fort Cobb. Farmers were employed
to instruct and assist them in the planting of corn, beans, peas, melons,
and other vegetables. Hazen's efforts in their behalf were greatly
appreciated by tribal members. One chief extolled him as "a good
man who aided us all he could."[47] On the whole, Hazen felt well
pleased with the farming progress made during the spring of 1869.
His successors would struggle to build on the foundation he had laid.

Continuing Indian raids were the most frustrating problem faced
by Hazen as commander of the Southern Indian District. He had
absolutely no sympathy for any participants in such excursions and
consistently advocated that strict measures be employed to deal with
the problem. Immediately upon his arrival on the reservation Hazen
stated that the "old and pernicious habit of marauding in Texas"
should be "checked at whatever cost." This, he advised, could not be
accomplished by the Indian agent who was powerless to do more than
cajole and issue hollow warnings, nor could it be done with the two
companies of troops he had on hand. The problem would only be
solved, he asserted, by the government's dictating its own terms and
then backing them up with the presence of a sufficiently strong military force. "Old gray headed men here laugh," Hazen said, "when
told the Government will punish, and say they have been told that
since they were children."[48]

Although unable to cope with the Texas raiders effectively because
of his small force, Hazen kept careful record of all individuals and
parties participating in such raids. He also attempted to recover stolen
property and locate white captives among the tribes. When Sheridan
arrived with his army in December he was presented with the evidence gathered against various members of the Kiowa and Comanche
bands. Hazen's information on robberies was documented with
reports prepared by McCusker, Alvord, Walkley, and residents of
Texas. Hazen believed that the guilty individuals had forfeited every
right under their treaties, as well as of "humanity," and recommended

to Sheridan that they be dealt with accordingly. He stated his views bluntly: "To hang all the principal participants in this outlawry, and to disarm and dismount the rest, with an ample force stationed among them is, in my opinion, the mildest remedy that promises a certain cure."[49] Sheridan hanged no one but promised sufficient troops to discourage or punish any such violations in the future.

The following spring, shortly after Sheridan had withdrawn from the area, small parties began once again to get the "roaming fever." They crossed the Red River and struck over a wide area of Texas. Colonel Grierson, commander at Fort Sill, attributed the renewed raiding activity to the scarcity and poor quality of the food supply. He agreed with the Indians who complained that Hazen's ration was insufficient, even when issued in full. The red men, he found, were usually without "a mouthful of food" for two or three days prior to each distribution. The quality of beef at the agency, in comparison to buffalo or young Texas steers, likewise left something to be desired. Grierson questioned the wisdom of buying low-standard beef just to save a few cents a day on an Indian. Such a policy, he complained, tended to drive them off the reservation, and the savings made were far exceeded by the financial expense required to get them back.[50]

When the raids first commenced in the spring, Hazen warned the Indians that troops would be used to hound down the outlaws and to mete out severe punishment. But when he later requested the deployment of troops, Grierson refused to take any significant measures. Thus his own strong threats of action against the guilty Indians could not be backed up. The old gray-haired men could laugh some more.

In his final report from Fort Sill, Hazen was highly critical of the military command for not supporting him in his effort to stymie the raiding activity. The lack of ability or desire to chasten, he contended, would be the downfall of the reservation system. Without it the Indian would continue to come and go as he pleased, and progress would be slow and uncertain.[51]

Hazen's services as Sherman's special agent were concluded on June 30, 1869. By that time Quaker agents were on hand to continue the work he had begun. Although he wished to see the army take over the Indian affairs, he felt confident that Lawrie Tatum and his assistants would administer the agency with efficiency and success, if given proper support. The Quakers, "with their industry, practical ability and known probity," would be a definite improvement over the previous system, which he considered a "burlesque upon the government and a swindle upon the Indian."[52]

W. B. Hazen demonstrated earnest application and marked efficiency in performing the varied and arduous duties associated with the placement of the Southern Plains Indians on reservations. A military agent without military authority and with duties only vaguely defined, he was forced to rely upon his own ingenuity and resourcefulness. In this period of close interaction he not only developed a more mature understanding of the Indians' problem but also became sympathetic to it. By providing for the needs of thousands of Indians during a difficult transitional period, he helped them accept the inevitable and adjust to their new and restricted way of life. In a period of less than a year only a small start could be made. Much still remained to be done and many of the high hopes held out for the reservation system were never realized. Nevertheless, the way was prepared for others to seek more effectively to lead the reluctant Indian along the white man's road. Given just treatment, careful guidance, and a "wholesome example of Christian morality," the Plains Indian, Hazen now believed, could successfully be absorbed into the life of the nation.[53]

VI

Superintendent of Indian Affairs

In May, 1869, Colonel Hazen was appointed commander of the Sixth Infantry Regiment and ordered to report to Fort Gibson, Indian Territory, on July 1. On June 30 the Headquarters of the Army issued a surprising supplementary order assigning him "by direction of the President" to also assume "the duties appertaining to the Office of Superintendent of Indian Affairs for the Southern Superintendency."[1] The Indian Bureau planned to discontinue the southern superintendency, encompassing the territory inhabited by the Five Civilized Tribes, after 1869. However, when it was discovered that a superintendent was required by law to fulfill outstanding treaty obligations, the commissioner obtained authorization to utilize Hazen in this position.

Ely S. Parker, commissioner of Indian affairs, on July 21 defined Colonel Hazen's assignment in the following general terms:

It is not intended that you should be burdened with the disbursement of moneys to the Indians, respecting which, the agents for the several tribes will receive instructions direct from this office, but you will be charged with the duties in regard to all matters where by treaty stipulations, or otherwise, the action of a Superintendent alone, or in conjunction with an agent is required. And also to render such other duty as the exigencies of the service may require.[2]

The problem demanding immediate action in the southern superintendency was the settlement of the Loyal Creek claims. At the outbreak of the Civil War the Creek Indian Nation was divided in its sympathies between the North and South; about one-half remained loyal to the Union, while the remainder, approximately sixty-five hundred cast its fortunes with the Confederate states. As a result of the civil strife in Indian Territory, the Loyal Creeks were forced to abandon their extensive property holdings and seek protection in the North. In their flight to Kansas during the winter of 1861–62, under the leadership of Chief Opothleyaholo, many lost their lives in attacks by both Indians and whites. Upon reaching Leroy, Kansas, the loyal faction went into camp for the remainder of the war. More than fifteen hundred of the men entered the Union Army.[3]

After the war the Creeks returned to their reservation where they found appalling devastation. Virtually all their property—houses, barns, fences, orchards, livestock, and horses—had been destroyed or lost. The government when negotiating at Fort Smith with the Five Civilized Tribes in September, 1865, assured the Indians that "those who have been loyal, although their nation may have gone over to the enemy, will be liberally provided for and dealt with."[4] A general treaty of "peace and amity" was signed at that time, but in 1866 separate "reconstruction treaties," which included provisions benefiting pro-Union tribal members, were negotiated.

By terms of the Creek treaty, signed on June 14, 1866, the government agreed to ascertain the losses sustained by the Loyal Creeks and provide payment. Article IV stipulated the procedure for the settlement of claims:

Immediately after the ratification of this treaty, the United States agree to ascertain the amount due the respective soldiers who enlisted in the Federal Army, loyal refugee Indians and freedmen, in proportion to their several losses, and to pay the amount awarded each, in the following manner, to wit: A census of the Creeks shall be taken by the agent of the United States for said nation, under the direction of the Secretary of Interior, and a roll of the names of all soldiers that enlisted in the Federal Army, loyal refugee Indians and freedmen, be made by him. The superintendent of Indian Affairs for the southern superintendency and the agent of the United States for the Creek

Nation shall proceed to investigate and determine from said roll the amounts due the respective refugee Indians and shall transmit to the Commissioner of Indian Affairs, for his approval, and that of the Secretary of the Interior, their awards, together with the reasons therefor. In case the awards so made shall be duly approved, said awards shall be paid from the proceeds of the sale of said lands [Article III] within one year from the ratification of this treaty, or so soon as said amount of one hundred thousand dollars can be raised from the sale of said lands to other Indians.[5]

Three years after negotiation of the 1866 Creek treaty, Hazen was appointed as superintendent to carry out these terms.[6]

On July 21, 1869, the commissioner of Indian affairs authorized Colonel Hazen and Captain A. F. Field, Creek agent, to begin the claims investigations "at the earliest day practicable." The investigation and determination of amounts to be paid were left to the discretion of Hazen. To defray the expenses of the officials, Congress appropriated the sum of $1,500.[7]

By mid-September Captain Field was concluding his census of the Loyal Creeks and in the following month claims hearings were begun. The initial investigations were conducted by Lieutenant S. P. Jocelyn of the Sixth Infantry, whom Hazen appointed "Assistant Superintendent of Indian Affairs for the Southern Superintendency." Leaving Jocelyn and Field to look after the Creeks, Hazen was free to organize the post administration at Fort Gibson and take a leave of absence. In December, after his return, Hazen personally conducted the final stages of the investigation.[8]

Under the supervision of Colonel Hazen, the work of the commission was typically thorough and efficient. Messengers were sent to all towns where there were Loyal Creeks to arrange a time and place for the presentation of claims. It was required that evidence be given under oath and verified by witnesses. At these hearings the claims of each individual were itemized in minute detail. Awards were made either on the basis of prevailing market prices or when these were not available, by standardized figures established by the investigators. On many miscellaneous articles the officers arbitrarily allowed one-half of the value claimed. An exhaustive memorandum of prices was compiled by Hazen to guide the investigators in making awards on claims. By December 19 the entire Creek territory had been canvassed by Jocelyn and Hazen but notice was given that claims would be accepted until February 1, 1870.[9]

On February 14, 1870, the Hazen and Field Commission forwarded its findings to the Indian Bureau. The comprehensive report included a general explanation of procedures and problems; a memorandum of prices; an abstract listing the claims, names of claimants, sex, age, amount claimed, amount awarded, and remarks as to type of claimant; individual vouchers for each claimant setting forth the wartime circumstances under which the claims arose and the amount, character, and value of property lost; and affidavits of witnesses as to the authenticity of the claims. When one notes that 1,523 separate claims were investigated and processed, the magnitude of the commission's work becomes apparent. The claims filed by the Indians amounted in the aggregate to $5,090,808.50. The awards made by Hazen and Field aggregated $1,837,035.41.[10]

In explaining their awards the commissioners stated:

The undersigned have been controlled in each case by an earnest desire to be just, and have awarded with that in view. . . . The amounts awarded may appear large, but in passing through the Creek country it becomes evident that they were a wealthy people, comparing favorably in their civilization and means with the settlers of the southwestern states.[11]

In a supplementary report dated April 30, Hazen transmitted the last of the printed vouchers and the census roll prepared by Field. He also recommended "the early adjustment of the respective claims, while the parties thereto can be easily found, and before the death or removal of claimants, and other accidents of time, render the payment complicated."[12]

The accuracy of the findings of Hazen and Field was never challenged by the government. On the contrary, Congressional committees examining the Loyal Creek claims in subsequent years uniformly recognized the thoroughness and exhaustive care with which the work was accomplished. The total awards thus made by the commission were reported by the commissioner of Indian affairs with the recommendation that payments be made according to the stipulations of articles III and IV in the 1866 treaty.[13] Secretary of the Interior Jacob D. Cox, after careful consideration of the treaty provisions, concluded that a sum of only $100,000 had been designated for payment of Creek claims. The Hazen and Field awards, he advised Parker, "greatly exceed the amount set aside by the terms . . . of the Fourth article . . . and that appropriated by Congress and I have therefore approved the amounts awarded by the Commission only so far as the sum placed at my disposal by the treaty and the act of Congress of July 15, will warrant, viz: $100,000." He declared that the awards would be "calculated upon a proratio basis by which each claimant will receive 5 444/1000 of one dollar, on the sum so awarded."[14]

In October, 1870, there was paid out to the claimants on these awards a total of $100,000 from funds obtained through the sale of Creek lands. The Indians apparently were told by J. A. Williamson, the agent authorized to make the disbursements, that the $100,000 was merely an advance payment and that the balance on the claims would be forthcoming later. Only after this assurance was given did the Creeks accept the reduced payments. Williamson reported that "Sand's party" and the Freedmen were "very bitter" toward the government and suggested that the Indian Bureau "use more than ordinary care in the selection of an agent for the Creeks."[15] The new agent, F. S. Lyon, reported "general dissatisfaction . . . with reference to the amount paid" on the claims. First the amounts had been "diminished by the commission," the Creeks grumbled, and then ridiculously slashed by the Interior Department. Destitute and discouraged they looked upon the whole procedure as a farce.[16]

It soon became obvious that the government intended to avoid further payment on the Hazen-Field awards. The Creek spokesmen protested vigorously and proved that loyal factions among the Choctaws, Seminoles, and Chickasaws had been compensated far more adequately than the individual Creeks for their losses. They argued that the intent had clearly been to treat them just as generously as the rest, and that to construe the treaty otherwise was a misinterpretation of its terms. As a result of persistent protests the claims of the Loyal Creeks were referred by the Secretary of the Interior to the United

States Court of Claims, which held, on June 4, 1884, that the United States was under no legal obligation to pay more than the $100,000.[17] Thus the meticulous efforts of the Hazen-Field Commission were nullified and an Indian faction that had suffered irreparable losses because of its loyalty to the United States government was not equitably compensated.

The Loyal Creeks received the same emphatic promises of payment for damages as the other Civilized Tribes when the general treaty was negotiated at Fort Smith in 1865. In the Creek treaty of 1866 the wording on claims differed from that used in the other "reconstruction" treaties; however, as the circumstances were the same in each case it must be presumed that the commissioners intended to compensate Loyal Creeks just as liberally as loyal Seminoles, Choctaws, and Chickasaws. Nevertheless, because of the terminology of the Creek treaty, the United States Court of Claims decreed that there could be no legal claims asserted beyond the sum of $100,000. The reason for this restrictive figure in the treaty, if, indeed, it was intended to be one, has never been satisfactorily explained. For thirty years Congress disregarded a solemn promise and moral obligation to the Loyal Creeks. Early in the twentieth century, when more sympathetic consideration was finally given to their claims, most of the original claimants were no longer alive to benefit from any belated humanitarian gestures.

An agreement with the Creek Nation, ratified by Congress on March 1, 1901, provided that the Loyal Creek claims should be submitted to the United States Senate for determination, and, in the event that any sum should be awarded to the Indians, provision should be made for its immediate payment. The award of the Senate was $1,200,000 and it proposed an amendment to the Indian appropriation bill providing funds for payment of the claims. The House refused to concur in that amendment. On March 3, 1903, Congress appropriated $600,000 for the purpose of paying the Loyal Creek Indians and freedmen after deduction of certain attorneys' fees. The act provided that this sum should be accepted by the Indians in full payment and satisfaction of all claims and demands growing out of the Hazen-Field investigations and that the payment of that sum should be a full release of the government from any such claim or claims. The Creek National Council, on May 23, 1903, agreed to accept the $600,000 under the terms of the act. Payments were made to claimants or heirs in 1904 by J. Blair Shoenfelt, Indian agent. In 1935 both the Senate and House committees on Indian affairs reopened the controversial case. Secretary of the Interior, Harold L. Ickes, reported to the committees that since the Senate sitting as a court of arbiters in 1901 "awarded the loyal Creeks $1,200,000 and as only $600,000 of such award has been paid, it would appear that the Government drove a hard bargain with the Indians. Hence it is believed that the Indians have a strong moral claim for payment of the balance of the amount awarded by the Senate." Bills were introduced in 1935 and again in 1937 to provide for such payment, but they were not enacted.[18]

Soon after the completion of the Loyal Creek claims investigation, President Grant appointed Enoch Hoag, superintendent of Indian affairs for the central superintendency, and Hazen to a commission to determine railroad construction rights through Indian country. Treaties with the Five Civilized Tribes and acts of Congress approved in 1866 provided for the construction of one north-south trunk line and one east-west line through the territory. The congressional statutes, passed July 25, 26, and 27, and as interpreted by the Secretary of the Interior, essentially authorized three railroad companies "to run a race, and the one first reaching the Kansas–Indian Territory border in the valley of the Neosho River was to have the right of way southward through the Indian Territory."[19] Only two companies—the Union Pacific, Southern Branch and the Kansas and Neosho Valley Railway—entered the contest. By the end of April, 1870, the latter company's line reached the southern border of Kansas near Baxter Springs, within the limits of the Neutral Lands. The Union Pacific, Southern Branch, having been renamed the Missouri, Kansas and Texas Railway Company, at that date had not completed its line to the state boundary; nevertheless, the company, without governmental approval, commenced construction in Indian Territory. On May 13 the commissioner of Indian affairs informed the company officials that they were trespassing on Cherokee lands and warned that no railroads could be built in the territory "until the right to do so had been passed by the Department or Congress." At the same time Super-intendent Hazen was given authorization to use troops, if necessary to force compliance with that regulation.[20]

Based on conflicting interpretations and claims, both railroad com-panies maintained they had won the right to build through Indian Territory into Texas. The Secretary of the Interior recommended to President Grant that he appoint superintendents Hoag and Hazen to settle that dispute and to determine which railroad "shall first fully comply with the conditions of the statutes . . . and to report to this Department when such complete fulfillment shall have taken place." He further recommended "that an Executive order be issued declaring that no railroad company shall be permitted to enter said Indian Ter-ritory . . . until such report shall have been received and approved by yourself, and a formal permission given." The recommendations of the Secretary were executed on May 23.[21]

The Hazen-Hoag Commission convened at Baxter Springs, Kansas, on June 10, and determined to conduct a thorough on-the-spot in-vestigation. The Kansas and the Neosho Valley Railroad, which had been reorganized under the name of Missouri River, Fort Scott and Gulf, was inspected from Baxter Springs south to its terminus at the state line. The commission established that the company's road had reached the border opposite the Quapaw reservation on April 30, 1870, but that it did not terminate in the Neosho valley as the terms stipulated. The inspection of the Missouri, Kansas and Texas on June 11 revealed that its line was likewise completed, touching the border a mile west of the Neosho River, near Chetopa, Kansas.[22]

On June 11 the commissioners received a telegram from Ely Parker which erroneously inferred that the President had decided to hear further arguments "on the matter of railroads through Indian Terri-tory."[23] On the basis of that information, and also because they ap-parently were persuaded that the Missouri River, Fort Scott and Gulf promoters "in good faith had spent much money," Hazen and Hoag permitted the company to submit written arguments on its own be-half. On June 13 the commission concluded its investigations and de-clared its findings in an official report to the commissioner of Indian affairs.

On the basic question of "which railroad had first fully complied with the provisions of the statutes and treaties," the commissioners reported as follows:

That the Union Pacific Railway, Southern Branch [Missouri, Kansas and Texas], reached the northern boundary of the Indian Territory, in the valley of the Neosho River on the west side and about one mile therefrom, at 12 M., the 6th day of June 1870, and that, at that time, there was no other railroad nearer than sixteen miles of that point.

That on the 9th day of June 1870, Governor James M. Harvey, of the State of Kansas, the officer specified by act of Congress to pronounce upon the completion of this railroad, certified over his official seal and signature, that the same was a first class completed railroad to the northern boundary of the Indian Territory.[24]

Hazen and Hoag officially declared that the Missouri, Kansas and Texas company, having met the prescribed stipulations, was entitled to build through Indian Territory. But the commissioners, at the same time, requested departmental consideration of the written arguments submitted by the Missouri River, Fort Scott and Gulf officials. And, while tacitly admitting that they were touching on matters beyond the scope of their assignment, they recommended that the "whole subject be reconsidered" in the interest of "the broadest equity to all parties." They also warned the department to expect trouble from the railroads in the future. "It has appeared," their report stated, "that the railroad companies place little value upon their right of way of 200 feet, through the Indian Country, but place great stress upon the lands they expect to acquire and settle along the lines of their respective roads." Hazen and Hoag "earnestly" recommended that the government strictly adhere to the policy of limiting construction to one north–south trunk line, with no land grants other than for the right-of-way. Permitting additional roads and land grants would lead to the "disintegration" of the territory "reserved by all the sacredness of treaty stipulations to the Indian tribes as their final home." This would be, in the opinion of the commissioners, "a breach of faith on the part of a powerful government towards its weak and unfortunate subjects, and very detrimental to the interest of both races."[25]

In reviewing the commissioners' report, Interior Secretary Cox disregarded the recommendation to reopen the railroad discussions. He declared that "this was beyond the instructions given to the commission." Arguments on the interpretation of statutes had been heard and considered previously, he wrote Parker, and there had been no intention "to re-open the case." The Secretary welcomed "any opinions" the commissioners might have on the subject, "on account of the thorough respect I have for their judgment," but emphasized that "the action of every commission appointed . . . should be strictly confined to the matters specifically submitted to them." Based on the commissioners' official determination of the issues in question, Cox announced he would recommend that the Missouri, Kansas and Texas railway "be held to have first complied with the conditions prescribed by law, under the interpretation given by this Department, and approved by the President," and that it, therefore, be granted the right to build through Indian Territory.[26]

In hearings held July 9–12, 1870, the Department of the Interior gave opportunity for interested parties to show cause why the Secretary's decision should not stand. Officers of the Missouri River, Fort Scott and Gulf line argued that an enclosure in the Hazen and Hoag report revealed that their rival's road was not a "first-class roadbed" as required by legislation. It was not mentioned that the document in question was supplied by James F. Joy, owner of the Missouri River, Fort Scott and Gulf, and did not represent the commission's own findings. Cox ruled that the certification by Governor Harvey stating it was a "first class road" must stand. The certification by the two commissioners that the Missouri, Kansas and Texas Railway Company was the only road within sixteen miles of the terminal designated, was not challenged. When the hearings ended, no evidence had been submitted to cause the Interior Department to change its initial decision.

On July 12 Cox forwarded the Hazen and Hoag report and his earlier recommendation to President Grant for his review. He also advised that before construction began, the company should be required to post bond that "they shall, in every particular, respect the rights of Indian tribes, and the individuals thereof, as guaranteed by the treaties . . . and statutes of the United States."[27] The recommendations of the Secretary were approved and implementation was authorized on July 20.[28]

The first Missouri, Kansas and Texas Railway ("Katy") passenger train entered the present state of Oklahoma as far as Big Cabin Creek on May 24, 1871, a few months before Hazen was transferred from Fort Gibson. The line through Indian Territory was completed by December, 1872.[29]

Although not expected to assume the full responsibilities of Indian superintendent, Hazen conveniently used the position as a forum to agitate for reforms in Indian Bureau management. He was especially critical of the "want of persistence" that characterized much of the Indian service, citing as a typical case in point the bureau's neglect of the Wichita Indians. In letters to Commissioner Parker, Hazen reviewed the program he had initiated in 1869 to re-establish those Indians on farms in the Washita valley, and deplored the fact that little had been done by his successors to carry the program forward. According to Hazen, some of the hostile bands around Fort Sill were getting better consideration from the Indian Bureau than the peaceful Wichitas, who had never caused the government any trouble. He urged that appropriate assistance be given the tribe and recommended that a separate reservation be provided them. His reports on the Wichitas were considered "worthy of careful attention" and, after further study, his recommendation was endorsed by the commissioner of Indian affairs. Hazen's correspondence, together with a report and recommendation from Parker calling for a reservation, was submitted to the Secretary of the Interior on February 17, 1870. The proposal was approved by the Interior Department and preliminary steps were authorized to determine a suitable location for the Wichita reservation. On February 26 Hazen, in cooperation with Enoch Hoag, was instructed to furnish the names of the Wichita bands, the number of Indians in need of government aid, and to suggest a site for their reservation.[30]

In May, 1870, subagent Jonathan Richards, agent Lawrie Tatum, and Lieutenant Jocelyn, the latter representing Colonel Hazen, held a council with the Wichitas. Agreement was reached on a proposed reservation in the Eureka valley, between the Keechei hills and the Washita River. Hazen and Hoag believed this area to be "substantially the reservation" originally selected for the tribe in 1858, but since included in the Kiowa, Comanche, and Apache reservation. On June 15 they recommended that about 500,000 acres in the Eureka valley be permanently designated for the Wichitas, since it "rightfully belonged to them," and suggested that the Kiowa, Comanche, and Apache tribes be compensated with lands to the southwest. This proposal concluded Hazen's direct involvement in securing a reservation for the Wichita tribe. By the time a slow-moving bureaucracy was prepared to take further action, he was transferred from Indian Territory. Nevertheless, on October 19, 1872, the government agreed to provide the Wichitas and affiliated bands a 743,610-acre reservation between the South Canadian and Washita rivers. Although this agreement was never officially ratified by Congress, the designated area attained sanction as the Wichita reservation.[31]

Hazen's final official function in the Indian service was to implement steps leading to the convening of a council of the Five Civilized Tribes for purposes of forming an intertribal government. His dual role as military commander and superintendent was terminated on August 22, 1870, following the merger of the southern and central Indian superintendencies.[32]

As the result of a strong recommendation by General Sherman, Hazen was granted an indefinite leave by the President to visit Europe and observe the Franco-Prussian War. He left the Indian Territory immediately following his release from the bureau assignment.[33]

As the last superintendent of Indian affairs for the southern superintendency Colonel Hazen worked diligently and cooperatively with the Secretary of the Interior and Indian Bureau officials. According to Commissioner Ely Parker, the officer's insight into Indian problems and his pertinent advice "materially guided" the bureau's policy toward the Indians of the Southwest. Unlike many army officers, Hazen was sufficiently enlightened to recognize that the "Quaker policy," was accomplishing some good, and in those areas he gave it his full support. In the case of the Indians under his jurisdiction the situation called for just treatment and sympathetic understanding. This Hazen sought to foster during his brief tenure as superintendent of Indian affairs in Indian Territory.[34]

VII

Casting Stones at the Establishment

From September to December, 1870, Colonel Hazen studied the tactics and organization of the contending armies in the Franco-Prussian War. While on this special assignment he visited several battle fronts and held personal interviews with Otto von Bismarck, General von Moltke, and other prominent officials in both Germany and France.

Early in 1871 the much-traveled officer joined the Sixth Infantry headquarters at Fort Gibson, Indian Territory, and resumed command of the regiment and post. Three of his ten regimental companies were garrisoned at Fort Gibson, while the remainder were scattered in one-company posts in Kansas, Arkansas, and Indian Territory. The major functions of the troops, numbering 513 enlisted men and 22 commissioned officers, were to police Indian reservations, build military roads, and generally maintain order along the "hither edge" of the frontier.[1]

On February 15, 1871, Hazen married Mildred McLean, twenty-one-year-old daughter of Washington McLean, owner of the *Cincinnati Enquirer*. This marriage provided a significant political and social connection for the ambitious Hazen, as the McLean family had considerable influence in Ohio Democratic circles. Colonel Hazen soon brought his young bride to Fort Gibson, where they moved into a comfortable residence built in 1867 for the commanding officer of the post.[2]

Orders were received in September to transfer the Sixth Infantry troops and headquarters to Fort Hays in western Kansas, to provide protection for the Kansas Pacific Railroad. Fort Gibson was vacated under command of Hazen on September 25, and on the thirtieth the regimental headquarters was officially established at Fort Hays. A small detachment was left at Fort Gibson to guard the facilities which were utilized temporarily as a military depot.[3]

With the Indian menace seemingly subsiding in the early 1870's—and with it the chance for military honors—Colonel Hazen faced the gloomy prospect of long-term routine garrison duty at isolated frontier posts. Prior to his transfer to Fort Hays he wrote pessimistically about his future in a letter to Representative James A. Garfield: "It is difficult to see ahead . . . in my profession, to conjecture what it has in store."[4] He was disturbed that Congress had, in 1869, eliminated twenty regiments of infantry and subsequently reduced the army from over fifty thousand enlisted men to a maximum thirty thousand. These reductions greatly restricted the chances of promotion for many regular officers who had retained commissions in the reorganized army after the Civil War. Although Hazen had sixteen years of seniority, there were a number of colonels who superseded him in the order of promotion. Furthermore, the brigadier general ranks were filled primarily by officers who still had many years of service before them.

Hazen realized that, short of attaining glory in Indian warfare, promotion or favorable assignments were usually dependent on special consideration from military superiors or political friends who effectively used their influence. His friendship with several Ohio political figures, especially Jacob D. Cox and James A. Garfield, had proved beneficial in the past, and he continued to nurture such contacts. The ties between Garfield and Hazen were especially close. While chairman of the House Military Affairs Committee, Garfield relied heavily on Hazen for advice on military legislation, and the two maintained an active correspondence until Garfield's death. Garfield's respect for Hazen is seen in a letter written in the fall of 1870 in which he stated:

The fact is, Hazen, that very few men in the army are thinking widely or deeply and I have faith in you, that you are working in the right direction and that the elements in you will bring out some noble results. For several years it has been a plan of mine, that you and I would yet be able to work together, each in his own field, so as to accomplish something worthy of our age and of the great nation we are proud to call our own.[5]

The two were to contribute to each other's careers in various ways in the years to come.

Hazen could also depend on sympathetic consideration from General Sherman. "Sherman is my friend," he told Garfield, "and would favor me in any possible way."[6] But he could not say the same for Sheridan, who had been elevated to the command of the Division of the Missouri in 1869 when Sherman became commander of the army. Their relationship had been strained since the Missionary Ridge engagement in the Civil War; Hazen's intervention on behalf of the Kiowas after the Battle of the Washita had further rankled Sheridan. Hazen privately admitted in 1871, "Sheridan and I have a sort of mutual dislike. I think him a selfish, weak unscrupulous man, admitting his dashing qualities as a leader in battle, but without a particle of administrative capacity."[7]

Not only was his divisional commander unfriendly, but Secretary of War William W. Belknap also seemed unfavorably disposed toward him. Hazen resented Belknap's refusal to approve him for duty in the East, which he had requested in order to facilitate research for a book he was writing on the organization of European armies. The Sixth Infantry commander complained to Garfield in January, 1872, that he had been rebuffed on several occasions by the Secretary and that the latter had "never turned his hand in the least thing to accommodate me." In the same letter he made the significant statement: "I have a shot or two in my locker for him, I have a great mind to let him have."[8] Thus with the influential Sheridan and Secretary of War Belknap both antagonistic toward him or, at best, maintaining a cool attitude, and with his own proclivity for "getting into hot water," Hazen had good reason to view his future with a degree of insecurity.

In February, 1872, Colonel Hazen revealed the nature of the "shots" he was reserving for the Secretary of War in the following letter and enclosure sent to Representative Garfield:

Fort Hays, Kansas, Feb. 4, 1872

My Dear Garfield:

Do you take any interest in Army matters since your new and laborous duties with a new committee?

The matter of post-traders has drifted into its worst possible shape. You know sutlers were abolished at the close of the war, as they, with their excessive privileges, ought to have been, and the Commissary Department required to furnish the necessary articles formerly kept by sutlers.

This law the commissaries have managed to evade.

The adjutant-General then published an order allowing any one to trade at a military post who should show fitness to the Department Commander. This was good enough for the troops, for it gave us the advantage of competition, but did not suit the traders, who have always sought exclusive privileges. So the last Army law [1870] embraced a clause giving the Secretary of War authority to appoint one, I think (perhaps one or more) traders at each military post "for the convenience of the travelling public." Mark the ingenuity of this wording. It gives it a civil character, takes from the post commander nearly all the control he formerly had over the traders, gives the trader full power over his tariff of prices, and as the Secretary of War refuses to appoint but one at a post, it makes him the old exclusive sutler of olden times, without any of the checks we formerly held over him. More still, they farm out their privileges, which formerly they could not do. I send you a case in point, perhaps the most outrageous in the Army. This part must be confidential so far as my name is concerned, as I cannot afford to quarrel with Mr. Secretary. Marsh is a personal and special friend of the Secretary through their wives, and Grierson [B. F.] who commands the post is a friend of the Secretary and the President, and don't want to make a row. I am always ready to cast stones at outrages, and this is a glaring one.

I am truly,
(Signed) W. B. Hazen[9]

The following enclosure represented Hazen's "case in point." The letter was written by Lieutenant Richard H. Pratt, who later founded Carlisle Indian School.

Fort Sill, I. T., Nov. 25, 1871

Dear General:

  I have incidentally learned that you have a desire to know whether a bonus is required from the traders here, for the privilege of trading, and have been urged to write you the facts in the case. As there seems to be no secret made of the matter, and as, in common with all others here, I feel it to be a great wrong, I think you will readily excuse the presumption which my writing, unasked by you, might indicate.

  I have read the contract between J. S. Evans, a Fort Sill trader, and C. P. or C. E. Marsh of 867 or 877 Broadway, N. Y. (Office of Herter Bros.) whereby J. S. Evans is required to pay the sum of $12,000 per year, quarterly, in advance, for the exclusive privilege of trading on this military reservation. I am correctly informed that said sum has been paid since soon after the new law went in force, and is now paid, to include some time in February. This is not an isolated case. I am informed by officers who were stationed at Camp Supply, that Lee and Reynolds paid $10,000 outright for the same exclusive privilege there. Other cases are talked of, but not corroborated to me; sufficient to state, the tax here amounts to near $40 per selling day, which must necessarily be paid almost entirely by the command, and you can readily see that prices of such goods as we are compelled to buy must be grievously augmented thereby. It not being a revenue for the Government, and Mr. Marsh being an entire stranger to every one at the post, it is felt by every one informed of the facts, to be, as I said before, a very great wrong.

(Signed) R. H. Pratt
U. S. A.[10]

  Representative Garfield responded to the disclosure immediately. "The case you state is a great outrage," he wrote Hazen, "and I am very sorry that you cannot let me say it in the House. But I will try to attack the trader system, in some effective way, without interfering with you."[11] Between February 13 and 16, Garfield showed Hazen's letter, "in confidence," to John Coburn, who had succeeded Garfield as chairman of the House Committee on Military Affairs. Coburn informed him that "similar facts" previously had come to his attention. Advising Hazen of his visit with Coburn, Garfield, in a letter marked "Private and Confidential," wrote: "His [Coburn's] information appears to implicate the Secretary of War, in these rascalities of the Post Traders." He stated further that "there appears to be a ring of Iowa Men, either relatives, or intimate friends of the Secretary, who are concerned in this business of Post Trading, and Coburn is apprehensive that it will appear that the Secretary is seriously implicated in the matter." Garfield assured Hazen that he had "enjoined upon him [Coburn] the utmost secrecy, in regard to your self, and the use of your name, in connection with the information you gave me." At the same time he asked Hazen whether he could, without "compromising" himself, provide the names of persons who might be summoned as witnesses before Coburn's committee "to develop the facts to which your letter alludes." Garfield considered the situation an "intolerable outrage" and declared, "Coburn and I have to day agreed that we will double teams, on the subject; and if we can get solid ground to stand on, will drive a six horse team through the whole establishment, if the facts warrant."[12]

Garfield also showed Hazen's disclosure to Eugene V. Smalley, a reporter for the *New York Tribune* who served as clerk for the House Military Affairs Committee. Smalley obtained permission to publish the essence of the letters in the *Tribune*, promising not to divulge his sources.[13] Appearing in the February 16 edition of the *Tribune*, Smalley's news story declared that according to "an officer stationed at Fort Sill, Indian Territory," post traderships "are systematically farmed out by those who obtain them from the War Department." The complete details of the Marsh and Evans contract were quoted from Pratt's letter. Although stating that the trader system in operation since 1870 had been recommended by the Secretary of War, the story did not charge Belknap with malfeasance; in fact, it stated that he had probably not been informed of the abuses. In an editorial in the same issue of the *Tribune*, however, the presumption was advanced that the War Department was involved in influence peddling:

Another of the multifarious ways and means of fleecing people, under the sanction of governmental influence, is brought to light. . . . Indian traders are rapacious and dishonest enough, but the military traders, who constructively sell goods at the military posts on the

*frontier, and live in "brownstone fronts" in New York City, are worse
if that be possible. It seems that one of the beauties of the semi-military
administration of affairs under which we live permits the appointment of purveyors, sutlers or traders, with exclusive privileges, at the
military posts, remote from settlements; and that these traders whose
monopoly is complete and amply intrenched, farm out their profitable
appointment at rates which pay them very handsomely for the "influence" with which they secure the job from headquarters. It must be
apparent that a New York concern which gets forty or fifty thousand
dollars a year for letting out a trader's post at a frontier fort, makes
the amount out of its political influence. The trader who buys the
selling business of the firm makes enough to pay his bonus and his
profits. Result is robbery of officers and soldiers. Will some humane
and enlightened statesman, not afraid of being called an adversary of
the Administration and the Republican party, see if this swindle cannot be broken up forthwith?*[14]

Secretary Belknap reportedly took a copy of the newspaper to President Grant and told him that if he believed the inferences concerning his department, he was "no longer fit to hold a place in the
Cabinet." To this the President is to have replied, "I do not believe
one word of it."[15]

In response to Garfield's request of February 16 for names of persons who could be subpoenaed to "develop the facts" of the Fort Sill
case, Hazen wrote as follows: "It would seem that Mr. Evans and
Mr. Marsh, and I would add, Reynolds, of Camp Supply, are possessed of the material information." Hazen requested that he be left
out "altogether," because he could not "afford to be the accuser of
the Secretary of War." He suggested that the committee consider the
information he had furnished as coming directly from Lieutenant
Pratt, or from Fort Sill. "I did not open this matter as a fight with
the Secretary," he said, "but with the subsistence department, whose
fault it all is for wilfully failing to carry out the law." Hazen stated
that information he had obtained from Reynolds revealed that Evans
went to Washington in 1870 to seek renewal of his trader's license,
but that Belknap told him that "he had concluded to give the appointment to a friend of his." When Evans remonstrated, declaring that

he had over seventy thousand dollars invested in the business, the Secretary reportedly told him that "if he was really so involved in the business as to make his continuance in it imperative, to come over to his own house and he would find the party there with whom he could arrange it." According to this story, Hazen continued, Evans went to Belknap's residence, "and there arranged with Marsh to give the bonus."[16] What Reynolds failed to relate, and what Hazen did not realize, was that the trader's license had actually been made out to Evans, who contracted to pay Marsh an extortionate sum for securing it for him. Hazen also included at this time an earlier and more complete letter from Pratt, which contained the information that Evans was to pay Marsh "so long as William W. Belknap is Secretary of War."[17] In concluding his letter, Hazen made this pertinent observation: "The worst outlook of the whole affair is, that Marsh is the Secty's special friend, with whom he and *his* stay when in N. Y."[18]

On March 2 Hazen requested permission to testify before the House Military Affairs Committee, then holding hearings on army-staff organization. His request to be summoned was in part motivated by personal considerations, as seen in a letter to Garfield: "It is very necessary for me to go East upon the subject of the publication of my book, much of which is pertinent to his [Coburn's] inquiry."[19] Apparently an agreement was reached among Garfield, Coburn, and Hazen that the latter would be subpoenaed to testify on army-staff organization and that the post trader subject would be raised incidentally during the questioning. Colonel Hazen appeared before the committee on March 22 under the assumption, as he later stated, that any information divulged on the Fort Sill post tradership situation would be treated confidentially.[20]

Having previously submitted his detailed opinions on army-staff organization in writing, Hazen was queried primarily on post traderships. He told the committee that in his frank opinion the purpose of the 1870 law was "to put the trader outside the control of the officers," making him subject only to the Secretary of War who made the appointments "of his own volition." The effect was to remove all control over prices since a single trader possessed a monopoly and was free to charge what the market would bear. In consequence, the prices were "extortionate," especially when the post trader rights were obtained for a large monetary compensation, as was the case at Fort Sill. Before coming to Washington to testify Hazen discussed the Fort Sill trading arrangements with J. S. Evans, who verified that he was obliged to pay Marsh $12,000 annually to retain the trading privileges at the post. Hazen volunteered no information directly implicating Belknap in the Marsh-Evans arrangements but presented sufficient evidence to indicate that the system as administered by the Secretary offered abundant opportunity for graft and corruption. Neither Coburn nor any of the other committee members raised any questions during the hearing that sought to establish the extent of Belknap's involvement.

In his testimony, Hazen emphasized that army commissaries were preferable to post traderships because they would result in "better goods at cheaper rates." He reminded the committee that a law passed in 1866 required the Commissary Department to furnish supplies regularly to the soldiers at cost, but the plan was never executed. Congress initially failed to appropriate money to defray the costs, but Hazen believed that since the Commissary Department had a surplus of appropriations on hand at the time, the law was enforceable. Instead, the Adjutant General issued an order reviving the post sutler or trader establishments. Since then, according to Hazen, the Commissary Department had made no attempt to execute the 1866 law, even though it was still on the books.

Hazen concluded his testimony by saying that rumors were prevalent that a great number of trading posts were farmed out under conditions similar to the arrangement at Fort Sill; however, Fort Sill was the only one on which he had positive knowledge. The practice, he insisted, should be prohibited immediately by legislation.[21]

A day or two following Hazen's appearance before the committee, Garfield privately informed General Irwin McDowell, commander of the Department of the East, of the Fort Sill case. McDowell immediately went to consult with Belknap. Although indignant when told of Hazen's candid criticism, the Secretary shrewdly suggested that McDowell draft an order on behalf of the War Department to convince the critics that abuses in the trader system were being rectified. McDowell thereupon prepared a draft which both Coburn and Garfield apparently regarded "as a complete remedy for the evils complained of."[22] On March 25 the order was officially issued by the War Department. It required post traders to "actually carry on the business themselves," and to "habitually reside at the station to which they were appointed." It forbade them to "farm-out, sublet, transfer, sell, or assign the business to others"; and it required the council of administration at each post, with the approval of the post commander, to establish rates and prices at which goods should be sold. Since Marsh was "farming out" his influence, not the business at Fort Sill, the departmental order did not affect his lucrative arrangement, nor, as was later revealed, Belknap's "take" of the proceeds. The *New York Tribune*, assuming that the post trader "swindle" was broken up, on March 27 praised the Secretary of War for his prompt action in correcting the abuses. Thus the heat was temporarily taken off Belknap and his cohorts.[23]

It is not clear just why Coburn and Garfield did not investigate the tradership corruption more thoroughly and pursue their earlier suspicions concerning Belknap's involvement. Perhaps they were disarmed by the Secretary's apparent eagerness to "correct" the abuses once they were exposed and, assuming that his departmental order had cleansed the system of all iniquity, were willing to let it go at that. Or, they may honestly have felt that there was insufficient evidence implicating Belknap directly to demand further investigation; as loyal Republicans they would not relish bringing embarrassment to the administration if it could be avoided. Furthermore, when Garfield was accused in September, 1872, of complicity in the Credit Mobilier scandal, he was, for sometime thereafter, in no position to launch a crusade against corruption in government. Whatever the circumstances, it is clear that the basic evidence on which Belknap was impeached in 1876 was readily accessible to high government officials in 1872.

What Colonel Hazen sought to avoid in his attack on the tradership system—arousing the ire of the Secretary of War—was not accomplished. Coburn made no effort to keep Hazen's testimony confidential, assuming that the officer wanted to remain anonymous prior to the hearings only. Belknap, upon learning that Hazen was responsible for stirring up the commotion, reportedly vowed to "send him to Hell." The Secretary later declared he could not recall making the

Ft. Davis, Texas, general view from North. Courtesy Western History Collections, University of Oklahoma Library.

Monument to Hazen's Brigade at Stone River erected in January, 1863. It is the oldest known Civil War monument. From Hazen, A Narrative of Military Service (1885).

A Cheyenne camp in Indian Territory during the early reservation period, about 1870. Courtesy Western History Collections, University of Oklahoma Library.

Cheyenne camp on the same reservation as above, about 1890. Forced acculturation had made little progress. Courtesy H. R. Voth Collection, North Newton, Kansas, Mennonite Library.

John Evans trading post, Fort Sill. Courtesy Fort Sill Museum.

William W. Belknap, Secretary of War, 1869–1876. The only cabinet officer (resigned) ever to be impeached and tried by the Congress of the United States. Courtesy National Archives.

George A. Custer, Montana Territory, 1874. He is sitting in front of a tent apparently provided by the Northern Pacific Railroad, inadvertently demonstrating a joining of forces by the military and business interests. Courtesy Northern Pacific Railway.

A painting of Fort Buford, Dakota Territory, looking south from the guard house, about 1872–73. Courtesy National Archives.

General David S. Stanley. Courtesy National Archives.

General William Babcock Hazen. Courtesy National Archives.

statement, however, Hazen soon had reason to believe he was being discriminated against by "those high in power for daring to tell the truth."[24]

Shortly after Hazen's return to Fort Hays, the Sixth Infantry was transferred to Fort Buford, a forlorn post in northern Dakota Territory. The military command decided to send a new regiment to the upper Missouri country, and the choice for this undesirable assignment lay between Gordon Granger and Hazen. The selection of Hazen's regiment was made by Sheridan, but there was speculation later that he had been influenced by high officials who wanted the aggressive officer put into isolation. Hazen, obviously distraught by this "banishment," complained to Garfield that at Fort Buford he would be "six months without mails" and "generally out of the world." Commenting on Granger's good fortune in not being selected, he said with apparent bitterness, "But you know he has been so loyal to the present administration . . . that he must be discriminated favorably."[25]

When the transfer order was received, Colonel Hazen was experiencing "a very painful hard time" with the wounds he had received in Texas. According to the post surgeon, the bullet "incapsulted" in his side had escaped from its bed causing "great nervous derangement" and "partial paralysis of the lower extremities." In a certificate dated May 8, 1872, Assistant Surgeon John Janeway expressed the "decided belief" that Hazen would "not be able to endure the extreme and continued cold of a winter on our northwestern frontier." But by that time Hazen was able to walk with the aid of a cane and indicated he would obey the order to move the regiment on May 10, despite the surgeon's efforts to dissuade him.[26]

The first group of regimental troops and the band left Fort Hays on the tenth, reaching the post at the mouth of the Yellowstone on June 1. After a temporary delay in Sioux City, Iowa, Hazen established his headquarters at Fort Buford on June 21. Six companies of the regiment were garrisoned at Fort Buford, two at Fort McKeen, and two at Fort Stephenson. Having lost forty-nine soldiers by desertion en route to Dakota Territory, the regiment comprised 497 men and 22 officers at the end of June, 1872.[27]

Tragedy struck the Hazen family soon after their arrival at Fort

Buford when their infant died. Hazen's own physical condition was such that the post surgeon pronounced him "quite unfit for duty." While en route to Dakota, Hazen submitted an application for sick leave, and on his own authority delayed at Sioux City, possibly hoping that the leave order would reach him there. However, his superiors disapproved of this procedure and possibly for that reason did not act on the request. On July 5 he renewed the application, this time requesting a leave of absence for thirty days, effective in the fall just prior to the closing of navigation on the Missouri River. "I believe my health for life, if not life itself, is involved," he wrote to departmental headquarters.[28] General W. S. Hancock, departmental commander, Department of Dakota, upon the basis of a recommendation from the medical director of the department, approved the leave, but with the stipulation that a medical certificate specifically recommending a change of climate be furnished.

Divisional Commander Sheridan, in reviewing the leave request, reluctantly gave his approval, but with the following endorsement:

> *The disability which Colonel Hazen now has seems to have come on him about the time his regiment was ordered to the Department of Dakota. I would regret very much to do injustice to Colonel Hazen, but must confess that he has done much injury to the discipline of the army by his reluctance to do duty with his regiment (which should be his pride), and I find it impossible to remove from my mind the impression that this reluctance is the foundation of his present disability.*[29]

This groundless supposition, which went contrary to the reports of four army medical officers, could only prejudice the military hierarchy against Hazen.

Meanwhile, Hazen continued to criticize the military establishment. During the summer of 1872 his book, *The School and the Army in Germany and France*, was released by Harper and Brothers. This publication, according to the *New York Tribune*, established Hazen as "one of the best military critics in the country," and stamped him as an outspoken exponent of army reform.[30] The work consisted of a detailed examination and comparison of the military and

educational systems of France and Germany, based on the author's
personal observations and research, and included some highly controversial comparative observations on the United States Army. Re-
calling that during the Civil War he had served twelve months under
a corps commander, and eighteen months under a division commander, "neither of whom during that time ever gave me a single
direction respecting the instruction of my command," and convinced
that the country had suffered incalculably "in consequence of the
indolence, ignorance, and shiftlessness of its officers," Hazen declared
it was high time that someone pointed out such glaring weaknesses
in military administration. Government and military officials could
profit greatly, he said, from a study of the successful German military
system. This was his purpose in writing *The School and the Army
in Germany and France*.[31]

Hazen's study included an attack on the staff corps, a popular
theme of line officers. In comparison with Prussia, Hazen maintained
that the American army had "an immense preponderance of 'staff'
both in numbers and in rank." Citing statistics to establish his point,
he declared that in the United States "we employ with our present
system as many officers or their equivalents, to administer the army
as we have fighting officers in it." Furthermore, by their numbers
and high military rank and the fact that the chief officers were stationed in Washington, the staff had become a powerful interest group
influencing legislation and executive action in their favor and against
the line. The nature of their duties brought staff officers into frequent
contact with general officers of the army, "with whom close relations
of friendship spring up, gaining them the favor and influence of these
high officers in all questions affecting their status." So politically
powerful had they become, said Hazen, "that we see its influence in
nearly every appointment to the staff, or advantageous transfer, in
which the law leaves discretion to the President." In fact, he averred,
so influential were the heads of staff departments that they had "nearly all gained independence of army control," bearing the same rela-
tion to the Secretary of War as the commander of the army. "The
staff departments," he charged, "are now substantially independent
bodies, instead of connected links of a great chain of military administration."[32]

Waste, extravagance, and lack of coordination resulted from the habitual and "insensible" arrogation of power by staff officers. As an example Hazen reported that in the spring of 1871 the surgeon general of the army had ordered the construction of a hospital at Fort Gibson, Indian Territory, not realizing that the post would be abandoned within a few months. Hazen, as commander of the fort, knew it would be discontinued, but his views on the subject did not count; at a cost of about twelve thousand dollars, the hospital was built. Tragically, when such errors were reported, "no especial notice" was taken by Washington officials. "There is a disposition among staff officers to stand by each other," Hazen charged, "which is apt to be stronger than the wish to serve the Government." He recommended that officers be held to a cash responsibility for careless or stupid misuse of public funds and property.[33]

The Quartermaster's Department was also mismanaged, the Sixth Infantry commander declared. Lacking vision and hamstrung by bureaucracy, the general efficiency of the entire operation was "open to grave question." The only purpose of all its "cumbrous machinery," he wrote, "seems to be to make places for a superabundance of officers, with so much rank as to unfit them for their legitimate duties." Hazen realized that the logistical organization of the western army was outmoded and warned that it would fail in case of a war.[34]

Some of Hazen's most serious charges were leveled at the Subsistence Department of the army. Discussing the law of 1866 requiring the department to furnish articles formerly sold by sutlers at the military posts at cost, Hazen stated:

This was very advantageous to the line, but the law was disliked by the Subsistence Department, because it added to their duties, and was considered by many degrading. A deliberate intention not to execute the law was soon manifested. The first excuse for not carrying it out was that Congress had made no special appropriation, and the adjutant-general published an order excusing ... compliance with the law, although the general appropriation for that department was so large that none was asked for during the following year. This was the entering wedge to kill the law.[35]

Since then the department had persistently failed "to perform its legal duty," resulting in a system whereby one trader was granted an unregulated monopoly. Closely following his presentation before the House Military Affairs Committee, Hazen deplored the farming out of traderships, and revealed the extortion racket that had developed at Fort Sill. Hazen's book was completed prior to his appearance before the Coburn committee and, therefore, did not reflect on the changes authorized by the War Department as a result of his agitation at that time. In this work the blame for the tradership evils was placed on the Subsistence Department, and not on the Secretary of War.[36] Hazen was to wage a long but unsuccessful fight to get the department to fulfill the law of 1866; his efforts served only to arouse antagonism among key staff members.

The "system of rewards for service" also received criticism. In Prussia, Colonel Hazen pointed out, it was virtually impossible for an incompetent or inefficient man to become or remain an officer, and promotions and duties were administered with justice and strict impartiality. Not so in the army of which he was a part, the uniformed author lamented:

We actually appoint men at the mere wish of influential persons, without any evidence of a single qualification; and it is not surprising that they sometimes possess none. ... The poorest shirk with us may hold his commission all his life if he does no flagrant act and signs his pay accounts regularly. ... With us duty goes for little, compared with personal favor. An officer may shirk for years, and then claim, by virtue of his rank, the best post of his grade in the service, to the exclusion of those who have all the while labored faithfully. The effect of any system that rewards alike those servants who do their duty and those who do not, can be readily imagined, and in the end will, as it should, destroy itself. In the Prussian army service is certain of due recognition and reward, and this is the strongest stimulus to its proper performance. With us, those who do honest, rough duty uncomplainingly are very likely to do it all their lives.[37]

Hazen concluded his "comparative observations" by declaring that "the centralized Washington administration" was in serious need of reform. "Unless these reforms can be brought about, and the country satisfied that our army is earnest, capable, and, above all, economical," he warned, "it will turn out that the staff has been and now is digging a grave in which the whole service must soon be buried." Hopefully the public, once made aware of the defects, would be satisfied with nothing short of the best military methods and system.[38]

The School and the Army attracted widespread attention in military and governmental circles. Congressman Garfield reported that he "was very greatly pleased with the spirit and character" of the work, and congratulated his friend on the "splendid reputation" it had given him.[39] A review in *The Nation* described the book as being "replete with matter of great interest and value both to the soldier and the statesman." Favorably impressed with the author's use of German and French documents, the reviewer stated that evidently no reliable source of information was neglected. Hazen's candid observations on the United States Army were said to "clearly point out certain vital defects in our own military establishment, the sad truth of which will come home to every one of our officers who has served in the field."[40] The *Army and Navy Journal* carried extensive excerpts from the work in its July 20 and 27 and September 28, 1872, issues. Obviously impressed with the book, the journal's editor observed:

The officers of our Army find so little to encourage them in undertaking literary ventures that the appearance of an elaborate work from the pen of one of them is a noteworthy event, and especially worthy of attention when the work proves to be so able and interesting as the one General W. B. Hazen has given to the public.[41]

Anticipating that there would be "abundant differences of opinion as to the justice of his special criticism," the editor offered the hope that Hazen would be answered by argument rather than by "abuse and aspersion of motive." The journal praised Hazen for "the moral courage to speak his whole mind without regard to personal consequences," and expressed the opinion that the armed services suffered from a "lack of intelligent, honest, and fearless criticism from those ... familiar with its wants and possibilities."[42]

Hazen undoubtedly expected his "bucking of the system" to arouse the hostility of a number of army men. There were reports that both Sherman and Sheridan took offense at some of his suggestions and comments. Coming on the heels of agitation stirred up over the War Department's mismanagement of post traderships, this criticism caused the outspoken officer to be considered by some as a chronic troublemaker. The charges against officers in the Subsistence Department involved Hazen in acrimonious debate, which ultimately required him to defend his accusations in court-martial proceedings. In retrospect, Hazen viewed the publication of his book as being responsible for his failure to be appointed to any active field command during the Indian wars of the 1870's.[43] Thus Colonel Hazen's readiness "to cast stones at outrages" had, by the end of 1872, made him a controversial figure—a reputation he continued to build throughout the rest of his lifetime.

VIII

The Arid Lands Controversy*

The career of W. B. Hazen from 1872 was almost continuously controversial. In 1873 an investigation of the large-scale construction program at Fort Buford was commenced by order of the military command. Accusations were made that Colonel Hazen on his own authority altered the plans recommended by the engineers and approved by staff officers. Apparently he ordered slight modifications in the plans for the commanding officer's quarters and relocated some of the buildings. Hazen said this was done in the interest of practicality and efficiency. After several thorough inspections, a series of charges and denials, and the compilation of reams of reports, the matter was dropped with a statement by Sheridan that the investigation was undertaken not because the changes were important but because it was necessary to teach Hazen a lesson.[1]

The operations of the Sixth Infantry Regiment during this period were unspectacular, being largely confined to escort and scouting duties. In June, 1873, Companies E, F, G, and detachments from several other companies left Fort Buford to become part of the Yellowstone expedition under command of Colonel David S. Stanley. The purpose of this expedition was to survey a route for the Northern Pacific Railroad west of Bismarck, then the western terminus of the line.[2]

Hazen was not impressed with the highly publicized plans of railroad officials and financier Jay Cooke to develop the Northern Plains into an agricultural empire. As early as 1866, in his inspection report

of the Department of the Platte, he had decried the false advertising
by commercial interests about the plains region. The appearance, in
1871, of a highly romanticized account of the resource values of the
land grant of the Northern Pacific line incensed him further. This
publication, entitled *The Northern Pacific Railroad; its Route, Resources, Progress and Business*, was issued by Jay Cooke and Company, the financial agent of the railroad firm. In this booklet and
subsequent releases, the promoters urged the public to buy with
"perfect safety" gold bonds of the company, which reputedly were
guaranteed "by an unreserved grant of land, the most valuable ever
conferred upon a great national improvement." The Northern Pacific's land grant was said to extend from Lake Superior "in a broad
fertile belt" through Minnesota, Dakota, Montana, Idaho, Oregon,
and Washington, terminating at Puget Sound. Clients were even
urged to sell their government bonds and invest in railroad bonds,
which offered a higher return.[3]

Hazen was disturbed by this distorted information circulated by
the railroad interests. Writing to Garfield on May 5, 1872, he said
that he was preparing a manuscript refuting the glowing claims made
for agricultural possibilities on the western plains. His imminent
transfer to Fort Buford would temporarily delay completion of the
work, but so certain was he that Jay Cooke was "perpetrating a grand
swindle in mortgaging his worthless bonds as if they were good,"
that he was determined to expose him.[4] Intermittently for two years
after this date Hazen collected data for an article describing and
evaluating the potential development of the plains region.

The orgy of railroad speculation typifying post–Civil War years
came to an end with the Panic of 1873 and collapse of Jay Cooke's
banking house and the Northern Pacific bonds which he had spon-
sored. The interest on the bonds of the road were paid, not from
earnings on the completed parts of the line, or from sales of the land
granted the company by the government, but by funds obtained from
new bond buyers. Now the coupons could not be paid, working hardship on holders, many of them clergymen, farmers, and small trades-
men. It was not long, however, before interested parties began to
promote ideas of reorganizing the Northern Pacific and completing
the line. Land agents intensified their promotional activities in behalf

Northern Plains "Mild Winter" Zone, from "Poetry and Philosophy of Indian Summer" (Harper's, December, 1873)

of the railroad. Concerted efforts were made in 1873 and 1874 to induce Russian Mennonites to buy company land in Dakota. The Northern Pacific Land Committee conducted a delegation of Mennonites on a grand tour of the line's holdings and offered extraordinary concessions designed to encourage the emigration of thousands of these renowned farming people. On August 20, 1873, G. W. Cass, president of the railroad, agreed to reserve all company land in Dakota "within fifty miles of the Red River until July 1, 1874," for Mennonite settlers. Furthermore, Michael Hiller, railroad agent, was instructed to petition Congress for legislation withdrawing public lands in that region from entry and reserving it for compact Mennonite settlements. Hiller, with a letter of endorsement from Jay Cooke, accompanied two of the German-Russian delegates to President Ulysses S. Grant's home on Long Island and urged special exemptions and privileges for the prospective immigrants. Early in 1874 Senator William Windom of Minnesota, a Northern Pacific stockholder, introduced a bill to authorize the temporary setting aside of 500,000 acres of land for Mennonite homesteads.[5]

In December, 1873, a pretentious article in *Harper's New Monthly Magazine*, entitled "Poetry and Philosophy of Indian Summer," extolled the fertility, climate—produced by an "aerial Gulf Stream"—and general virtues of the Northern Pacific's great "Fruitful Garden." Hazen viewed the article as a propaganda effort in behalf of speculators seeking to recover their fortunes, and wrote a lengthy letter to the *New York Tribune* disparaging the company's land west of Minnesota. Dated January 1, 1874, Hazen's letter was published on February 7 under the bold headline, "WORTHLESS RAILROAD LAND." In his introductory paragraphs, Hazen stated that for two years he had been "an observer of the effort upon the part of the Northern Pacific Railroad Company to make the world believe this section to be a valuable agricultural one." He, along with others, had "kept silent although knowing the falsity of their representations, while they have pretty fully carried their point in establishing a popular belief favorable to their wishes." Noting that these "shameless falsehoods" were still being circulated, even in reputable periodicals, he expressed "a feeling of shame and indignation . . . that any of our countrymen . . . should deliberately indulge in such wicked deceptions."

Since his post of duty was then in the railroad's so-called "Northern Tropical Belt," where nature stared him in the face "with its stubborn contradictions," he had decided to end his silence and put the "contradictions" on paper. Practical farming experience, in addition to many years of observation as a military officer on the frontier, he said, further authorized him to speak on the subject.

Presenting a table of temperatures and rainfall at Fort Buford from 1867 to 1873, Hazen characterized the expanse west of the hundredth meridian to the Sierras as a region of extreme cold in winter and general drouth in summer. The annual variation of temperature was approximately 130 degrees. While admitting that the Indian summers were "beautiful beyond description," he ruefully warned that this hardly made up for the "terrific winter storms" which took the lives of both man and beast. "Not a winter had passed since this post was established in 1866, but some poor soldier of its garrison has lost life or limb by freezing." Indian scouts informed him that similar conditions of cold and aridity extended north into Saskatchawan, Canada.

Except for occasional wet years, rainfall amounts were held to be insufficient for general agriculture. Hazen even cast doubt on the value of the land for grazing purposes, saying that in order to supply his post with nine hundred tons of hay in 1872 it had been necessary to search an area of some twenty-four hundred square miles. His views on the value of the lands west of the hundredth meridian were stated bluntly and pessimistically:

> ... excepting the very limited bottoms of the small streams, as well as those of the Missouri and Yellowstone, from a few yards in breadth to an occasional water-washed valley of one or two miles, and the narrow valleys of the streams of Montana already settled, and a small area of timbered country in north-west Idaho (probably one-fiftieth of the whole), this country will not produce the fruits and cereals of the East for want of moisture, and can in no way be artificially irrigated, and will not, in our day and generation, sell for one penny an acre, except through fraud or ignorance; and most of the land here excepted will have to be irrigated artificially. ... The country between the one hundredth meridian and the Sierras—the Rio Grande to the British possessions—will never develop into populous States because of its want of moisture.[6]

Hazen expected his dim appraisal to "meet with contradiction," but declared that "the contradiction will be a falsehood." The facts could all be substantiated by reading the reports of General Gouverneur K. Warren of the Engineer Corps and Professor Ferdinand V. Hayden, who had made accurate scientific explorations of the country. Hazen cautioned his readers not to accept at face value the descriptions of "enthusiastic travelers and discoverers," or the testimony of "men of distinction" who were given guided tours "during the fruitful months of the year to the Red River of the North, to the rich valleys of Montana, or to the enchanting scenery of Puget Sound." Their reports, while perhaps accurate on those points, were "valueless" as far as providing a general description of the lands encompassing the Northern Pacific's grant.

Hazen was not opposed to western railroad building per se. Rather, he was raising his voice against the unethical practices of many railroad promoters. "I would prefer to see these roads based upon honesty and the needs of the country, commensurate with their cost." He could see no difference, he said, between the man who draws a check upon a bank where he has no money "and selling bonds secured by lands that have no value." In conclusion, Hazen's *Tribune* letter warned the bondholders of the Northern Pacific Railroad that the only way they could avoid a total loss on their investment was to change their bonds into "good lands now owned by the road in the valley of the Red River of the North, and East of that point."[7]

Colonel Hazen's evaluation of the Northern Pacific's undeveloped lands, featured in one of the nation's foremost newspapers, aroused considerable controversy. "Authorities" in the East and West rose up to accuse him of hostility to a great interest, ignorance of the subject, and even bribery. Typical of the stream of critical reaction—coming from western editors, congressmen, railroad officials, military men, and other interests—were extended rebuttals by John Osborne Sargent and George A. Custer.

Sargent, who called himself an "ex-surveyor general" with forty years experience on the frontier, attacked Hazen in a thirty-two page pamphlet entitled "Major General Hazen Reviewed."[8] Beginning on a caustic note, the writer theorized that "there are some useful and in other regards respectable members of society, who are unhappy unless they can see their names in the newspapers." Hazen belonged in that class of "monomaniacs," Sargent said. Reviewing his qualifications for speaking on the subject of western lands, Sargent noted that Hazen had "traveled some" in Europe, had authored a book "which no one could wish his worst enemy to have written," and then minimized, through a series of inaccurate statements, the veteran frontier officer's experience in the West. By this means Sargent sought to show that Hazen had "no real personal knowledge of the country involved." Furthermore, Sargent said he had "found no record" of the Warren and Hayden reports cited by Hazen as substantiating his facts.

Stating that the *Tribune* letter was not only an attack on Cooke's Northern Pacific Railroad, but on the "New Northwest" as well, Sargent sought to refute the "barren lands" characterization. General Land Office reports for 1870–71 were quoted to "prove" the richness of land in Dakota, and reports of surveyor generals in Montana, Idaho, and Washington were cited to verify the abundance of good lands in those territories. The optimistic evaluation of W. Milnor Roberts, chief engineer of the Northern Pacific, was given with the reassuring remark that the author "set the highest value upon his testimony." The same confidence was placed in the glowing descriptions of Martin Maginnis, delegate from Montana Territory. For the readers who might wish further "objective" and "reliable" analyses, Sargent mentioned the names of W. S. Hancock, Sheridan, and others who either had "or would no doubt if asked make favorable statements on the area." In conclusion it was said that Hazen's attack "on the integrity of the promoters of the Northern Pacific Railroad is as reckless and wanton as his penny valuation of the territory described is preposterous."[9]

Perhaps the most effective—and certainly among the most influential—spokesman of western interests in this controversy was Lieutenant Colonel George A. Custer. Having achieved prominence through the Battle of the Washita and a series of articles on his western career in *Galaxy*, Custer now turned his writing skill on Hazen's description of the Northern Plains. The result was a nine-column "Letter to the Editor" which appeared in the *Minneapolis Tribune* of April 17, 1874.

The editorial bias of the *Minneapolis Tribune* was reflected in the following headline build-up given to Custer's letter: "THE NORTH-WEST"; "General G. A. Custer in Reply to General Hazen"; "Personal Observations and Experiences vs. Prejudice and Unfounded Rumors"; "The Lands of the Northern Pacific in Dakota and Montana"; "Gen. Custer Describes what He and Hundreds of Others Saw Last Summer"; "And Refutes General Hazen's Sweeping Condemnation"; "The Country Rich with Agricultural and Grazing Lands"; "Wheat, Corn, Oats, Potatoes, Vegetables of all Kinds, and many Varieties of Fruits Grow Luxuriantly, are Excellent in Quality, and Yield Enormously."[10]

Custer insisted in his letter from Fort Abraham Lincoln, Dakota Territory, that since he "passed and repassed over every mile" of the proposed route of the Northern Pacific between the ninety-second and one hundred eighth parallels, and was stationed in the heart of its lands at Fort Abraham Lincoln, he possessed better "facilities" for observation than Hazen. Professing "too high a regard for General Hazen to insinuate even that he would knowingly publish that which is not strictly founded on truth," he, nevertheless, proposed to prove that his fellow officer's statements were "not founded on facts, but are exactly the reverse and were written in ignorance therof."

The lands around Fort Buford, about a hundred miles north of the projected railroad, were worthless, Custer conceded. But that was not true of the company's lands situated more favorably to the south. Nor did the reports of "Indian scouts and half-breeds" concerning the "unknown and uncared for region of the Saskatchawan," have anything to say about the quality of land between Bismarck and Tacoma. "Facts brought to light by the ill-fated North Pole expedition are almost as applicable to the question under consideration as the vague ideas and opinions which are endeavored to be put forth concerning the Saskatchawan country." Custer, apparently unaware that in 1866 Hazen, as acting inspector general of the Department of the Platte, had officially inspected the Upper Missouri country, chided him for not informing his readers that he had "never been nearer to the lands or route of the Northern Pacific Railroad, extending from the Missouri to the Yellowstone rivers, than he was when he penned his remarkable letter, viz., over one hundred miles distant." A major contention by Custer was that conditions near Fort Buford were not typical of conditions along the surveyed route of the Northern Pacific. His own observations of the area in question, he said, basically agreed with the representations made by the line's promoters.

Custer's impressions of the country were gained while a member of the military escort accompanying the railroad's surveying party to the Yellowstone in the summer of 1873. Tracing in great detail the route of this expedition, Custer said that from Fort Rice to the Little Missouri his command had marched over a "beautiful and rolling country," and camped "every night, with a single exception, where wood, water and grass were to be had." Near the Little Missouri River he had encountered the Bad Lands which "General Hazen would have his readers to believe is a fair sample of the lands through which the Northern Pacific railroad is to pass." Although the Bad Lands bounded the river on both sides, Custer had reportedly discovered that the river valley itself possessed "an immense area of rich bottom land, covered at that time with a luxuriant growth of the finest pasture and capable of sustaining a dense population." Beyond the Little Missouri to the Bad Lands of the Yellowstone, grazing, wood, and water were found "in ample quantities." The Bad Lands of the Yellowstone, he admitted, represented an "exceptional strip of waste tract." "It may offer a partial explanation of General Hazen's statements," Custer said, "to assume that his personal knowledge of the country of which he writes . . . is confined to that portion made up of these 'bad lands,' which entirely surround and hem in Fort Buford." He repeated that Hazen had undoubtedly never ventured "ten miles from his post in the direction of the Northern Pacific Railroad." Thus, Custer continued, if Hazen had written that for purposes of agriculture and grazing, the Bad Lands would never be worth "a penny an acre," all parties would agree with him; the commander of Fort Buford ignorantly assumed that the entire region was as barren as his immediate surroundings.

Between the Yellowstone and the Musselshell in Montana, Custer's party passed through a section of country "entirely unknown to white men—not even excepting General Hazen." All along the way, and especially in the Musselshell valley, he had found good water and grass.

Summarizing his findings on the surveying jaunt, Custer declared that the entire territory between the Missouri and Yellowstone, excluding the Bad Lands, constituted "as fine a grazing area" as he had ever seen. "As far as the eye could reach," there was "an almost unbroken sea of green, luxuriant, wavering grass, from six inches to one foot in height." Water was not only generally good "but abundant." He assured the farmer and stockman that wood, water, and grass existed in sufficient quantities to make the area a most desirable location. His own optimistic evaluation of the country, Custer claimed, was supported by professional members of the Yellowstone expedition "and by hundreds of men composing my command."

Custer also contended that Hazen deliberately distorted statements in Professor Hayden's report on the productivity of Montana lands. Quoting from the report, he ingeniously cited passages reflecting favorably on specific locations in the Territory. The Flathead Lake area and the valley of the Bitter Root, according to Custer's interpretation of Hayden, offered excellent agricultural possibilities. "By proper efforts this entire [Bitter Root] valley can be brought under cultivation, affording a rich agricultural area of at least 400,000 acres." Indeed, Custer continued, farms in Montana already at that time offered examples of productivity that clearly disproved Hazen's contention that the only agricultural lands in the Territory were confined "to the narrow valleys of the streams." And as for grazing lands, Hayden was reported to have written that Montana "is the best grazing section of the Rocky Mountain region."

On conditions around Fort Abraham Lincoln, Custer offered the experiences of Brevet Major General William P. Carlin to prove that successful gardening and tree culture was practical in the region. He also argued that the winters were not nearly as severe as Hazen had indicated. His own comments on the winters in that northern climate must have strained the credulity of even his most ardent fans.

> *I have never had occasion to wear an overcoat, [he wrote] rarely wear gloves, or if so very light ones, and have never felt the unpleasant effects of cold weather. Often . . . I have lain down in the open air and slept comfortably, this too in the months of December and January. Nor has mine been an exceptional instance. . . . The beautiful properties of this clime can scarcely be overestimated; no diseases of malarial, or pulmonary character are known.*[11]

Custer ended his lengthy discourse with a final sweeping denunciation of what he called "Gen. Hazen's misrepresentations." He endorsed the Northern Pacific Railroad as an enterprise worthy of national support:

General Hazen . . . writes of a section of the country which he has
never seen, and of which he has no personal knowledge. . . . I ask the
impartial reader to compare the statements of Gen. Hazen with those
contained in this letter, and then judge whether his universal denun-
ciation of a large and valuable portion of the public domain, and of
those who are endeavoring, honestly as I believe, to develop its untold
resources, is either just or merited. . . . The beneficial influence which
the . . . Railroad, if completed, would bring in the final and peaceable
solution of the Indian question . . . might well warrant the general
government in considering this enterprise one of national importance,
and in giving to it at least its hearty encouragement.[12]

Editorializing on the Hazen-Custer debate, the *Minneapolis Trib-*
une in a typical western Chamber of Commerce approach stated:

General Hazen's condemnation of the Northern Pacific lands, and
of the Northwest generally, was made up of prejudice and rumors
of an exceptional character, while General Custer speaks from per-
sonal observation and experience, and brings abundant corroborations
for any assertion he makes. His letter is an able vindication of the
country, and we trust his statements will be given as wide publicity
as the false *and* groundless *misstatements of General Hazen.*[13]

A few days later the *Tribune* declared that "every statement made by
Hazen, intended to injure the country," was refuted by "facts and
figures which can not be controverted."[14] Voicing agreement with
this view was the editor of the *Bismarck Tribune* who declared that
"the wild assertions of General Hazen, relating to the Northern Pacific," were effectively answered by Custer, "who has taken up the
statements of Hazen in detail, proving their falsity."[15] The May 13,
1874, issue of the Bismarck newspaper published an abridgment of
Custer's letter under the heading "Custer's Raid. Now the Dashing
Cavalry General goes for the scalp of Hazen."
    Representative of the "pro-Hazen" press reaction was this comment
by the *Cincinnati Commercial*:

General W. B. Hazen, who has been in exile at Fort Buford for

*some years . . . is not only one of the true heroes of the great war of
the North and the South, but an old Indian fighter, and in addition
to writing the most instructive book (with perhaps the exception of
Moltke's) on the Franco-Prussian war, he has done the country
service in exposing the criminal falsifications of speculators about the
American Siberia which is his place of exile.*[16]

Somewhat surprisingly an important western newspaper, the *Omaha
Herald*, defended Hazen in this controversy. The editor, formerly an
admirer of Custer, printed a strong attack on the general's reply to
Hazen.

Hazen refused to back down before the onslaughts of his critics.
Writing to Garfield on May 20, 1874, he urged the congressman to
speak out against the Northern Pacific Railroad which, he noted, "has
introduced their bill for Congressional aid and in the manner it was
plain to me, three years ago they would do." Commenting on Custer's
letter, he declared that the lieutenant colonel had based his observations on the experiences of one year, and that it had been far above
average in rainfall. His description, therefore, although "most honestly written," had no value as far as providing "an example of the
general usefulness of the country." Defending his basic thesis on the
High Plains Hazen wrote:

*The rainfall in 1872 and 1873 was 22 inches each year, while in the
five preceding years (as far back as our post records go,) it was but
10 inches each year. If you will take the trouble to call the meteorological records of the Government at the Surgeon General's office you
will see that the rain fall in that region does not exceed an average of
15 inches annually, and you also know, or can easily learn that this is
entirely inadequate to any successful general agriculture. No more
than you, do I believe that the Cookes are bad men, but they are and
have been laboring under a most fatal delusion which have successfully carried a large portion of the nation with them about this country. . . . I will repeat again, and will thoroughly prove before I am
done, that with small exceptions, say one fiftieth, or one hundredth
of the whole, the area bounded by the Rio Grande and 49th parallel
and the 100th meridian and Sierra Nevada Mountains, is neither a*

security to a bond or worth one penny an acre, and will not be in our day and generation.[17]

Hazen emphasized that it was of the utmost importance that Congress secure the facts about the "interior country" before providing further funds or support for railroad construction into that area. In his opinion there was "no national call" or need for the Northern Pacific to push its expensive project forward; rather, he saw it as "the work of speculators to make money for themselves."[18]

Indicating his motives for attacking the railroad in the first place, Hazen said:

I have written with . . . a great deal of feeling in this matter, for I know fully of what I write, and am appalled at what the Government may do, if it act upon the knowledge that now pretty securely rules concerning this interior country, for to make these grants of money can lead not only to great waste of national treasure, but great burdens to the national government. It besides fosters a spirit created by the war for dealing in great financial schemes which demoralizes honest business and robs the prudent of their money.[19]

Garfield was urged to join his crusade against the machinations of speculators and vested interest groups: "Do not keep silent . . . but try to husband the little commercial integrity still left us in the opinion of the world."[20]

In response Garfield assured Hazen that there was no chance that Congress would pass any legislation that session "by which the United States will be saddled with any further burdens of the Northern Pacific Railroad." He confessed that he had at one time possessed "some faith in the scheme" but during his visit to Montana in 1872 had become "perfectly disenchanted of any enthusiasm or faith in the matter." Since then he had done all he could to prevent people from investing their money in the bonds of that road. He promised Hazen that if the issue came to the floor of the House, which he doubted, he would use his letter to combat it.[21]

A further and more detailed expression of Colonel Hazen's views on the West appeared in January, 1875. The article written for the

North American Review was entitled "The Great Middle Region of the United States, and its Limited Space of Arable Land," and it is described as the "most scientific description of the country [plains region] put in print up to that date."[22] Hazen began research for the article while at Fort Hays, and before the end of 1873 a major portion of the manuscript was written. As a result of the attacks of Custer and others—questioning his judgment and veracity—Hazen lengthened the work to refute some of the claims made by his critics in response to the February, 1874, *Tribune* letter.

Hazen asserted that reliable information on the resource value of the West was deplorably small. "Of the value and capabilities of the great middle country," he wrote, "much is said and little is known." He intimated that he subscribed neither to the "Great American Desert" view nor the "Fruitful Garden" school of writers; rather, he believed the truth lay somewhere between the two extremes. It was his purpose to provide a detailed description of the country "between the Mississippi Valley and California," including information on climate, rainfall, topography, and soil, as well as a critical analysis of agricultural possibilities.[23]

A persistent theme stressed throughout was the general barrenness of the land beyond the hundredth meridian to the Sierra Nevada. The problem was not in the soil, he noted, but rather in the lack of sufficient rainfall. "Wherever pure water can be found for irrigation, even in the most arid and unpromising soil, the most abundant crops can be raised." But he warned that the amount of water available for irrigation was "exceedingly limited," and the "success of artesian wells is not promising." Debunking the popular theory that rainfall followed civilization, Hazen noted: "The natural laws that govern these phenomena are too broad and general to be affected by the slight results of civilization already found there. The wish is father to the thought." He pointed out that along the ninety-eighth meridian the annual rainfall ranged generally from twenty-five to thirty inches, and on the hundredth meridian from twenty to twenty-five. Although aridity ruled out general agriculture, he believed the grazing facilities to be "exceedingly valuable." Successful stock raising, however, would require a heavy outlay of capital to provide protection and food for stock in the winter, especially on the Northern Plains.[24]

The American people should be informed, Hazen insisted, of one crucial fact; they should be informed that only a limited amount of good agricultural land was left in the West for settlement.

> . . . we are rapidly approaching the limit of time [he wrote] when the landless and homeless can acquire both lands and homes by merely settling on them. We have reached the border all along, from Dakota to Texas, where land for nothing is no cheaper than good land at thirty dollars an acre. Not but that there is yet a great deal of good land for pre-emption in all the extreme frontier States; yet in all these States some settlements have reached the border, and from the 100th meridian to the Sierra Nevada Mountains, a distance of twelve hundred miles, there is not more than one acre to the hundred that has any appreciable value for agricultural purposes, or that will for the next hundred years sell for any appreciable sum. Moreover, for one hundred miles before reaching that meridian there is comparatively little good land. The authorities for this statement are believed to be impeachable. My personal observations have been of the strictest character, accompanied by careful statistical study. I have served in every State and Territory on both the eastern and western frontier, excepting Arizona and Alaska, and in all of these I have seen the land tried in gardens and in fields. There is no fault of soil anywhere. The fault is in the want of water. It is possible that, at some remote period, the good lands of the country may be so densely populated as to cause many to seek a precarious existence by such meagre farming as is possible in this region; but until then, the occasional great stock-grower, the scattered groups of miners, and the fortunate farmer, or groups of them, in the narrow valleys, who can control a little water for irrigation, will comprise the population.[25]

His view that the West beyond the ninety-eighth meridian was not capable of sustaining a large population would shock many people, Hazen predicted. Special interest groups were for years practicing "a system of misrepresentation" about the value of western lands, leading people to assume there was an almost limitless frontier for agricultural expansion. The government on its part was negligent, he believed, in not determining accurately the agricultural potential of the great middle region. Hazen thought it strange that Washington sent out expeditions year after year "to gather up, describe, and publish all that could be found out relative to beasts, birds, insects, fishes, and every conceivable creeping, crawling, or flying creature, also correct reports of its geology," but never charged any one "to learn and report that most important of all items, 'whether it is good for agriculture.'" He previously suggested to Garfield, a member of the House Appropriations Committee, that a clause be added to each measure appropriating funds for western explorations stipulating that recipients "report precisely upon the agricultural capacities of the country." That was the greatest national interest in those expeditions, he said, "and there is the least said of it."[26]

To illustrate the tactics of "misrepresentation" about western lands, Hazen cited the practices of the Northern Pacific Railroad Company:

> *By issuing a series of misrepresentations of the climate on a part of their route; by causing the press to publish, as editorials or current news, the statements of the company; by producing attractive displays of vegetable products at fairs, grown no one knows where, certainly in none of the country mentioned as bad in this article; by a specious literature, as magazine articles, so artfully written as to hide their intent; by engaging the religious press and church influence of the country,—they have succeeded, to a large extent, in deceiving the people.*[27]

Another manipulation "employed with marked success" was the securing of large military escorts to accompany surveying expeditions, "to be known and written about as acting in the interests of the road." Hazen was, no doubt, referring to the Yellowstone expedition of 1873 and the Black Hills expedition of 1874 which Custer accompanied and publicized in the press.

To sustain his charge of deceptive advertising appearing in the guise of news stories, Hazen quoted from an article published in *The Nation*, on August 22, 1872. This news release, distributed by Northern Pacific promoters, appeared earlier in the *New York Daily Bulletin*, and presumably in other publications as well. Hazen took exception to the following "facts" presented in the release: that "long

trains of emigrants" were following the track of the Northern Pacific
Railroad builders, "so that the country is filling up with a rapidity
which is destined to increase into the largest population"; that "operations are now centered in Montana, where track-laying progresses
at the rate of three miles a day"; that "in Dakota the climate is
genial" and the soil "admirably adapted to the cultivation of grain";
that "natural water-springs can be found almost anywhere by excava-
tions ten or twelve feet beneath the surface"; that "of the soil fully
nine-tenths is arable land"; and that the railroad had converted the
Indian savages into friends, thereby "amicably settling for the United
States government, at once and forever, the Indian question on the
most difficult and threatening portion of the frontier."[28]

Such claims and statements were flagrant falsehoods, the irate officer told *North American Review* readers. In fact emigration along
the Northern Pacific at that time had not extended beyond the line of
the Red River; "track-laying" had not reached "nearer to any point
in Montana than two hundred and fifty miles"; the statements on
climate, availability of water, and amounts of arable land were utterly
ridiculous—"It would be difficult to invent so many falsehoods in so
few words"; and the railroad, not having even reached the hostile
Sioux country, had done nothing to pacify the Indians.

Returning to the main thrust of his controversial *New York Tribune* letter, Hazen emphasized the effects of such heedless ethics:

*These advertisements, asking and advising the people who have
safely invested their savings in government securities to exchange
them for the securities of these roads, with the promise of a higher
rate of interest, have induced thousands of the poor and needy of the
country, who have put by the little earnings of a lifetime in safe
securities, and those holding funds in trust, to exchange them for
these bonds, having a present security of land at two dollars an acre
that has no available value. If these roads ought to be built, can there
be any sufficient reason why they should be built upon a basis of de-
ception and fraud?*[29]

The Sixth Infantry commander personally questioned the necessity
or practicability of building five transcontinental lines at that time.

"Military or state considerations" certainly did not require more than one or two. Addressing himself to the bombastic reaction to his earlier highly publicized observations on the Northern Plains, Hazen noted that "much has been said and published which requires comment or reply." By reference to a rainfall chart, dating back to 1867, he demonstrated that the Dakota country in 1873 had received the most rainfall on record, a total of twenty-one inches. Over ten inches of precipitation had fallen from May through August. The unusually wet summer resulted in "an extraordinary growth of vegetation such as has seldom been seen here." Custer, and other "authorities" on the West, some of whom Hazen accused of being paid by the Northern Pacific Railroad Company, unknowingly had been misled by the unusual season. "These writers," he explained, "have committed the error so commonly and innocently committed by thousands who undertake to enlighten mankind. They have substituted an example for a general principle. They . . . pursued the idea that other seasons had been and would be, like the one they described. In this was their error, since they wrote of the most exceptionally fruitful year on record." General Custer's personal knowledge of the Dakota country was based on one year's experience, Hazen reminded readers, and "the experiences gained in a single season are quite as apt to mislead as to instruct."[30]

Extensive meteorological data on the entire plains region were reviewed by Hazen. It seemed "to establish beyond question an insufficient rainfall for successful agriculture in those regions west of the 100th meridian," despite periodic wet cycles. Colonel Alfred Sully, a veteran of Northern Plains service, was quoted in support of this view, and he declared that "all practical and intelligent men who have a true knowledge of the country, formed upon long experience, and who have no other interest in it than to truthfully represent it," were of the same opinion. Granted, there were "places and spots" where with "great labor, a rainy season, or other favorable circumstances," encouraging results might be obtained. But the average farmer, "whose margin of profits is small at the best, cannot bear such uncertainty," and to lure him beyond the hundredth meridian "faster than he would naturally find his way with his eyes open, from

the continuous borders of the settlements, will lead to his disappoint-
ment and misery."[31]

Never reluctant to engage in controversy, Hazen concluded his
treatise with a sharp thrust at Jay Cooke:

> *The plan of "placing" the lands of the Northern Pacific Railroad*
> *"where they would do the most good" was varied by Jay Cooke from*
> *the example of his illustrious predecessor in this, that while Oakes*
> *Ames undertook to place them directly with congressional repre-*
> *sentatives, Jay Cooke, more radical and shrewd, endeavored to place*
> *his with the people, until enough had been so placed as to assure such*
> *interest in the road as would compel Congress to subsidize it. If this*
> *scheme is ever to be meritorious, and be able to stand upon its boasted*
> *land grant, why is it not so now? It can never have more acres of land*
> *to the mile of road than it has at present nor can it ever again—*
> *should construction go on—have as many acres of good land to the*
> *mile as it has now. . . . Until there shall arise some more palpable rea-*
> *son in its favor than has, as yet, been produced, it is an act of simple*
> *duty to record a protest against the plan.*[32]

After his *North American Review* article appeared, and when provoked by critics who questioned his motives and honesty, Hazen published *Our Barren Lands*, a detailed rebuttal in defense of his views
and reputation.[33] In this publication Hazen stood firm on his contention that there could be no general agriculture along the line of
the Northern Pacific west of the Missouri, nor in the entire region
bounded by the hundredth meridian on the east, the Sierra Nevada
Mountains on the west, and Canada and Mexico on the north and
south, excepting only some valleys where irrigation was possible. His
claim of February, 1874, that the Northern Pacific's lands were no
security for money had already been verified, he contended. Hazen
supported his estimate of the worthlessness of that land by a letter
from General Sully, embracing experience from 1863 to 1870; one
from Lieutenant H. H. Crowell for the season of 1874; reports from
officers of the International Boundary Survey for the same year; those
of newspaper correspondents in the Black Hills expedition with Cus-

ter; statements from the Lewis and Clark journals; and the testimony of numerous officers and farmers in 1874.

Repeating statistics and arguments presented in his earlier writings, Hazen sought to show that Custer's reports, based on limited observations made during a period of above average rainfall, were neither valid nor accurate. Comparing Custer's report on the Black Hills expedition with reports written by newspaper correspondents who accompanied him, the author found:

Where Gen. Custer saw plenty of water, the correspondents noticed it stagnant, and for 155 miles they saw not a drop of it running. Where the General saw grass in abundance for his stock, the citizens noticed the country was all dried up, and the good grass only in occasional patches; and where the commander saw wood for fuel, the others noticed that it grew scraggily and sparsely, and only near the water.[34]

These contradictory perceptions, Hazen said, were presented by him "with no unkind intent to General Custer, whom I genuinely admire." He wished merely to show the man's "peculiar tendencies" and his "standpoint of observation" so that readers could properly interpret his writings. Custer's enthusiasm was declared to be "a most admirable trait when properly directed, but it often deals with colors so bright that facts are transformed into fiction."[35]

Charges were made by several "letter writers," including Thomas L. Rosser, a divisional engineer of the Northern Pacific Railroad, and W. Milner Roberts, the line's engineer-in-chief, that Hazen possessed no personal knowledge of the country and that his impressions were based on "unfounded rumors." Meeting this accusation squarely, the infantry commander stated that he had served six years at different times, beginning in 1855, in every state and territory to be penetrated by the railroad. For eight years longer he had been on duty in other sections of the "interior country." His facts were drawn "largely from the archives of the government, from the official reports of its officers, from its recorded tables of rain-fall extending over a period of fifty years, from the reports of explorers from Lewis and Clarke down," and from other reliable authorities. "Such testimony," he declared, "is not usually classed as unfounded rumor." To the contention that conditions at Fort Buford were not typical of conditions in the railroad's forty million acres, it was stated that no appreciable difference in annual rainfall averages existed and that according to the isothermal lines, what was true climatically of Fort Buford was practically "true of all the section of country lying along the road in Dakota." Custer's citations from Hayden's reports on Montana, it was charged, failed to note that the professor always associated irrigation with agriculture and that the "good land" referred to in the reports was usually pasture land.[36]

Hazen's stated objective was to describe the true character of the yet unknown middle region, "that others may not be injured by what I conceive to be misrepresentations about it." The stories of a "Tropical Belt," a "Continental Wheat Garden," and a country with a "climate and soil that will produce in abundance all the cereals and fruits of the Atlantic States," were "puerile inventions," he averred. Westward migration had reached its "outposts" and should be warned to halt. "It is time that one and all clearly understood the truth that animal and vegetable life can not be sustained on these barren lands." With sufficient amounts of arable land available elsewhere there was "no need to go so far to find so little." Hazen concluded his rather combative fifty-three page pamphlet with an urgent appeal: "Hereafter let emigration to these places known not to be arable, be emphatically discouraged."[37]

Western lands and railroads were not the only subjects of disagreement between Hazen and Custer.[38] In the February, 1874, issue of *Galaxy*, Custer gave an account of the winter campaign of 1868, including Hazen's action in preventing an attack on the Kiowa camps along the Washita River. Custer expressed the belief that Colonel Hazen had been guilty of bad judgment, saying that it was surprising to find an experienced military officer who "could be so . . . completely deceived" as to the real character of the Indians.[39]

Hazen defended his actions in a thoroughly documented, privately published pamphlet entitled, "Some Corrections of 'My Life on the Plains'" (1875). The essence of the material appeared earlier in the *Army and Navy Journal*.[40] Hazen explained his role as Sherman's special agent at Fort Cobb, detailing the accurate surveillance that had

been maintained over the friendly Kiowa and Comanche bands under
his charge. The documents Hazen reproduced showed, contrary to
Custer's assertions, that the Kiowas as a tribe did not participate in
the Battle of the Washita. On the night of November 26, the chiefs
Custer assumed had joined in that fight were sleeping at Fort Cobb;
they did not leave for their camps up on the Washita until mid-
morning of the twenty-seventh, several hours after the battle was
fought. Failure to protect the Indians from Custer's attack would
have violated a sacred agreement made with them at Fort Larned and
the directives given him by General Sherman.[41]

Hazen's "corrections" extended to Sheridan's account of the incident also. In a statement published in 1872 the divisional commander
had expressed the following opinion:

> *Had it not been for Colonel Hazen, who represented that these
> Indians [Kiowas] were friendly, when I followed their trail, without
> missing it for a moment, from the "battle of Washita" until I overtook
> them, the Texas frontier would be in a better condition than now, and
> we would be free from embarrassment.*[42]

Sheridan's statement that he had followed the trail of the Kiowas
"from the Battle of Washita until I overtook them" was in error, as
Hazen pointed out:

> *The facts are he was not at the battle nor did he visit that section until
> December 10th, thirteen days afterwards, when he followed a trail, no
> one then knowing when it was made, until he came up with the
> Kiowas. This was the trail made by the Kiowas when first hearing of
> my arrival at Cobb.*[43]

Obviously incensed, Hazen declared that the official documents
revealed the false imputations and "mischievous errors" propagated
by Custer and Sheridan were unwarranted. Custer and Sheridan,
however, were not convinced; they never altered their original ver-
sion of that episode.

W. B. Hazen showed considerable intrepidity in attacking western
railroads and eastern financiers, and in quarreling publicly with na-

tional military heroes. As he probably expected, this served to keep
his name before the public. And the caustic criticisms of Lieutenant
Colonel Custer—his sharp-tongued former pupil at West Point—followed by his own combative literary defense, not only gave publicity
to their respective works but enhanced their disputatious reputations.

Although overly pessimistic in his predictions about the future of
the "Great Middle Region"—he did not foresee new dry-farming techniques, the introduction of hardy varieties of seeds, and extensive irrigation projects—Hazen's writings on the West in the midseventies
contributed to the public's knowledge of the area. Official explorations
by Clarence King, F. V. Hayden, George M. Wheeler, and John W.
Powell had covered only limited areas by 1875, and their reports were
not readily accessible to the general public. Eventually seven volumes
were produced by the Wheeler Survey, twelve by the Hayden, and a
considerable number by the Powell Survey, thereby furnishing a
wealth of accurate information on the area long known as the "Great
American Desert."[44] Meanwhile, the Hazen-Custer controversy
served to publicize the Dakota country, created widespread interest
in the entire Great Plains province, and pointed up the need for
thorough studies of the agricultural potential of the area. Hazen's
statements of caution to would-be settlers were at least partly justified
by events in the decades following his publications, during which time
hundreds of emigrants were wrecked in hopes and fortune by ventur-
ing across the hundredth meridian into the inhospitable limits of the
arid lands.

Belknap Brought to Bay

During the winter of 1875–76 the ring began to close round the weak and corrupt Secretary of War, William W. Belknap. As a result of the 1874 congressional elections the House Military Affairs Committee was reorganized, with Democrat Hiester Clymer as chairman. Under his leadership, an investigation was quietly begun into the persistent rumors of corruption in the War Department. Hazen was probably the source of many of these rumors; it is known that in January, 1876, in response to a request from Clymer, he forwarded information pertinent to the investigation of the committee.[1] On February 10, 1876, the *New York Herald* demanded a full investigation into suspected corruption and graft in Belknap's office, and followed it up with charges that the Secretary was farming out traderships in the West.[2]

Ever since 1872 Hazen and Belknap had been at odds. In the fall of 1874 Hazen confidentially told James A. Garfield that Belknap "is very bitter about my report of the farming out of the Sutlerships. Smalley, the clerk of the Military Committee, had the information I gave published in the *Tribune* with such embellishments as he saw fit, and so describing his authority as to at once connect me. . . . The Secty [Belknap] has of course never forgiven me."[3] In 1875 the Secretary had spurned an effort at reconciliation, refusing to acknowledge a letter from Hazen in which he apologized for some unkind remarks. The officer's inability to be transferred from Fort Buford, where the climate presumably had an adverse effect on his old wounds, was blamed on Belknap. The colonel was also convinced that Belknap was undermining his reputation with the officers and men in his regiment. Thus Hazen had ample cause for contributing to a campaign against the Secretary of War.[4]

On March 2, 1876, the Committee on War Department Expenditures, headed by Clymer, reported that it had found "uncontradicted evidence of the malfeasance in office by General William W. Belknap, then Secretary of War."[5] The evidence revealed that in the summer of 1870 the socially ambitious and free-spending wife of Secretary Belknap, in return for hospitality, had offered to obtain a post tradership for Caleb P. Marsh. Mrs. Belknap intimated that she would not be averse to accepting some of the presumably lucrative proceeds of the business. Marsh, a New York contractor, visited Washington and applied for the Fort Sill tradership. Belknap was willing to appoint Marsh, but when John S. Evans, the holder of the license, pressed for reappointment, he brought the two together to negotiate an arrangement. Marsh, who obviously held the upper hand, agreed to let Evans retain his highly profitable position for a consideration of $12,000 a year, payable in quarterly installments. In the fall of 1870 the first payment of $3,000 was received. Marsh sent one-half of the amount to Mrs. Belknap.

After the death of Mrs. Belknap in December, 1870, Marsh sent half of the quarterly payments to Belknap himself. If the Secretary happened to be in New York when the installments were due, he obtained the money in person. If not, the quarterly remittance was mailed to him. Belknap soon married Mrs. Bowers, the sister of his deceased wife, who shared in the payments. In 1872, following Hazen's disclosure of the contractual arrangement at the Fort Sill trading establishment and his complaint about the cost of goods, Evans found it expedient to lower his prices. As a result it became impossible to pay the extortionate sum and still make a profit. Marsh, thereupon, agreed to reduce his claim to $6,000 annually and thereafter cut in half his payments to the Secretary of War. In total, Marsh received about $40,000 of which $20,000 was delivered to the Belknaps.[6]

The Committee's report, with a demand for impeachment, was presented to the House in the afternoon of March 2. Belknap, having been informed early that morning by a friend on the committee, had tendered his resignation in a move to forestall impeachment. President Grant accepted the resignation shortly after ten o'clock "with great regret," not even asking the reason for such precipitate action. News of the Committee's disclosures was followed by a spate of rumors on Capitol Hill that the former secretary had committed suicide. James Garfield, reflecting the trepidation of the Republican party, confessed in his diary that for a while "I almost wished they were true."[7]

In reporting the Belknap scandal, the *New York Times* stated that "one of the most extraordinary features of the case is the lateness of the disclosure." The newspaper learned that the details of the Marsh-Evans contract were "brought to the attention of prominent officers in Washington" more than three years previously, and that in early 1876, the chairman of the House Committee on Military Affairs received "the facts and the names of necessary witnesses" to establish the truth of the charges against Belknap. According to the *Times*, "General Hazen, an officer of high character," having furnished the information, was "banished to the most distant command in the North-west as punishment for his indiscretion."[8]

When the scandal broke Colonel Hazen was in Mexico City, having obtained a leave of absence for the treatment of a chronic ear inflammation. As soon as he heard that the House had voted impeachment proceedings, he wrote to Clymer that a study of the records would reveal that in 1872 he provided the House Military Committee "the same information as that upon which your investigation is now founded." His testimony then had "only referred to the blackmailing of the post-traders and not the final disposition of the money," but the *New York Tribune*, in publishing his evidence, had "added the presumptive disposition which is now proven to have been true." Belknap, according to Hazen, had denied the charge of misuse of political influence and neither the President nor Congress had seen fit to pursue the matter, "leaving it a question of veracity between the Secretary and myself." "I have waited patiently four years," Hazen wrote, "never doubting but I should be finally vindicated, although at times feeling very heavily the weight of the displeasure of those high in power for daring to tell the truth." Referring to the information he had sent Clymer in January, Hazen released him from the restriction he had imposed that his name not be used in connection with the committee's investigation.[9]

Hazen's letter to Clymer was published in the *Cincinnati Commercial* and reprinted on March 30 in the *New York Times* and the *New York Tribune*. Insinuations by the press that the House Military Affairs Committee in 1872 had covered up the Secretary's wrongdoing brought a heated denial from John Coburn, the former chairman:

I never heard of or saw any accusation against the Secretary of War, [*he wrote to the* Commercial] *so far as this matter of post traders was concerned, until recently. . . . If Hazen knew of these crimes could he not have told them* [*the Democrats*] *if the Republicans refused to listen? But the fact is, Hazen when examined . . . said not a word against Belknap. If he knew of the crimes, and concealed them when sworn to tell the whole truth, he is not the frank and honest man I believe him to be. . . . Gen. Hazen never intimated in the remotest degree that the Secretary of War was guilty of a corrupt disposition . . . or even of the slightest misconduct, and he does not pretend to say in his letter that he did so before the committee.*[10]

The fact that the hearings were published was sufficient proof, Coburn emphasized, that there was no attempt to suppress information. He emphatically denied that he or his committee had either individually or collectively "any knowledge of the crimes of the late Secretary of War of which he now stands accused."[11]

The *New York Tribune* called Coburn's reply to the *Cincinnati Commercial* a "remarkably impudent letter." Coburn, according to the *Tribune*, by indirection sought "to injure Hazen's word." In a precisely accurate analysis of the situation the newspaper stated:

Neither the Tribune *of February 16, 1872, nor Hazen in his letter to Coburn, nor the writer from Fort Sill quoted in the* Tribune *alleged that the Secretary of War was cognizant of the swindle; but the name and address of Marsh, and the particulars of his contract, with the price, were correctly given, and the Committee was invited to inquire further and put a stop to the outrage, which it declined to do.*[12]

Hazen's letter unwittingly embarrassed Garfield as his early connection with the case was now revealed in the press. In an open letter to Coburn the congressman explained and defended his actions in 1872. Garfield admitted that Hazen had disclosed to him the terms of a contract between Marsh and Evans and that he had urged Coburn "to go to the bottom of the case, but not to disclose Hazen's name." However, he failed to mention Coburn's expression of concern that an investigation might appear to implicate Belknap, who was known to be a friend of Marsh. Garfield said that Hazen was "willing to testify on the subject" and that he subsequently appeared before Coburn's committee. But he emphasized that nothing *"in the testimony"*[13] of Hazen "indicated or suggested any corruption on the part of the Secretary of War." Garfield was technically correct but he failed to reveal the pertinent fact that Hazen's letters to him clearly suggested connivance on Belknap's part. Garfield reported that, following Hazen's testimony, the War Department, after consulting Irwin McDowell, issued its circular forbidding the "farming out" of post traderships, "which appeared to us both [Coburn and Garfield] to cover the whole case." Clymer's investigations now showed "that General Hazen was mistaken in supposing that Marsh was the Post Trader. The fact now appears to be that Evans was the Post Trader, and paid Marsh for securing the appointment—so that the Departmental order did not reach that feature of the case." Garfield said that the "attempt to make it appear that the testimony was suppressed, is, of course a sham; for Hazen's testimony was printed by Congress." Furthermore, he declared, the "attempt to make it appear that I did not do my whole duty is absurd and that Hazen suffered thereby, likewise."[14]

In continuing its aggressive investigation of Belknap's corrupt management of traderships, which even struck the President's own brother, the Committee on War Department Expenditures summoned George A. Custer to testify. In his appearance before the committee on April 4, Lieutenant Colonel Custer declared that Belknap, in an effort to forestall criticism or adverse reports, had invoked a "gag rule" on military officers. Thus, after March 15, 1873, no officers were permitted to write a member of Congress relative to military measures, except by prior approval of the secretary, and all their visits to Washington were subject to close scrutiny.[15] To exemplify Belknap's determination to safeguard his conduct from exposure, Custer referred to the "exile" of Colonel Hazen. For daring to send a communication criticizing the post tradership system, he told the committee, Hazen was sent to a lonely outpost in Dakota, about a thousand miles to the west of St. Paul. In response to Clymer's question on the state of civilization at Fort Buford, Custer said that "except the civilization that he takes with him, there is none whatever there."[16] He added that Hazen's wife, a daughter of Washington McLean, "represents a good deal of the civilization that he takes with him when he goes to Fort Buford." Questioned as to whether Hazen was a "meritorious officer," Custer surprisingly enough replied, "Very. He has always rendered conspicuous services ever since he has been in the service. . . . I heard General Sherman, in speaking of him the other day, say that he considered him one of the most meritorious officers in the service."[17] On the basis of those complimentary remarks it appears that the feud between the two officers, if, indeed, there ever was one, had been settled. Their common interest in dethroning Belknap may have been a contributing factor.

The impeachment trial of Secretary Belknap began on April 17. Because of Hazen's close association with the case, he was naturally summoned to appear as a witness. After a long debate the Senate decided, in late May, that it had jurisdiction over Belknap even though he had resigned his office. The trial, which President Grant believed was being conducted for "partisan purposes," dragged on through June and July. Colonel Hazen first testified on the tenth of July. A number of military officers had previously paraded across the stand as a great cloud of witnesses to give Belknap ringing character recommendations. Hazen held no truck with this Grant-like display of misguided loyalty. In his testimony he readily verified that in 1872 he had revealed the irregular arrangement at Fort Sill and that he was the source of the *New York Tribune* article that publicized the Marsh-Evans contract. He stated that prior to his appearance before the Military Committee he wrote either an official or unofficial letter to the War Department complaining about the traderships in general but received no reply. His reason for writing Garfield instead of Belknap on the Fort Sill matter was that he "believed it would receive no attention if sent to the Secretary of War."[18]

During the course of the questioning, House manager John A. McMahon sought to show that Belknap, even though aware of accusations of corruption in the tradership at Fort Sill, failed to check into the reports. He stated that Hazen had not officially charged the Secretary with misconduct or libeled his character in any way; what he had done was to call attention to a "monstrous grievance" which needed correction. But Belknap, instead of endeavoring as the Secretary of War to correct these evils, had cloaked them, not even bothering to inquire of the officer who had made the charges.

He shuts his eye to the transaction [McMahon stated] and goes nowhere for information.... He knew that General Hazen was the man who was responsible for this statement, and yet he neither corrects the abuses nor calls upon General Hazen in any shape or form.... He becomes very indignant because instead of the matter being represented to him, the Secretary of War, it was represented to a Military Committee. The fact of the matter was known when it was represented to the Military Committee ... yet that sore, that disgraceful corruption, that cancer upon the body politic was never probed into, never cut out, until finally it grew so rotten that it fell to pieces of its own accord.[19]

The counsel for the defense countered by maintaining that Belknap was under no responsibility to inquire of Hazen since the latter had not reported through official military channels. He might as well inquire of "any man on the street" as of Hazen if he were to check out all rumors. It was declared that the Secretary had questioned General B. H. Grierson, commander of Fort Sill, about the subject, and implied that he had therefore fulfilled his duty. McMahon replied that Belknap's letter to Grierson was so general that it never even touched the heart of the problem.[20]

In cross-examination, Hazen repeated his claim that he sent "an official or unofficial letter" on the trader system through the proper channels, and assumed that it was on file in the Secretary of War's

office. He also said that he offered "to give information in regard to
the post traderships" before being subpoenaed by the Military Committee. In an effort to show a lack of consistency on Hazen's part,
the defense introduced a letter he had written to Belknap on September 12, 1875. In the letter Hazen maintained that his actions in 1872
had been misinterpreted "by one or two enemies of high rank in the
army." He sought to imply that he had not criticized Belknap's management of post traderships, although he confessed that he had made
some intemperate statements about him "to either Coburn or Garfield," for which he apologized. Hazen explained that when summoned in 1872 "to give evidence upon staff organization," the subject of post traders was raised. When this occurred, the letter stated,
"I at first remonstrated, on the ground that I had not reported the
matter to you because I believed the Commissary Department would
defeat any action in that direction." Here was proof from the witness
himself, the defense charged, that he had not reported the Fort Sill
matter to military officials; yet he now at the trial said he had reported it.[21]

Referring to prosecution charges made earlier in the trial that
Hazen had been exiled to the "arctic" because of his disclosures, the
defense asked the witness if he were responsible for such reports.
Hazen replied that his friends had arrived at that conclusion but that
he had never made such statements. He admitted that he thought
that the Secretary felt unkindly toward him but appeared reluctant
to cite any specific "unkind acts" committed. Generally Belknap's
counsel sought to show that Hazen followed a devious course toward
the defendant and that he was motivated by personal considerations.[22]

Hazen was recalled to the stand on July 11 by the House manager
to permit him to correct a part of his previous day's testimony. The
officer stated that upon investigation he found that his letter to the
War Department complaining about post traders was written after,
instead of before, the committee hearings of 1872. Defense counsel
Matthew Carpenter questioned Hazen sharply. He demanded to
know if the witness "has not been pretty active now in the press and
in all ways setting this thing [impeachment] going?" "Somewhat
so," Hazen admitted. "Is that any portion of the duty of the colonel
of a regiment?" Carpenter pointedly asked. "No more his duty than

that of any citizen," was the tart rejoinder.[23] Then, beginning to "hit below the belt," the counsel asked the cutting question, "Is it true that you are unpopular in the Army?" To this Hazen replied, "I do not know that it is," but declared the belief that Belknap sought to make him so. Revealing that the Belknap camp held Hazen chiefly responsible for the Secretary's downfall, Carpenter told the Senate:

[Hazen] has been laboring for months to get this impeachment for his own vindication. [His motives] are utterly groundless . . . he has violated all the proprieties and all the duties of his official station by the hand he has taken in the matter and his anxiety to fan public sentiment against General Belknap, who has never done him an injury in his life-time . . . all that has been done by him has been not in line of his duty, but in violation of it, against the President of the United States, the Commander-in-Chief of the Army, and . . . his charges are wholly untrue.[24]

McMahon, who earlier had reminded Carpenter that Belknap was on trial, and not Colonel Hazen, responded to his outburst by declaring that "the counsel has imbibed the sentiment and the feeling of the client in this case in regard to, I would say, the distinguished witness who is upon the stand."[25]

The *New York Tribune*, reporting on Hazen's testimony at the trial, observed that the veteran western commander "bears the ill-will of the defense for having started the first steps in this action, and it is not strange that it strives to put him in the worst possible attitude." The reporter pointed out that only a part of the circumstances connecting Hazen with the case could be produced as evidence, "and they receive a color to suit the vindictive temper of the counsel."[26] In an editorial on July 14 the *Tribune* vigorously defended Hazen against the efforts of Belknap's lawyers and others to discredit him:

Attacks on General Hazen for alleged inconsistencies in his course about the post-tradership frauds seem to us to come with poor grace from those who profess to wish that these frauds should be stopped and their guilty authors punished. Nobody doubts that General Hazen started the exposure, that he was thereupon directly or indirectly per-

secuted by the War Department for it, or that it is the earnest desire now of General Belknap and his astute counsel in falling themselves, to drag down General Hazen also if possible. It does not seem the part of good citizens to give them the slightest help. It is quite possible that after standing exile for two or three years, with domestic affliction entailed in consequence, with torture from old wounds, General Hazen may have grown a little weary of a fight which seemed hopeless, and have done his best to get on good terms again with the Secretary under whom he had to serve. Let those who wouldn't have been tempted to do likewise throw the first stones.[27]

The evidence against Belknap was conclusive. Marsh reluctantly swore to all the damaging evidence. Evans, Pratt, and Reynolds, the same people Hazen four years earlier had said were "possessed of the facts to develop the case," and many other witnesses unraveled the sordid details of the extensive sale of post traderships throughout the West. Hazen's testimony was crucial in establishing that Belknap had been made aware of Marsh's lucrative operation at Fort Sill and that he had not acted to terminate it. The defendant's contention before the Senate that he had no idea why Marsh was giving him quarterly "gifts" was preposterous; the further statement that he never bothered to inquire of the donor the reason for his gratuity made it even more so. Yet on August 1, Belknap was acquitted, not because two-thirds of the senators considered him innocent of the articles of impeachment, but because twenty-three members insisted that the Senate lacked jurisdiction.[28] As might have been expected, the scandal-ridden Grant administration, after some feeble motions, soon abandoned all moves to prosecute Belknap in criminal court. Nevertheless, as a result of the exposure of Belknap's malfeasances, the military and Indian traderships were brought under careful scrutiny and were gradually made more responsible in their operations.

X

Vindication and Farewell to the Barren Lands

In August, 1876, following the Belknap trial, Hazen returned to Fort Buford. An elaborate campaign against the Sioux, in which Custer had already lost his life, was in progress on the Northern Plains. Despite his highly successful record as an Indian fighter, Hazen was not utilized in the massive effort to crush Sitting Bull and his intrepid allies.

Meanwhile James Garfield and Washington McLean were collaborating on plans to "better" Hazen's "position in the army."[1] It was probably their recommendation to the new Republican president, Rutherford B. Hayes of Ohio, that resulted in Hazen's appointment, in June, 1877, as military attaché to the United States legation in Vienna, Austria. The primary purpose of the assignment was to secure an American military observer of the Russo-Turkish War, which erupted in April, 1877. Hazen's widely acclaimed book on the organization of European armies and his longstanding interest in military science made him well qualified for the position. The *Cleveland Leader* observed that Colonel Hazen's selection "is everywhere commended as one of the very best that could have been made. It secures to our Government not only a capable and discriminating observer of the military operations in Turkey, but likewise a man who will put on record fearlessly and truthfully what he sees." The *Leader* assumed that "General Hazen's present conspicuous and flattering appointment shows that whatever the feeling of his superiors may have once been toward him, he is now in high favor at Army Headquar-

ters, as he abundantly deserves to be." Hazen was praised as "a gentleman, a scholar and a gallant soldier, whose integrity is as spotless as
that of Bayard himself."[2]

Hazen received notification of his appointment on July 8 and left
immediately thereafter for Ohio and Washington, D.C. Prior to his
arrival in the nation's capital, Colonel David S. Stanley of the Twenty-
Second infantry, encouraged by William Belknap, preferred charges
against him, alleging that he had committed perjury in the Belknap
impeachment trial. Stanley contended that Hazen had sworn falsely
in declaring that he had been subpoenaed by the House Military
Affairs Committee in 1872 to testify on military organization plans
rather than on the Fort Sill tradership. Hazen's statement that he was
assured his testimony before the committee would be kept secret was
likewise alleged to be false. Charges relating to Hazen's Civil War
record were also presented. Stanley bore a longstanding grudge
against Hazen dating back to the Civil War; his demand for a court-
martial now threatened to prevent Hazen from carrying out the
coveted European assignment.[3]

On July 31, Hazen, served with a copy of the charges, personally
answered the allegations to the satisfaction of the Secretary of War
and President Hayes. On the following day the President announced
"that the interest of the public service will not be subserved by a
prosecution of these charges."[4]

Hazen wrote Garfield that "evidently there had been no intention of
putting me on trial." He had found both the President and the Secretary of War "very kindly disposed" and his letter of appointment and
instructions "already made out." Voicing bitterness about Stanley's
actions, Hazen said: "He has dogged me for five years. He has repeatedly broken his written pledge to quit it and has been let off by
me, on the idea that his talk was merely the doings of a drunken sot.
Clear cases of drunkenness on duty can be made out but it would look
like going out of my bailey wick to do this." Declaring that he did
not desire to initiate court-martial proceedings, Hazen, nevertheless,
intimated that it might be necessary to take action against him after
he returned from Europe.[5]

W. B. Hazen's European service extended from September, 1877, to
June 24, 1878. The highlight of his mission was an observation tour

of the Russo-Turkish front in the Danubian-Balkan area during the fall of 1877. Upon the completion of his foreign assignment Hazen received a thirty-day delay en route and a four-month leave which he used to tour Europe with his wife and infant son. He returned to America on November 10, 1878.[6]

Shortly after his return to the United States, Hazen became entangled in one of the most remarkable court-martial cases in American military history. Colonel Stanley, undaunted by the failure to press charges against Hazen in 1877, proceeded aggressively to attack him in the press. The *St. Paul Pioneer Press*, hostile to Hazen because of his literary war against the Northern Pacific Railroad, gave early support to the assault. William Belknap, associated with a law firm in Iowa, aided in the dissemination of Stanley's various printed allegations. On March 14, 1879, F. L. Hosmer, a reporter for the *New York Times*, published an interview with Stanley in which the officer repeated his charges of perjury against Hazen and also accused him of cowardice in the Civil War. Shortly thereafter, supported by a clique of Hazen's enemies, Stanley once again requested a court-martial against the controversy-plagued officer. Stung by the vicious public attack on his character, Hazen retaliated by formally requesting that Stanley be arraigned by a court-martial on the charges of publishing and circulating libelous material against him.[7]

For several years General Sherman had tried unsuccessfully to bring about a rapprochement between the two western commanders. On March 19, 1879, he reluctantly recommended "that both Generals Stanley and Hazen be arraigned by the same court-martial on the charges made." Entertaining "not only respect but personal affection" for both officers, and recognizing that there was "too much personality in the whole matter," Sherman apparently wished to remain as neutral as possible in the controversy. By ordering the officers to be tried jointly by the same court, he put them "on equal footing." Both men would have the opportunity to prove their sundry charges.[8]

Sherman's recommendation was approved by President Hayes, despite the fact that W. M. Dunn, judge advocate general, ruled that the charges against Hazen "are all outlawed by the military statute of limitations, the 103rd article of war; the most recent alleged offenses, charged therein, being stated to have been committed on July 10th

1876."[9] This exceeded the two-year limitation for prosecuting cases. Apparently, through a devious process of reasoning, Sherman and Hayes had concluded that they could circumvent the statute of limitations by trying the men jointly. Hazen could not comprehend the decision to have him court-martialed in utter disregard of the statute of limitations. It was the equivalent of decreeing that every man could interpret the law to suit himself, he protested.

They permit this man [Stanley] to pursue me in his drunkenness and falsehood, to be joined by disgraced politicians, contractors, the Staff, and the petty quarrels of my own command . . . aided by the complicity of ex-Secretary Belknap. . . . It is positively a triumph of wrong in many forms.[10]

The general court-martial, under the direction of Major General Winfield S. Hancock, was ordered to convene in early April at Fort Columbus, New York Harbor. Stanley's charges against Hazen were summarized as follows by the *New York Tribune*:

1. *That General Hazen was guilty of disgraceful conduct at the battle of Shiloh, deserting the brigade. . . .*
2. *That General Hazen was guilty of imposture in causing a monument to be built at Stone River . . . on ground which his forces did not occupy during the battle.*
3. *That General Hazen kept out of danger at the battle of Pickett's mills. . . .*
4. *That in his official report of the action of his brigade at Mission Ridge, General Hazen falsely claimed that it was first upon the ridge, and that it captured certain guns which were in fact captured by other troops.*
5. *That General Hazen swore falsely as a witness before the Senate in the Belknap impeachment trial in regard to the purpose for which he was subpoenaed before the House military Committee, and made false statements as to the unwillingness of the Subsistence Department to comply with the law requiring it to furnish sutler's supplies to the Army.*[11]

The charges preferred against Stanley stated that he had committed libel in accusing Hazen in print of cowardice, imposture, and falsehood. Specifications of libel were made under two charges: "I. Conduct unbecoming an officer and a gentleman"; and "II. Conduct to the prejudice of good order and military discipline."[12]

Convening on April 10, the court decided to try Stanley first in the extraordinary and highly publicized proceedings. Judge Advocate Major D. G. Swaim was charged with the prosecution, and R. T. Merrick served as private counsel for Hazen. The members of the distinguished court-martial board were Major General Hancock, Brigadier General John Pope, Brigadier General C. C. Augur, Brigadier General R. B. Marcy, Colonel Israel Vogdes, Colonel J. H. King, Colonel N. W. Brown, and Colonel B. H. Grierson.

The complexity of the case was discerned by a *Tribune* reporter who explained that, although Stanley was technically the defendant the real defendant was Hazen, whose military record and character were assailed by Stanley. "In trying Stanley for accusing Hazen for cowardice and falsehood, the Court was in reality trying Hazen too; for Stanley's defense was that the charges he had publicly made were . . . capable of proof. Thus his defense was a direct attack on Hazen." The *Tribune* speculated that if Stanley succeeded in establishing his charges it would "ruin Hazen with the Army and destroy his brilliant record." However, if Stanley failed, it "would put him in the unenviable position of having given currency, presumably from unworthy motives, to slanders upon a brother officer calculated to reflect irreparable injury upon his reputation."[13]

To establish the charge of cowardice at Shiloh,[14] Colonel Stanley's witnesses were Colonel A. McD. McCook, Brigadier General Thomas J. Wood, retired, and Surgeon Robert Murray. All three testified that they had seen Hazen at Pittsburg Landing about noon on the second day of the engagement. They contended that Hazen had deserted his men in the thick of battle and taken refuge at the river bank to get out of danger. The judge advocate offered evidence explaining Hazen's accidental separation from his brigade, and officers of his command who were near him in the action attested to his gallant conduct.

Wood also testified that in the Battle of Stone's River Hazen's brigade had not fought on the ground where a monument was later erected "to the fallen" of his command. He sought to show that his own division had maintained that position and that Hazen had been engaged some three hundred yards away. Swaim rebutted Wood's evidence by the testimony of Robert Kimberly, who had been Hazen's adjutant general. Kimberly swore that Hazen's forces seized the Round Forest position, where the monument was later erected, at about 10:00 A.M. on December 31, 1862, and held it until ordered to withdraw later that night. This was corroborated by General J. M. Palmer, Hazen's division commander, who stated that none of Wood's troops held the ground during the time of the battle. Benson J. Lossing, a prominent historian, testified that General George H. Thomas had informed him that Hazen's troops had held the most important point on the field and that the monument stood upon that point.

In defense of his allegations against Hazen's conduct at Pickett's Mills, Stanley offered testimony from Wood and Colonel Daniel Bowman. Their accounts were contradicted by Kimberly and Colonel W. M. Beebe of Hazen's wartime staff.

Lieutenant General Philip Sheridan was Stanley's star witness on Missionary Ridge. Reading from his official report on that engagement, he reiterated the contention that his division reached the crest of the ridge before Hazen's brigade and that the latter appropriated guns captured by his men. Sheridan refused to be drawn into a discussion on his disagreement with Hazen's policy toward the Indians on the Washita in 1868. When asked if he recalled Hazen's contradiction of his account "on some phase of the dealings with the Kiowas," he replied that he did not, "as he had a lot to do with them at the time."

Kimberly described in detail the charge of Hazen's brigade up Missionary Ridge; the capture of a battery at the top; the turning of one of the guns to the right along the crest in front of Sheridan, who was only half-way up the hill; and the capture of eighteen pieces of artillery in its own front. After receiving Kimberly's testimony, the court decided to hear no more evidence on the Civil War, even though the prosecution had much more to present.

The testimony given by Hazen at the Belknap impeachment trial was presented by the defense to sustain and justify the charge of perjury. Stanley sought to prove that Hazen in 1872 had been called to testify before the House Military Committee on post traders' abuses and not, as he had said at the trial, and earlier in a letter to Belknap, on army-staff organization. His stated claim to a pledge of secrecy from John Coburn was also disputed. The defense believed that the testimony of Coburn would cinch their case since it possessed a letter he wrote to Matthew Carpenter in 1876 supporting Stanley's charges on those points. Subsequently, however, Congressman Garfield— prodded by Hazen—had refreshed Coburn's memory on the initial promise of secrecy given Hazen and on the "official" purpose of his appearance before the committee.[15]

Thus at the Stanley-Hazen trial Coburn testified that the main topic of his committee hearings in 1872 had been army-staff reorganization, adding only that Hazen was summoned to testify on post traderships as well. He declared that it had been his understanding that Hazen wanted secrecy on the Fort Sill business only prior to the hearings since "he had volunteered information in advance of an inquiry." Coburn admitted that "he might have talked" to Hazen prior to his testimony but did not recall giving any promise of secrecy at that time.

Eugene Smalley, clerk of the committee in 1872, testified that the members contemplated subpoenaing Hazen before he requested it because of his knowledge of army organization. He said that Hazen had not introduced the post trader issue into the inquiry, but did not recollect that the officer protested against testifying on the subject. He knew of no "open assurance" given him of secrecy, but observed that it was possible "some member may have given him that private assurance." Henry Slocum, who had been a member of the committee in 1872, confirmed that the discussion on abuses in the tradership system "came up incidently" in the hearing. He knew of no understanding that Hazen's testimony was to be confidential and recalled no "remonstrance" on his part against testifying on the topic. William Belknap, who was in constant attendance at the trial,[16] identified a letter he had received from Hazen explaining his testimony in the hearings. He admitted that he had been provoked with Hazen but claimed to have done several favors for him in spite of that fact.

Hazen contended before the court that Coburn had given him assurances that his name and testimony would not be revealed. "Before beginning to testify," he said, "I referred to a letter I had received from General Garfield, telling him [Coburn] of the secrecy which General Garfield had promised, and he made the remark to me, 'Go on and testify; that will be alright.' I supposed that he understood that assurance until he wrote the Carpenter letter." Under questioning Hazen said, "I do not insist that it was an assurance, but I always so understood and believed and never heard the contrary" until after the Belknap trial.

The prosecution's attempts to submit Garfield's letter containing Coburn's pledge of secrecy and Hazen's letter requesting the opportunity to participate in the army-staff hearings were overruled by the court. Garfield was prepared to uphold Hazen's position as a prosecution witness, but his evidence was likewise considered inadmissible. The judge advocate vigorously protested these strange and arbitrary rulings by the court, but to no avail.

It was also alleged by Stanley that Hazen's oft-repeated assertions were untrue that the Subsistence Department was flagrantly obstructing the law providing for the furnishing of soldiers' stores. Marcus Simpson and Thomas Haines of the commissary staff testified that their department was not budgeted monies nor had they received appropriations or directives from the War Department to fully execute the law of 1866. Other commissary officers said that so far as they knew there was no opposition to carrying out the law. The judge advocate, however, proved that three lists of stores prepared by the inspector general of the army never were supplied. The contention was made that if the Commissary Department had cooperated with the inspector general the law would have been faithfully executed.

On May 5, following closing arguments, the Stanley case was submitted to the court for its decision. The trial had been characterized throughout by personal denunciations and vicious acrimony. Many of Hazen's fellow officers in the Civil War rose up in judgment against him as old battles were refought and petty disputes revived. Colonel Hazen's aggressive and outspoken manner and his criticism of the so-called "bummer" element in the army, had made him unpopular in certain military quarters. Unfortunately the trial brought into the open much harbored ill will on both sides and left scars that could never be healed.

A mass of testimony offered by Hazen's counsel had been arbitrarily ruled out during the trial. Excluded was evidence seeking to establish Hazen's creditable record in the Civil War, vital correspondence with Garfield, and documents showing that Stanley had on several occasions admitted that his charges against Hazen were untrue. The court ruled time and again that such testimony was either cumulative or that it did not relate to the precise points in Hazen's conduct which had been called in question by Stanley. In ruling out evidence, it was frequently stated that the testimony might properly be introduced during Hazen's trial.

On June 18 the findings of the court-martial board were announced by Sherman in General Court-Martial Order No. 35. The court's verdict on charge I, "Conduct unbecoming an officer and a gentleman," was "not guilty, but guilty of conduct to the prejudice of good order and military discipline." Stanley was found "guilty" on charge II, "Conduct to the prejudice of good order and military discipline." The sentence recommended by the court was that Stanley "be admonished in General Orders by the General of the Army." This was the lightest sentence possible under the regulations. The board also ruled that since the military statute of limitations prohibited the trial of any officer for offenses committed more than two years before the order for the assembling of a court, Stanley's charges against Hazen could not legally be heard. Sherman, who two months earlier had disregarded the statute of limitations provision, concurred in the court's findings and ordered that "this trial and judgment of Colonel Stanley must stand as the final decision of all matters raised in the controversy."[17]

W. M. Dunn, the judge advocate general, joined Swaim in criticizing the court-martial board's handling of the trial, and recommended that the court be reconvened to renew the inquiry. Dunn charged that while Stanley, the defendant, was given full liberty to present evidence assailing Hazen's reputation, the prosecution consistently was prevented from submitting evidence crucial to their case. Swaim and Dunn also protested the light sentence meted out by the court. Stanley's offense, they said, was one of the most serious that could be committed against a fellow officer. However, Dunn's views and recommendations for the reconvening of the court were rejected.[18]

Commenting on the findings of the court the *New York Tribune* stated: "While the verdict is not as radical in its condemnation of General Stanley's conduct as General Hazen's friends would perhaps have been glad to have it, it is nevertheless a victory for the latter." The prohibition against future prosecution would not be a "hardship," for Hazen, the newspaper editorialized, "inasmuch as by the decision of the court-martial he has secured a substantial vindication."[19]

The *Tribune* did not reflect Hazen's attitude. He vehemently protested his "muzzling" in letters to Garfield, and blamed Sherman for "selling him out." He had already taken steps to prosecute Stanley in criminal court, hoping thereby to win a clear-cut vindication on the charges so dramatically publicized during the trial. This was seemingly forever denied him by Sherman's order that the issues not be revived by either party. Hazen's long friendship with the general of the army was now in jeopardy as he appeared bent on challenging the order against further prosecution. For two years following the trial Hazen, by various means, including an appeal to the President, sought a repeal of Sherman's order. Provoked by Hazen's accusations of injustice, Sherman told Secretary of War William A. Ramsey:

No man should know better than he, that for years I endeavored to act as a mutual friend, between him and Colonel Stanley, trying to prevent this very result. . . . I infer he now wishes to teach me an old lesson, older than any of us, that he who interferes in a personal quarrel must expect the kicks and cuffs of both.[20]

Labeling Hazen's appeal to the President as "ungenerous, unofficer-like and unusual," Sherman with characteristic frankness warned "if General Hazen insists on reviving this controversy he will regret it to the last day of his life."[21] In 1881, Hazen finally gave up the fight and withdrew his request for the repeal of General Order No. 35. This apparently paved the way for a renewal of friendly relations between Hazen and Sherman.

Following the climactic verdict in the Stanley trial, Hazen was ordered to resume active command of the Sixth Infantry Regiment, still headquartered at Fort Buford. The beleaguered colonel's spirit, as he traveled back to the Dakota Country, was undoubtedly low. His prospects for the future appeared as barren as the lands he had described and in which he seemed destined to serve out his career. But political developments in the spring of 1880 foreshadowed a dramatic change in fortunes.

The Republican party, meeting in convention in June, 1880, nominated James A. Garfield for President. The Democratic party's nominee was Major General Winfield S. Hancock. During the summer and fall Hazen, while on detached service in Washington, D.C., actively campaigned for his friend. In July, after personal discussions with Grant, Sheridan, and George A. Forsyth, he assured Garfield that he definitely had the support of those three influential figures. He could not report as positively on Sherman, "since his words did not always appear to me as coming from the heart." Nevertheless, he believed that the general, although understandably not wishing to commit himself publicly, favored him also.[22]

Hazen also wrote his brother-in-law, John McLean, editor of the traditionally pro-Democratic *Cincinnati Enquirer*, urging him "to do what he could" to further Garfield's campaign. Garfield and the McLeans had commenced a friendly relationship in 1875 as a result of their mutual interest in Hazen. Hazen promised Garfield that if the *Enquirer* did not do "all it should," he and his wife would personally see to it. The newspaper apparently "did what it should," with the resulting loss of about five thousand daily subscribers, according to a confidential postelection report.[23]

As the prospects of Garfield's election brightened in late summer, Hazen visualized possibilities of future advancement in rank and position. He entertained faint hopes of being nominated quartermaster general upon the retirement of Brigadier General Montgomery C. Meigs, but in the wake of the controversy-laden Stanley trial this did not appear likely. On August 24, 1880, the sudden death of Brigadier General Albert James Myer, chief of the Army Signal Corps, opened a staff position subject to presidential appointment.

Colonel Hazen immediately set his sights on securing the nomination, hoping the appointment would be delayed until after the election. On September 24 he informed Garfield that he wanted the Signal Corps post. In late October, Hazen asked Garfield to speak privately to President Hayes on his behalf when the latter passed through Ohio on his return from a western trip. He appeared fearful that Hayes might commit himself to some other candidate for the position unless Garfield acted promptly.[24]

On the evening of Garfield's thumping electoral victory in the presidential election, Hazen managed an informal interview with President Hayes. The Chief Executive gave the impression that he felt obligated "to please the Shermans," and contemplated appointing Nelson Miles as chief signal officer. Miles had married a niece of General Sherman's. Hayes promised Hazen, however, that he would confer with the President-elect before making the important appointment. Hazen suggested to Garfield that Miles "could have the Inspector Generalcy in place of Marcy, who must be retired soon."[25]

On November 5, Hazen again appealed to Garfield, stating that on the basis of his record no officer had better claims to the Signal Corps position than he. "I want the place," he wrote, "because it gives me new work, which to me is new life. The want of work is strangulation and death."[26] With the posting of this earnest plea Hazen returned to the West to rejoin his regiment, garrisoned since July, 1880, at the White River agency in Colorado.

On December 6, following two separate consultations with President-elect Garfield, Rutherford B. Hayes announced Hazen's promotion to the rank of brigadier general and appointment as chief signal officer. The glad tidings reached Hazen at Rawlins, Wyoming, on that same day. On the seventeenth, after a speedy confirmation, the fifty-year-old army veteran assumed his new duties in Washington.

Hazen's nomination predictably resulted in some resentment and open criticism. The *New York Tribune*, however, considered his selection an excellent choice, stating:

Among the colonels in active service it would be impossible to designate one better fitted by mental powers, scholarly habits and scientific tastes to fill the service. There is opportunity enough to make it more thorough and accurate, which a vigorous man, not fond of running in old ruts, will early see.[27]

On Christmas Day, 1880, Hazen gratefully acknowledged Garfield's influence in swinging the nomination to him:

I wish to thank you heartily for your kind and efficient action, which turned the question in my favor. And in thanking you, I wish to thank you all, for I believe your mother and your wife were my active good willers all the way through. To them as well as you—my gratitude is deep and lasting.[28]

Then, revealing his characteristic zest for undertaking new responsibilities, he concluded with the words, "I like my work, and the field opens larger every day."

W. B. Hazen's career from 1877 to 1880 was highlighted by his Vienna assignment and the bitter quarrel with D. S. Stanley and his coconspirator, W. W. Belknap. Although accorded great fanfare, the unique Stanley-Hazen court-martial trial brought credit to none of the leading principals in the case. Hazen thought by bringing Stanley to trial he could once and for all publicly and officially disprove the recurring charges of cowardice, perjury, and misrepresentation raised against him. The main result was to give wider circulation to the scandalous accusations. Since the court excluded much testimony favorable to Hazen, while permitting damaging evidence, and since only one-half of the trial as originally planned was held, his side of the story did not get a thorough review. Furthermore, several Eastern newspapers, including the *New York Times*, displayed an obvious anti-Hazen bias in their coverage of the proceedings. Thus in retrospect Hazen's insistence on a court-martial against Stanley was ill conceived. Convinced that he had been unable to state his case effectively in court, Hazen in 1885 produced *A Narrative of Military Service*, a documented work devoted in part to the defense of his Civil War record and personal reputation. His designation as chief signal officer in 1880 made up for any loss of prestige he may have suffered as a result of the public quarrel with Stanley. The appointment to that high-level and challenging staff position in Washington was a deserving reward for long and faithful military service. Possessed with the indomitable spirit of the frontier and a broad background of varied experiences gained in the trans-Mississippi West, William B. Hazen was prepared to utilize fully the new opportunities of service that were now his.

XI

Hazen in the West: An Appraisal

Brigadier General W. B. Hazen's appointment as chief signal officer terminated twenty-one years of military service in the West. Under his administration the Signal Corps was organized efficiently and recorded many noteworthy advances in performance and service. In 1884–85 Hazen became the center of a national controversy rising out of the disastrous Lady Franklin Bay Polar Expedition commanded by Adolphus W. Greely. Although found guilty by a court-martial for unduly criticizing his superior, Secretary of War Robert T. Lincoln, the finding did not hurt his career. On January 16, 1887, Hazen died suddenly as a result of kidney poisoning. Colonel John H. Janeway, surgeon, United States Army, certified that Hazen's bullet wound suffered in 1859 caused "diaphragmatic spasm and neuralgia of the diaphragm" and that the movement of the bullet which remained in his body, together with diabetic complications, caused his illness and death.[1] Hazen's only surviving son, John McLean Hazen, died in 1898, at the age of twenty-two. His widow, Mildred McLean Hazen, married Admiral George Dewey in 1899.

William B. Hazen's life does not fit the stereotyped picture of a blood and guts, hell-raising, wenching, and whisky-guzzling frontier soldier. He was refined, scholarly, and apparently happily married to a cultured lady of society. He toured Europe three times prior to 1880, socializing with many high military and government officials, including Otto von Bismarck. Well informed on public issues and a good conversationalist, he moved with equal facility in Washington's high society or in camp circles on the rough frontier. His contribution to the West was not made as a glamorous Indian fighter, but came through conscientious and intelligent performance of service that brought credit to his profession at a time when avarice and mediocrity typified much of the military system.

Unspectacular—but important—in the story of the West was Hazen's role in establishing three important frontier army posts. In 1856, as the commanding officer at Grand Ronde, Oregon Territory, he selected the site and began construction of a post later called Fort Yamhill. In 1869, on the basis of a recommendation from Hazen and B. H. Grierson, Fort Sill was established at its present location. The major construction of Fort Buford, Dakota Territory, established in 1866, occurred after Hazen assumed command in 1872.

Hazen's bravery and zeal in leading five successful expeditions against Indians in Texas, in which he recovered captives and many stolen goods, won him the plaudits of frontier citizens, five military citations, and a brevet. He was the first officer since the Seminole War to be breveted for service against Indians.

Hazen played a major role in placing the Southern Plains Indians on their reservations in 1868–69. His contribution, often overlooked because of the public fascination for the more glamorous exploits of Custer, was at least equally important. He was the key arm of the military in preventing the peaceful bands from joining the hostiles in the winter campaign of 1868. His judicious administration at Fort Cobb and Fort Sill, his courage and firmness in the face of danger, and his far-sighted plans for the bands under his jurisdiction won him the praise of military superiors, Indian Bureau officials, and even some words of approbation from Indians. In an assignment requiring considerable initiative and ingenuity, it is doubtful whether a more competent or responsible officer could have been found than W. B. Hazen.

Although Hazen believed in severe punishment of hostile Indians for their depredations, he felt just as firmly that the peaceful should be treated honorably and with justice. It was in this context that as a temporary superintendent of Indian affairs he initiated a successful movement to secure farming lands for the dispossessed Wichita Indians. Also during his superintendency in 1870–71, a thorough and honest determination was made of the claims of Loyal or Union

Creeks for losses sustained during the Civil War. The Hazen-Field
investigations laid the basis for what could have been a reasonable and
equitable settlement; unfortunately legal technicalities and congressional opposition dealt the Indians still another defeat. They were
forced to settle for only a small fraction of the sum Hazen established
as a just award.

A courageous act of far-reaching import was Hazen's exposure of
the post tradership corruption at Fort Sill in 1872. Culminating in the
impeachment of Secretary of War William W. Belknap four years
later, his agitation helped induce long-needed reforms in the military
and Indian tradership system. The early history of the tradership
scandals including the short-lived investigation undertaken by representatives John Coburn and James Garfield, after receiving damaging evidence from Hazen, has heretofore generally escaped historical
attention. While other officers and politicians either closed their eyes
to graft in the War Department, or else were unable to distinguish
between extortion and rugged individualism, Hazen's convictions
would not permit him to remain silent. As a result his career suffered
directly and indirectly. Statements at the Belknap trial and Belknap's
close collaboration with D. S. Stanley in his efforts to defame Hazen's
character indicate that he held the latter significantly responsible for
his apprehension and fall into disrepute.

The Belknap scandals were a striking example of the general moral
laxity of the times. An even larger offense against the American
people was the wholesale looting of the West by railroad corporations
and speculators. In official reports, periodical articles, pamphlets, and
letters to congressmen and the press, Hazen called attention to this
more subtle form of extortion. His personal campaign against the
questionable operations of Jay Cooke and the Northern Pacific Railroad, which he began in 1872, reached its climax in 1874 and 1875.
Just how much effect Hazen's writings had on the railroad's promotional efforts is difficult to evaluate. The violent reaction of the road's
supporters would seem to indicate a clear recognition of his potential
influence with Congress, which was periodically being asked to bail
out the railroad, and with the gullible public, which was being asked
to finance further expansion.

Hazen's article in the *North American Review* in 1875 on the

"Great Middle Region" was one of the most detailed and scientific descriptions published by that date of the public domain between the hundredth meridian and the Sierra Nevadas. His pessimistic evaluation of the agricultural potential of the region coincided with the analysis John Wesley Powell gave the House Committee on Public Lands in 1874.[2] It should be noted that Hazen's article had been written in 1873, although it was not published until a year after Powell announced his conclusions on the arid lands to the congressional committee. The latter's celebrated *Report on the Lands of the Arid Region of the United States* was not published until 1878.[3]

In seeking to repudiate the "myth of the great fruitful garden," being foisted on the nation by speculators and railroad corporations, Hazen went too far in the opposite direction, dismissing most of the high plains as incapable of sustaining substantial settlement. Nevertheless, he correctly predicted that undependable rainfall would pose an insoluble problem for a generation or longer. Time and again, between 1870 and 1890, settlers crossed the hundredth meridian in periods of relatively high rainfall, only to be driven back by the dry cycle which inevitably followed. Not until new seeds and new techniques of farming were introduced was agriculture feasible on the Great Plains. Once native Americans, Russian-Mennonites, with their hardy Red Turkey wheat, Scandinavians, and other intrepid pioneers got a toe hold in the sod, they refused to be driven out of even the most inhospitable corners. Even so the western farmer has faced a continuing fight to survive in the arid lands. Periodic drouths and the growing concern over water shortages in the West are indicative of the fact that the final chapter in the struggle between man and the desert has not yet been written.

Hazen's writings on the West were intended to counter the misrepresentations of railroad barons and their financial and literary agents. He did not criticize sound and legitimate railroad expansion based on the economic needs of the West. Neither did he seek to halt the westward movement. Rather, he wisely cautioned that the advance beyond the ninety-eighth meridian should proceed "naturally" with "eyes open" and not be stampeded by greedy and irresponsible propagandists.

While most of the military commanders after the Civil War appear to have been content to reminisce about the glories of the past, General Hazen was concerned about the army's future. His study of the European armies convinced him that the western army was woefully lacking in modern tactical or logistical organization and that the cumbersome military administrative system would be seriously hamstrung in a war with a foreign power. His carping criticism of the low professional military standards and suggestions for army reform, published in *The School and the Army in Germany and France,* and repeated before congressional committees, met with opposition in some military quarters and complete indifference in others. In general the military leadership lacked the initiative to creatively build for the future.

A militarist imbued with the highest traditions of West Point, Hazen gained the reputation of being an army "watch dog." As his career advanced he came to be recognized as an able man and a dangerous enemy. Displaying neither fear nor favor he exposed graft and corruption, waste and inefficiency, negligence and shoddy performance of duty wherever he found it. He was always willing "to cast stones at abuses," and those who dared cross him did so at their own peril. Not always judicious, he at times displayed an irritating air of superiority and occasionally wrote and acted rashly. Quick to point out mistakes in others, he found it difficult to accept criticism.

Hazen's qualities made him both friends and enemies, and involved him in almost constant controversy. There were those in the army who held no truck with the likes of Hazen, and he was the victim of persistent and malicious attacks. On the other hand, proponents of army reform, realistic Indian policies, and old-fashioned honesty and integrity in the civil and military departments of the government had high regard for Hazen. General William T. Sherman said in 1883 that Hazen's "military record from the day of his first commission is perfect, and is such as any man may be proud of. He is an officer of the highest professional attainments and of the best possible habits."[4] James A. Garfield relied extensively on Hazen for advice on military affairs in the post–Civil War years. Whitelaw Reid, a prominent editor and champion of reform in the "Gilded Age," admired Hazen's courage in exposing corruption regardless of personal consequences. In 1880 he singled out the veteran officer as "a representative of the element in the Army which studies hard and works hard, believes that an officer has something to do in time of peace besides drinking whiskey and playing cards, and does not think the old saying need ever be verified that a full colonelcy and complete imbecility come to a man at the same time." He deplored the fact that some petty-minded individuals were determined to downgrade his record of solid achievement.[5]

Most of the controversies that attended William Babcock Hazen's career have faded into relative obscurity. His life and contributions, however, form a colorful and noteworthy chapter in the history of the western frontier.

Abbreviations Used in Notes

AAG   Assistant Adjutant General
AGO   Adjutant General's Office
NA   National Archives
OJAG   Office of the Judge Advocate General
RG   Record Group
USAC   United States Army Command

Notes

Chapter I
A Shavetail in the Pacific Northwest

1. William B. Hazen to Thomas Corwin, March 13, 1851, Records of War Department, Adjutant General's Office, United States Military Academy File, 1851, Letters Received, National Archives, Washington, D.C., Record Group 94 (hereafter cited as AGO, NA, RG 94); Eben Newton to Charles M. Conrad, Secretary of War, August 15, 1851, AGO, Letters Received, NA, RG 94; *The Register of Cadet Applicants, 1850–51*, AGO, Engineer Department, NA, RG 94. William B. Hazen was born at Hartford, Vermont, on September 27, 1830, but his parents, Stillman and Ferona Fenno Hazen, moved the family to Hiram, Ohio, in 1834.

2. W. H. Tucker, *History of Hartford, Vermont*, 362; Military Academy Merit Rolls, 1855, United States Military Academy File, 1855, AGO, NA, RG 94.

3. Regular Army Organization Returns, Fourth Regiment United States Infantry, October, 1855, AGO, NA, RG 94; Post Returns, Fort Reading, California, November, 1855, AGO, NA, RG 94.

4. William M. Colwig, "Indian Wars of Southern Oregon," *Oregon Historical Quarterly*, Vol. IV (1903), 228; Alice Applegate Sargent, "A Sketch of the Rogue River Valley and Southern Oregon History," *Oregon Historical Quarterly*, Vol. XXII (March, 1921), 3; Stephen Beckham, *Requiem for a People*, 9.

5. Frances Victor, *The Early Indian Wars of Oregon*, 269, 273–74; C. F. Coan, "The Adoption of the Reservation Policy in Pacific Northwest, 1853–1855," *Oregon Historical Quarterly*, Vol. XXIII (March, 1922), 3.

6. Robert Carlton Clark, "Military History of Oregon, 1849–1859," *Oregon Historical Quarterly*, Vol. XXXVI (March, 1935), 23–24, 59; Robert W. Frazer, ed., *Mansfield on the Conditions of the Western Forts 1853–54*, xxiv–xxvi; 35 Cong., 2 sess., *House Exec. Doc. No. 93*, 22–23.

7. George Crook, *General George Crook: His Autobiography* (ed. by Martin F. Schmitt), 7, 10; Clark, "Military History of Oregon 1849–1859," *Oregon Historical Quarterly*, Vol. XXXVI (March, 1935), 21.

8. 35 Cong., 2 sess., *House Exec. Doc. No. 47*, 11; 33 Cong., 1 sess., *Sen. Exec. Doc. No. 1*, 11, 6.

9. Commissioner of Indian Affairs, *Annual Report of the Commissioner of Indian Affairs for the Year 1856*, 264 (hereafter cited as Commissioner of Indian Affairs, *Report*, with the applicable year added); Coan, "The Adoption of the Reservation Policy in Pacific Northwest, 1853–1855," *Oregon Historical Quarterly*, Vol. XXIII (March, 1922), 8, 14–15.

10. H. O. Lang, *History of the Williamette Valley*, 360.

11. *Ibid.*, 376–77; Victor, *Early Indian Wars of Oregon*, 343–44.

12. Post Returns, Fort Lane, Oregon Territory, December, 1855, AGO, NA, RG 94; Major G. I. Rains to the Adjutant General, December 13, 1855, Records of the War Department, United States Army Commands, Letters Received, Department of the Pacific, NA, RG 98 (hereafter cited as USAC, Letters Received, Department of the Pacific, NA, RG 98).

13. Hubert Howe Bancroft, *History of Oregon*, II, 388; Captain A. J. Smith to Major E. D. Townsend, AAG, January 8, 1856, USAC, Letters Received, Department of the Pacific, NA, RG 98.

14. *Ibid.*

15. Report of First Lieutenant Edmund Underwood to Captain A. J. Smith, January 8, 1856, enclosure in *ibid.*; Bancroft, *History of Oregon*, II, 389; Rodney Glisan, *Journal of Army Life*, 277.

16. Smith to Townsend, February 12, 1856, USAC, Letters Received, Department of the Pacific, NA, RG 98.

17. Joel Palmer to Brevet Major General John E. Wool, December 1, 1855, 34 Cong., 1 sess., *House Exec. Doc. No. 93*, 23.

18. *Oregonian*, October 20, 1855, in Clark, "Military History of Oregon, 1849–1859," *Oregon Historical Quarterly*, Vol. XXXVI (March, 1935), 30.

19. Palmer to Wool, December 1, 1855, 34 Cong., 1 sess., *House Exec. Doc. No. 93*, 24–25.

20. 34 Cong., 3 sess., *Sen. Exec. Doc. No. 5*, 153.

21. Palmer to Wool, December 1, 1855, 34 Cong., 1 sess., *House Exec. Doc. No. 93*, 24–25; C. C. Royce, comp., "Indian Land Cessions in the

United States," Bureau of American Ethnology, *Eighteenth Annual Report*, II, 812–13; Coan, "The Adoption of the Reservation Policy in Pacific Northwest, 1853–1855," *Oregon Historical Quarterly*, Vol. XXIII (March, 1922), 4.

22. George H. Ambrose to Palmer, December 2, 1855, 34 Cong., 1 sess., *House Exec. Doc. No. 93*, 120; Bancroft, *History of Oregon*, II, 398–99.

23. Palmer to Wool, November 1, 1855, 34 Cong., 1 sess., *House Exec. Doc. No. 93*, 113; Smith to Townsend, January 5, 1856, USAC, Letters Received, Department of the Pacific NA, RG 98.

24. Nathan Ford to Ambrose, December 18, 1855, Records of the Oregon Superintendency of Indian Affairs, 1848–73, MSS, Letters Received, NA, RG 75, Microcopy 2, Roll No. 14, University of Oklahoma Division of Manuscripts, Bizzell Library, Norman, Oklahoma (hereafter cited as Oregon Superintendency, Letters Received, NA, RG 75); Ambrose to Palmer, January 7, 1856, Oregon Superintendency, Letters Received, NA, RG 75; Smith to Townsend, January 5, 1856, USAC, Letters Received, Department of the Pacific, NA, RG 98; Lang, *History of the Willamette Valley*, 435.

25. Ambrose to Palmer, January 7, 1856, Oregon Superintendency, Letters Received, NA, RG 75.

26. Post Returns, Fort Lane, Oregon Territory, January, 1856, AGO, NA, RG 94; Smith to Townsend February 12, 1856, USAC, Letters Received, Department of the Pacific, NA, RG 98; Crook, *Autobiography*, 31.

27. Smith to Captain D. B. Jones, AAG, February 23, 1856, USAC, Letters Received, Department of the Pacific, NA, RG 98.

28. Ambrose to Palmer, January 31, 1856, and February 24, 1856, Oregon Superintendency, Letters Received, NA, RG 75; Smith to Jones, February 12, 1856, and February 23, 1856, USAC, Letters Received, Department of the Pacific, NA, RG 98.

29. Crook, *Autobiography*, 31; Ambrose, "Journal of the Removal of the Rogue River Tribe of Indians," Oregon Superintendency, Letters Received, NA, RG 75 (hereafter cited as Ambrose, Journal, NA, RG 75).

30. Frazer, ed., *Mansfield on the Condition of the Western Forts 1853–54*, 114; Ambrose, Journal, NA, RG 75.

31. Ambrose to Palmer, February 29, 1856, Oregon Superintendency, Letters Received, NA, RG 75; Smith to Jones, March 3, 1856, USAC, Letters Received, Department of the Pacific, NA, RG 98; Crook, *Autobiography*, 31; Ambrose, Journal, NA, RG 75; A. F. Hedges to R. B. Raymond, October 9, 1856, Records of the Oregon Superintendency of Indian Affairs, 1848–73, MSS, Letters Sent, NA, RG 75, Microcopy 2, Roll No.

6, University of Oklahoma Division of Manuscripts, Bizzell Library (hereafter cited as Oregon Superintendency, Letters Sent, NA, RG 75).

32. Ambrose, Journal, NA, RG 75; Smith to Jones, March 3, 1856, USAC, Letters Received, Department of the Pacific, NA, RG 98.

33. Ambrose to Palmer, March 3, 1856, and March 6, 1856, Oregon Superintendency, Letters Received, NA, RG 75; Ambrose, Journal, NA, RG 75; Frazer, ed., *Mansfield on the Condition of the Western Forts 1853–54*, 114, 185.

34. R. B. Metcalf to Palmer, March 8, 1856, Oregon Superintendency, Letters Received, NA, RG 75; Palmer to George Manypenny, Commissioner of Indian Affairs, April 11, 1856, Oregon Superintendency, Letters Sent, NA, RG 75; Ambrose, Journal, NA, RG 75.

35. Ambrose, Journal, NA, RG 75; William B. Hazen to Colonel S. Cooper, adjutant general, March 31, 1856, USAC, Letters Received, Department of the Pacific, NA, RG 98.

36. Lang, *History of the Willamette Valley*, 434–35.

37. Hazen to Cooper, March 31, 1856, USAC, Letters Received, Department of the Pacific, NA, RG 98.

38. Metcalf to Palmer, April 10, 1856, Oregon Superintendency, Letters Received, NA, RG 75; John F. Miller, Indian agent, to J. W. Nesmith, July 20, 1857, in Commissioner of Indian Affairs, *Report for 1857*, 361, 363, 367.

39. Palmer to Manypenny, April 11, 1856, Oregon Superintendency, Letters Sent, NA, RG 75.

40. "Petition from Citizens near Grand Ronde Reservation," enclosure in James A. Campbell and others to Palmer, March 28, 1856, Oregon Superintendency, Letters Received, NA, RG 75; Metcalf to Palmer, April 3, 1856, Oregon Superintendency, Letters Received, NA, RG 75.

41. A. D. Babcock to Palmer, April 21 and April 30, 1856, Oregon Superintendency, Letters Received, NA, RG 75.

42. Palmer to Manypenny, April 11, 1856, Oregon Superintendency, Letters Sent, NA, RG 75; Colonel George Wright to Hazen, March 21, 1856, Letter Book, Headquarters, Northern District, Department of the Pacific, 1856, AGO, NA, RG 98; Palmer to Wool, April 14, 1856, Oregon Superintendency, Letters Sent, NA, RG 75.

43. Palmer to Wool, April 19, 1856, Oregon Superintendency, Letters Sent, NA, RG 75.

44. John Ostrander, teacher, to John F. Miller, July 21, 1857, in Commissioner of Indian Affairs, *Report for 1857*, 87; Philip H. Sheridan, *Personal Memoirs of P. H. Sheridan, General, United States Army*, I, 108

(hereafter cited as Sheridan, *Personal Memoirs*); Glisan, *Journal of Army Life*, 380.

45. Palmer to Manypenny, April 11, 1856; Palmer to J. S. Rinearson, April 3, 1856; Palmer to Metcalf, April 11, 1856; and Palmer to Wool, April 14, 1856, Oregon Superintendency, Letters Sent, NA, RG 75.

46. Wool to Palmer, April 19, 1856, Oregon Superintendency, Letters Received, NA, RG 75.

47. M. C. George, "Address Delivered at Dedication of Grand Ronde Military Block House at Dayton City Park, Oregon, August 23, 1912," *Oregon Historical Quarterly*, Vol. XV (March, 1914), 65.

48. Order No. 6, Headquarters, District of Southern Oregon, Department of the Pacific, July 4, 1856, AGO, NA, RG 98; Post Returns, Grand Ronde Coast Reservation, July, 1856, AGO, NA, RG 94; Oscar Winslow Hoop, "History of Fort Hoskins, 1856–1865," *Oregon Historical Quarterly*, Vol. XXX (March, 1929), 349.

49. Post Returns, Fort Yamhill, August, 1856, AGO, NA, RG 94; *Outline Index, Military Forts and Stations, Reservation Division*, AGO, NA, RG 94.

50. Jacob P. Dunn, *Massacres of the Mountains*, 177.

51. Smith to Major W. W. Markell, AAG, September 19, 1856, USAC, Letters Received, Department of the Pacific, NA, RG 98; Headquarters, Department of the Pacific, to Smith, December 3, 1856, Letter Book, Department of the Pacific, 1856, AGO, NA, RG 98.

52. Philip Sheridan reportedly "lived with" a Rogue River Indian girl who was "as graceful as a deer and as slender as a fawn." Fred Lockley, ed., "Reminiscences of Mrs. Frank Collins, Nee Martha Elizabeth Gilliam," *Oregon Historical Quarterly*, Vol. XVII (1916), 367.

53. Glisan, *Journal of Army Life*, 375–76.

Chapter II
Scouting Indians on the Texas Frontier

1. A. B. Bender, *The March of Empire*, 130–35; W. C. Holden, "Frontier Defense, 1846–1860," *West Texas Historical Association Year Book*, Vol. VI (June, 1930), 41.

2. Holden, "Frontier Defense, 1846–1860," *West Texas Historical Association Year Book*, Vol. VI (June, 1930), 41–42; Colonel M. L. Crimmins, "The First Line of Army Posts Established in West Texas in 1849," *West Texas Historical Association Year Book*, Vol. XIX (1943), 121–24;

William H. Leckie, *The Military Conquest of the Southern Plains*, 16; Carl Coke Rister, *The Southwestern Frontier, 1865–1881*, 49.

3. Charles J. Kappler, *Indian Affairs, Laws and Treaties*, II, 322–23, 363–64, 445–47; Lena Clara Koch, "The Federal Indian Policy in Texas, 1845–1846," *Southwestern Historical Quarterly*, Vol. XXVIII (April, 1925), 263–65.

4. Report of R. B. Marcy and R. S. Neighbors to P. H. Bell, September 30, 1854, in Dorman H. Winfrey, ed., *Texas Indian Papers, 1846–1859*, III, 186–90; R. B. Marcy, *Thirty Years of Army Life on the Border*, 170; Koch, "The Federal Indian Policy in Texas, 1845–1846," *Southwestern Historical Quarterly*, Vol. XXVIII (April, 1925), 100, 104; 35 Cong., 1 sess., *House Exec. Doc. No. 2*, 551; Holden, "Frontier Defense, 1846–1860," *West Texas Historical Association Year Book*, Vol. VI (June, 1930), 55–58; Rupert Norval Richardson, *The Comanche Barrier to South Plains Settlement*, 245, 257.

5. Walter Prescott Webb, *The Texas Rangers*, 151; H. R. N. Gammel, comp., *The Laws of Texas: 1822–1897*, IV, 949–50; Brevet General D. E. Twiggs to Lieutenant Colonel L. Thomas, July 6, 1858, in 35 Cong., 2 sess., *Sen. Exec. Doc. No. 1*, 11, 258; Twiggs to Hardin R. Runnels, September 9, 1858, in Webb, *Texas Rangers*, 160.

6. W. J. Hughes, *Rebellious Ranger Rip Ford and the Old Southwest*, 142–46; Richardson, *The Comanche Barrier to South Plains Settlement*, 238.

7. Regular Army Organization Returns, Eighth United States Infantry, May, 1858, AGO, NA, RG 94; M. Steck, Indian agent, to Colonel James L. Collins, superintendent of Indian affairs, New Mexico, August 10, 1858, in 35 Cong., 2 sess., *House Exec. Doc. No. 2*, 548; Frank D. Reeve, "The Apache Indians in Texas," *Southwestern Historical Quarterly*, Vol. L (October, 1946), 210; Washington Seawell to Brevet Major General D. E. Twiggs, Commanding Department of Texas, June 24, 1858, in an endorsement on W. B. Hazen to Lieutenant and Adjutant William E. Dye, June 22, 1858, AGO, Letters Received, Department of Texas, NA, RG 94.

8. W. B. Hazen to Lieutenant and Adjutant William E. Dye, June 22, 1858, AGO, Letters Received, Department of Texas, NA, RG 94.

9. *Ibid.*

10. General Order No. 5, Headquarters of the Army, New York, New York, November 10, 1859, by command of Brevet Lieutenant General H. L. Scott, AGO, NA, RG 94. The Mescalero outlaws that eluded Hazen continued their depredations for several more years. They and their kins-

men found the Guadalupe Mountains a strategic vantage point for raiding the cattle herds driving northward along the Texas–New Mexico
border. Finally, in 1863 a substantial number of these Indians were
rounded up and assembled on a reservation at the Bosque Redondo on the
Upper Pecos in New Mexico. Reeve, "The Apache Indians in Texas,"
Southwestern Historical Quarterly, Vol. L (October, 1946), 211.

11. Regular Army Organization Returns, Eighth United States Infantry, August, 1858, through November, 1859, AGO, NA, RG 94.

12. Hazen to Captain R. P. Maclay, May 23, 1859, AGO, Letters Received, Department of Texas, NA, RG 94.

13. General Order No. 5, Headquarters of the Army, New York, New
York, November 10, 1859, by command of Brevet Lieutenant General H.
L. Scott, AGO, NA, RG 94; Francis B. Heitman, *Historical Register and
Dictionary of the United States Army from 1789 to 1903*, Vol. I, 517.

14. Regular Army Organization Returns, Eighth United States Infantry, June–September, 1859, AGO, NA, RG 94; *Dallas Herald*, August 21,
1858.

15. Hazen to Maclay, October 7, 1859, in W. B. Hazen, *A Narrative
of Military Service*, 431.

16. The men sent on the mission to Fort Clark arrived at the post on
November 4. The following morning the post commander, Brevet Major
William H. French, sent Assistant Surgeon W. J. H. White and an escort
of twenty men to the battle site with a wagon and relief supplies. Mounted
on unshod mules and slowed by rough country the relief detail reached
the location on November 8.

17. Second Lieutenant W. B. Hazen, Report of the Operations of a
Scout, October and November, 1859, to Captain J. Withers, AAG, Headquarters Department of Texas, December 20, 1859, AGO, Letters Received, Department of Texas, NA, RG 94.

18. Copy of surgeon's certificate, R. L. Brodie, assistant surgeon, U.S.A.,
January 23, 1860, an enclosure in Hazen to Adjutant General's Office,
Washington, D.C., March 16, 1860, AGO, Letters Received, NA, RG 94;
Special Order, No. 11, Headquarters, Department of Texas, December 12,
1859, AGO, NA, RG 94.

19. Lieutenant Colonel J. E. Johnston to the Assistant Adjutant General, Headquarters of the Army, November 14, 1859, AGO, Letters Received, NA, RG 94.

20. General Order No. 16, Headquarters, Department of Texas, October 30, 1860, in Crimmins, "Colonel Robert E. Lee's Report on Indian
Combats in Texas," *Southwestern Historical Quarterly*, Vol. XXXIX

(July, 1935), 23–24. Lee commanded the Department of Texas from February 20 to November 27, 1860; General Order No. 11, Headquarters of the Army, November 23, 1860, AGO, NA, RG 94.

    21. Cited in Hazen, *A Narrative of Military Service*, 436.

    22. Copy of surgeon's certificate, R. L. Brodie, assistant surgeon, U.S.A., January 23, 1860, an enclosure in Hazen to Adjutant General's Office, Washington, D.C., March 16, 1860, AGO, Letters Received, NA, RG 94.

    23. Twiggs to Colonel L. Cooper, Adjutant General's Office, Headquarters of the Army, November 9, 1859, in an endorsement on Brevet Major William H. French to Lieutenant J. A. Washington, AAG, Headquarters, Department of Texas, November 5, 1859, AGO, Letters Received, Department of Texas, NA, RG 94.

Chapter III
The Civil War Years

    1. W. B. Hazen, *A Narrative of Military Service*, 1; Mark M. Boatner III, *The Civil War Dictionary*, 390; Frederick Whittaker, *A Complete Life of Gen. George A. Custer*, 44.

    2. W. H. Tucker, *History of Hartford, Vermont*, 363; Hazen, *Narrative of Military Service*, 2.

    3. Hazen, *Narrative of Military Service*, 3–10.

    4. *Ibid.*, 15, 20–21.

    5. *The War of the Rebellion: A Compilation of the Official Records of the Union and Confederate Armies*, 1 series, VII, 426.

    6. Robert Underwood Johnson and Clarence C. Buel, eds., *Battles and Leaders of the Civil War*, I, 485.

    7. Hazen, *Narrative of Military Service*, 24.

    8. Johnson and Buel, eds., *Battles and Leaders*, I, 487.

    9. Hazen, *Narrative of Military Service*, 25.

    10. *Ibid.*, 26–28; Major General W. B. Hazen to Colonel R. H. Ramsey, AAG, December 29, 1865, Records of the War Department, AGO, Commission Branch, NA, RG 94. This communication is entitled "Summary of the Official Service of Major General W. B. Hazen U.S. Volunteers during the War of the Rebellion." Hereafter this source will be cited as "Summary of Hazen's War Service," AGO, Commission Branch, NA, RG 94.

    11. The Union losses were 13,000, the Confederate 10,700.

    12. Transcript of the Stanley-Hazen Trial, Records of the War De-

partment, OJAG, General Courts Martial, 1812–1938, NA, RG 153 (hereafter cited as Stanley-Hazen Trial, OJAG, NA, RG 153).

13. Brigadier General William Nelson to Major General D. C. Buell, April 10, 1862, cited in Hazen, *Narrative of Military Service*, 34–35.

14. Hazen, *Narrative of Military Service*, 30–32, 36.

15. "Summary of Hazen's War Service," AGO, Commission Branch, NA, RG 94.

16. Benson J. Lossing, *The Pictorial Field Book of the Civil War*, II, 542–43; T. L. Livermore, *Numbers and Losses in the Civil War in America, 1861–1865*, 97; "Summary of Hazen's War Service," AGO, Commission Branch, NA, RG 94; Hazen, *Narrative of Military Service*, 72.

17. Lossing, *Pictorial Field Book of the Civil War*, II, 544.

18. Hazen, *Narrative of Military Service*, 72–73.

19. Lossing, *Pictorial Field Book of the Civil War*, II, 546–47; John Fiske, *The Mississippi Valley in the Civil War*, 172.

20. Comte de Paris, *History of the Civil War in America*, II, 525; Lossing, *Pictorial Field Book of the Civil War*, II, 547.

21. Livermore, *Numbers and Losses in the Civil War in America, 1861–1865*, 97.

22. John Fitch, *Annals of the Army of the Cumberland*, 223.

23. Lossing, *Pictorial Field Book of the Civil War*, II, 546.

24. Hazen, *Narrative of Military Service*, 98.

25. *Ibid.*, 103.

26. *Ibid.*, 118; Johnson and Buel, eds., *Battles and Leaders*, III, 644.

27. Lossing, *Pictorial Field Book of the Civil War*, II, 135–36.

28. "Summary of Hazen's War Service," AGO, Commission Branch, NA, RG 94; Hazen, *Narrative of Military Service*, 132.

29. *Ibid.*, 120–21, 147.

30. Livermore, *Numbers and Losses in the Civil War in America, 1861–1865*, 105–106; Francis B. Heitman, ed., *Historical Register and Dictionary of the United States Army from 1789 to 1903*, I, 517.

31. Hazen, *Narrative of Military Service*, 152–53.

32. Jacob D. Cox, *Military Reminiscences of the Civil War*, II, 17; Report of Brigadier General W. F. Smith to Major General George H. Thomas, November 4, 1863, cited in Hazen, *Narrative of Military Service*, 161–62.

33. Cox, *Military Reminiscences of the Civil War*, II, 18–19.

34. Cited in Hazen, *Narrative of Military Service*, 159–60.

35. *Ibid.*, 168–70.

36. "Summary of Hazen's War Service," AGO, Commission Branch, NA, RG 94.

37. Hazen, *Narrative of Military Service*, 176, 178.

38. This extract from Sheridan's report is cited in Hazen, *Narrative of Military Service*, 235.

39. Hazen, *Narrative of Military Service*, 180–235. See also Cox, *Military Reminiscences of the Civil War*, II, 114.

40. Hazen, *Narrative of Military Service*, 179.

41. Sheridan, *Personal Memoirs*, I, 320.

42. Richard O'Conner, *Sheridan the Inevitable*, 140.

43. Hazen, *Narrative of Military Service*, 239–40; Cox places the responsibility for the arrest on Sheridan. See Cox, *Military Reminiscences of the Civil War*, II, 114.

44. "Summary of Hazen's War Service," AGO, Commission Branch, NA, RG 94.

45. *Ibid.*; an interview with Hazen reported in the *New York Tribune*, May 10, 1879.

46. Hazen, *Narrative of Military Service*, 299–300.

47. "Summary of Hazen's War Service," AGO, Commission Branch, NA, RG 94; Hazen, *Narrative of Military Service*, 297, 290.

48. Hazen, *Narrative of Military Service*, 298–99.

49. *Ibid.*, 326; "Summary of Hazen's War Service," AGO, Commission Branch, NA, RG 94; William Tecumseh Sherman, *Memoirs, Written by Himself*, II, 171–72.

50. Hazen, *Narrative of Military Service*, 319–20.

51. Report of William T. Sherman in George Ward Nichols, *The Story of the Great March from the Diary of a Staff Officer*, 329–31; John A. Carpenter, *Sword and Olive Branch*, 75–76; an interview with Hazen reported in the *New York Tribune*, May 10, 1879.

52. "Summary of Hazen's War Service," AGO, Commission Branch, NA, RG 94; an interview with Hazen reported in the *New York Tribune*, May 10, 1879.

53. Nichols, *Story of the Great March*, 89–91.

54. Report of Sherman in *ibid.*, 92; Hazen, *Narrative of Military Service*, 333.

55. Nichols, *Story of the Great March*, 92.

56. *Ibid.*

57. Hazen, *Narrative of Military Service*, 336–37.

58. *Ibid.*, 337.

59. Sherman, *Memoirs*, II, 287.

60. Hazen, *Narrative of Military Service*, 353.

61. "Summary of Hazen's War Service," AGO, Commission Branch, NA, RG 94; Carpenter, *Sword and Olive Branch*, 80–81.

62. Hazen, *Narrative of Military Service*, 360–61.

63. *Ibid.*, 375, 379; "Summary of Hazen's War Service," AGO, Commission Branch, NA, RG 94.

64. Cited in *Washington Post*, March 16, 1885.

65. *Ibid.*

66. *New York Tribune*, May 10, 1879.

67. Hazen, *Narrative of Military Service*, 353.

68. Cox, *Military Reminiscences of the Civil War*, II, 114.

Chapter IV
Inspector-General, Department of the Platte

1. General P. Cooke, commanding, Department of the Platte, to Adjutant General, U. S. Army, April 1, 1866, Records of the War Department, AGO, Letters Received, Department of the Platte, NA, RG 94. Hereafter this series of records will be cited as AGO, Letters Received, Department of the Platte, NA, RG 94; W. B. Hazen to Assistant Secretary of War, June 7, 1866, Records of the War Department, AGO, Commission Branch, NA, RG 94.

2. Dee Brown, *Fort Phil Kearny*, 18–22; Francis Paul Prucha, *A Guide to the Military Posts of the United States, 1789–1895*, 152. The department was modified on August 11, 1866, by the creation of the Department of Dakota.

3. George E. Hyde, *Red Cloud's Folk: A History of the Oglala Sioux Indians*, 117–18; James C. Olson, "The 'Lasting Peace' of Fort Laramie," *The American West* (Winter, 1965), 52.

4. Prucha, *Guide to Military Posts*, 24–25; 50 Cong., 1 sess., *Sen. Exec. Doc. No. 33*, 51.

5. Hazen to Brevet Major H. G. Litchfield, AAAG, Department of the Platte, October 16, 1866, 39 Cong., 2 sess., *House Exec. Doc. No. 45*, 6; Robert A. Murray, "The Hazen Inspections of 1866," *Montana the Magazine of Western History*, XVIII (January, 1968), 25–26.

6. Robert G. Athearn, *Sherman and the Settlement of the West*, 67–68.

7. Hazen to the Adjutant General, August 10, 1866, AGO, Letters Received, Department of the Platte, NA, RG 94; Brown, *Fort Phil Kearny*, 63, 95.

8. Brown, *Fort Phil Kearny*, 103; Hazen to Litchfield, October 16, 1866, 39 Cong., 2 sess., *House Exec. Doc. No. 45*, 6. Two companies of the Second Cavalry were ordered to report to Colonel Carrington in August to assist in the protection of the Bozeman Trail, 40 Cong., 1 sess., *Sen. Exec. Doc. No. 13*, 36.

9. Hazen to Litchfield, October 16, 1866, 39 Cong., 2 sess., *House Exec. Doc. No. 45*, 6.

10. 50 Cong., 1 sess., *Sen. Exec. Doc. No. 33*, 17–18.

11. Brown, *Fort Phil Kearny*, 105; Grace R. Hebard and E. A. Brininstool, *The Bozeman Trail*, I, 286.

12. Brown, *Fort Phil Kearny*, 97, 105, 148; 50 Cong., 1 sess., *Sen. Exec. Doc. No. 33*, 23; Hazen to Litchfield, October 16, 1866, 39 Cong., 2 sess., *House Exec. Doc. No. 45*, 6.

13. Hazen to Litchfield, October 16, 1866, 39 Cong., 2 sess., *House Exec. Doc. 45*, 2–3.

14. *Ibid.*, 3–4.

15. *Ibid.*, 5.

16. *Ibid.*, Robert M. Utley, "A Chained Dog: The Indian-Fighting Army," *American West*, Vol. X (July, 1973), 19–21.

17. Hazen to Litchfield, October 16, 1866, 39 Cong., 2 sess., *House Exec. Doc. No. 45*, 5–6.

18. 40 Cong., 1 sess., *Sen. Exec. Doc. No. 13*, 7; James C. Olson, *Red Cloud and the Sioux Problem*, 58–76.

19. Hazen to Adjutant General, U.S. Army, October 20, 1866, AGO, Letters Received, Department of the Platte, NA, RG 94.

Chapter V
Sherman's Agent on the Washita

1. Ray Allen Billington, *Westward Expansion*, 654–55.

2. For a detailed discussion of the Chivington atrocity see Stan Hoig, *The Sand Creek Massacre*.

3. Charles J. Kappler, *Indian Affairs, Laws and Treaties*, II, 887, 893.

4. George E. Hyde, *Red Cloud's Folk*, 137.

5. Commissioner of Indian Affairs, *Report for 1867*, 2.

6. *Ibid.*, 4; *United States Statutes at Large*, XV, 17. Although couched in more moderate language, this was the same policy Hazen had advocated in his inspection report of 1866.

7. William Tecumseh Sherman, *Memoirs, Written by Himself*, II, 435.

8. Kappler, *Indian Affairs, Laws and Treaties*, II, 977–78, 983–89; Donald J. Berthrong, *The Southern Cheyennes*, 298.

9. George W. Manypenny, *Our Indian Wards*, 204.

10. *United States Statutes at Large*, XV, 222.

11. O. H. Browning to W. T. Sherman, August 6, 1868, in Commissioner of Indian Affairs, *Report for 1868*, 82–83.

12. General Order No. 4, August 10, 1868, Headquarters, Division of the Missouri, in *ibid.*, 85.

13. Sherman to Browning, August 11, 1868, in *ibid.*, 85–86.

14. Thomas Murphy to Charles E. Mix, September 19, 1868, in *ibid.*, 75; Sherman to J. M. Schofield, September 17, 1868, in *ibid.*, 77.

15. *Annual Report of the Secretary of War for the Year 1868*, 4; P. H. Sheridan to W. B. Hazen, September 19, 1868, in W. B. Hazen, "Some Corrections of 'Life on the Plains' " (privately published pamphlet, 1875), reprinted in *Chronicles of Oklahoma*, Vol. III (December, 1925), 300; Hazen to Sherman, June 30, 1869, in Commissioner of Indian Affairs, *Report for 1868*, 388.

16. Hazen, "Some Corrections of 'Life on the Plains,' " *Chronicles of Oklahoma*, Vol. III (December, 1925), 300–301; Hazen to Sherman, November 10, 1868, The Sherman-Sheridan Papers, University of Oklahoma typescript (hereafter cited as S-S Papers); Sheridan to Sherman, October 15, 1868, the Papers of Philip H. Sheridan, Division of Manuscripts, Library of Congress, Washington, D.C. (hereafter cited as the Sheridan Papers).

17. Hazen to Sherman, November 10, 1868, S-S Papers; Commissioner of Indian Affairs, *Report for 1868*, 258; Hazen to Sherman, June 30, 1869, in *Report for 1869*, 388; Captain Henry E. Alvord to Hazen, October 30, 1868, S-S Papers.

18. Commissioner of Indian Affairs, *Report for 1868*, 258; Edward W. Wynkoop to Peter Cooper and others, December 23, 1868, Sheridan Papers; *New York Tribune*, December 24, 1868.

19. Alvord to Major James R. Roy, October 30 and November 5, 1868, S-S Papers.

20. Captain J. B. Rife to S. T. Walkley, September 24, 1868, Letters Received by the Office of Indian Affairs, 1824–81, MSS, Central Superintendency, Kiowa Agency, Microcopy 234, Roll No. 375, NA, RG 75, University of Oklahoma Division of Manuscripts, Bizzell Library (hereafter cited as Letters Received, Central Superintendency, Kiowa or Wichita Agencies, NA, RG 75, with the proper microcopy and roll numbers); Henry Shanklin to Hazen, October 11, 1868, S-S Papers; Alvord to Roy,

November 5, 1868, S-S Papers; Charles J. Brill, *Conquest of the Southern Plains*, 131; Hazen to Sherman, November 7, 1868, S-S Papers.

21. Hazen to Sherman, November 7, 1868, S-S Papers.

22. *Ibid.*, November 10 and November 22; Hazen, "Some Corrections of 'Life on the Plains,'" *Chronicles of Oklahoma*, Vol. III (December, 1925), 302–303.

23. Sheridan to Brevet Major General W. A. Nichols, AAG, December 24, 1868, Sheridan Papers.

24. Hazen to Sherman, November 22, 1868, S-S Papers.

25. Sherman to Hazen, October 13, 1868, in Hazen, "Some Corrections of 'Life on the Plains,'" *Chronicles of Oklahoma*, Vol. III (December, 1925), 303.

26. Hazen to Sherman, November 22, 1868, S-S Papers.

27. Berthrong, *The Southern Cheyennes*, 231–32.

28. Hazen to Sherman, December 31, 1868, Sheridan Papers.

29. Hazen to James A. Garfield, January 17, 1869, the papers of James A. Garfield, Division of Manuscripts, Library of Congress, Washington, D.C. (hereafter cited as Garfield Papers).

30. Hazen to Sherman, June 30, 1869, in Commissioner of Indian Affairs, *Report for 1869*, 389, 398; Henry Shanklin to Commissioner of Indian Affairs, January 9, 1869, Letters Received, Central Superintendency, Wichita Agency, NA, RG 75, Microcopy 234, Roll No. 929.

31. Hazen to Sherman, November 10, 1869, S-S Papers.

32. *Ibid.* An investigation later revealed that Walkley had participated in a scheme whereby he encouraged the Caddoes to steal Texas cattle which he then purchased for five cents per pound. The agent sold the cattle to the government for nine cents a pound to be used for Indian rations. A. G. Boone to N. G. Taylor, Commissioner of Indian Affairs, January 26, 1869, Letters Received, Central Superintendency, Kiowa Agency, NA, RG 75, Microcopy 234, Roll No. 376.

33. Hazen to Sherman, June 30, 1869, in Commissioner of Indian Affairs, *Report for 1869*, 389–90, 393–94.

34. Hazen to Sherman, November 22, 1868, S-S Papers.

35. Sherman to General E. D. Townsend, January 4, 1869, Division of the Missouri, Letters Sent, 1868–71, Records of the War Department, U.S. Army Commands, NA, RG 98.

36. Hazen to Roy, November 26, 1868, S-S Papers.

37. *Ibid.*; Hazen to Sherman, June 30, 1868, in Commissioner of Indian Affairs, *Report for 1869*, 390, 395.

38. Hazen to Sherman, December 14, 1868, S-S Papers.

39. Hazen to the officer commanding troops in the field, December 16, 1868, Sheridan Papers.

40. George H. Shirk, "Campaigning With Sheridan: A Farrier's Diary," *Chronicles of Oklahoma*, Vol. XXXVII (Spring, 1959), 90. Cloud Chief is located about nine miles east of Cordell, Oklahoma.

41. Report of Operations of the Command of Brevet Major General George A. Custer, from December 7 to December 22, 1868, Sheridan Papers; George A. Custer, *Wild Life on the Plains and Horrors of Indian Warfare*, 257; Sheridan to Sherman, December 19, 1868, in Manypenny, *Our Indian Wards*, 235; Sheridan, *Personal Memoirs*, II, 334; Hazen, "Some Corrections of 'My Life on the Plains,' " *Chronicles of Oklahoma*, Vol. III (December, 1925), 297–98, 316–18.

42. Quoted in W. S. Nye, *Carbine and Lance*, 72.

43. Sheridan to Nichols, December 24, 1868, Sheridan Papers; Hazen, "Some Corrections of 'My Life on the Plains,' " *Chronicles of Oklahoma*, Vol. III (December, 1925), 310; Berthrong, *The Southern Cheyennes*, 338–39; William H. Leckie, *The Military Conquest of the Southern Plains*, 114–26.

44. DeBenneville R. Keim, *Sheridan's Troopers on the Borders: A Winter Campaign on the Plains*, 231, 255–56; Nye, *Carbine and Lance*, 75, 78, 84–86, 102; Sheridan to Sherman, January 8, 1869, Sheridan Papers; Hazen to Sherman, June 30, 1869, in Commissioner of Indian Affairs, *Report for 1869*, 392; W. Eugene Hollon, *Beyond the Cross Timbers*, 147.

45. Boone to Commissioner of Indian Affairs, December 13, 1868, Letters Received, Central Superintendency, Kiowa Agency, NA, RG 75, Microcopy 234, Roll No. 375; Hazen to Sherman, June 30, 1869, in Commissioner of Indian Affairs, *Report for 1869*, 382–83.

46. *Ibid.*, 384–85; Hazen to Sherman, November 7, 1868, S-S Papers; Hazen to Interpreter Philip McCusker, January 20, 1869, Letters Received, Central Superintendency, Wichita Agency, NA, RG 75, Microcopy 234, Roll No. 929; Wichita Files—Farmers, Oklahoma Historical Society, Indian Archives, Oklahoma City, Oklahoma.

47. International Council File, May, 1875, Oklahoma Historical Society, Indian Archives, Oklahoma City, Oklahoma.

48. Hazen to Sherman, November 10, 1868, S-S Papers.

49. Hazen to Sheridan, December 24, 1868, enclosure in Sheridan to Nichols, December 27, 1868, Sheridan Papers.

50. B. H. Grierson to the Assistant Adjutant General, Department of the Missouri, April 7, 1869, Sheridan Papers.

51. Hazen to Sherman, June 30, 1869, in Commissioner of Indian Affairs, *Report for 1869*, 393.

52. *Ibid.*, 394.

53. *Ibid.*, 396.

Chapter VI
Superintendent of Indian Affairs

1. Special Order No. 157, June 30, 1869, Headquarters of the Army, Washington, D.C., Letters Sent by the Office of Indian Affairs, 1824–81, MSS, Finance and Miscellaneous, NA, RG 75, Microcopy 21, Roll No. 93, University of Oklahoma Division of Manuscripts, Bizzell Library. Hereafter this series of records will be cited as Letters Sent, NA, RG 75, with the proper microcopy and roll numbers.

2. E. S. Parker to William B. Hazen, July 21, 1869, Letters Sent, NA, RG 75, Microcopy 21, Roll No. 91.

3. 55 Cong., 1 sess., *Sen. Doc. No. 68*, 4; 76 Cong., 1 sess., *Sen. Report No. 110*, 3.

4. 76 Cong., 1 sess., *Sen. Report No. 110*, 3; 55 Cong., 1 sess., *Sen. Doc. No. 68*, 4.

5. 55 Cong., 1 sess., *Sen. Doc. No. 67*, 2.

6. Parker to Hazen, January 10, 1870, Letters Sent, NA, RG 75, Microcopy 21, Roll No. 93.

7. Parker to Hazen and Parker to A. F. Field, July 21, 1869, *ibid.*, Roll No. 93.

8. Field to Parker, September 12, 1869, Field to Parker, November 18, 1869, Hazen to Parker, October 11, 1869, and Hazen to Parker, January 19, 1870. Letters Received by the Office of Indian Affairs, 1824–81, MSS Creek Agency, NA, RG 75, Microcopy 234, Roll No. 232, University of Oklahoma Division of Manuscripts, Bizzell Library. Hereafter this series of records will be cited as Letters Received, Creek Agency, NA, RG 75, with the proper microcopy and roll numbers.

9. Hazen to Parker, February 14, 1870, *ibid.*; memorandum of prices observed in making awards on claims of Creeks, enclosure in *ibid.*

10. Parker to J. D. Cox, March 16, 1870, 41 Cong., 2 sess., *House Exec. Doc. No. 217*, 2; as late as 1937 government officials relied upon statements showing awards were $1,836,830.41. J. George Wright, an inspector in the Department of the Interior, in 1905 discovered an error had apparently been made in footing the total. He reported the error to the Department's secretary on April 5, 1905, listing the correct total as given

above. For some unexplained reason the inaccurate figure continued to be cited. George Wright to the Secretary of the Interior, April 5, 1905, Department of the Interior, Office of Indian Affairs, File No. 83595-1903, Creek-Special Series A, Box 4, NA, RG 75.

11. Hazen to Parker, February 14, 1870, Letters Received, Creek Agency, NA, RG 75, Microcopy 234, Roll No. 232.

12. *Ibid.*, April 30, 1870.

13. Parker to Cox, March 16, 1870, 41 Cong., 2 sess., *House Exec. Doc. No. 217*, 1–2.

14. Cox to the commissioner of Indian affairs, September 5, 1870, Letters Received, Creek Agency, NA, RG 75, Microcopy 234, Roll No. 232.

15. J. A. Williamson to Parker, October 11, 1870, *ibid.*; memorials of S. W. Peel and Isparhecker, former chief Muskogee (Creek) Nation, presenting the claims of the Loyal Creeks, 57 Cong., 1 sess., *Sen. Doc. No. 420, 5.*

16. F. S. Lyon to the commissioner of Indian affairs, October 20, 1871, Commissioner of Indian Affairs, *Report for 1871*, 576.

17. Petition of the delegates of the Creek Nation, 45 Cong., 2 sess., *House Misc. Doc. No. 38*, 1–5; Thomas Connor et al. v. the United States, 19 U.S. Court of Claims, 675–81; 55 Cong., 1 sess., *Sen. Doc. No. 67, 4.*

18. 76 Cong., 1 sess., *Sen. Report No. 110*, 1–8.

19. Cox to President U. S. Grant, May 21, 1870, Letters Received, Southern Superintendency, NA, RG 75, Microcopy 234, Roll No. 839.

20. Parker to Levi Parsons, president of Union Pacific Railway Southern Branch, May 13, 1870, Parker to Hazen, May 13, 1870, Letters Sent, Land and Civilization, NA, RG 75, Microcopy 21, Roll No. 96.

21. Cox to Grant, May 21, 1870, and endorsement by U. S. Grant, May 23, 1870, Letters Received, Southern Superintendency, NA, RG 75, Microcopy 234, Roll No. 839.

22. Enoch Hoag and Hazen to Parker, June 13, 1870, Letters Received, Southern Superintendency, NA, RG 75, Microcopy 234, Roll No. 839.

23. Parker to Commissioners Hoag and Hazen, June 11, 1870, Letters Sent, Finance and Miscellaneous, NA, RG 75, Microcopy 21, Roll No. 96.

24. Hoag and Hazen to Parker, June 13, 1870, Letters Received, Southern Superintendency, NA, RG 75, Microcopy 234, Roll No. 839.

25. *Ibid.*

26. Cox to the commissioner of Indian affairs, July 2, 1870, *ibid.*

27. Cox to Grant, July 12, 1870, *ibid.*

28. Endorsement by U. S. Grant, July 20, 1870, in *ibid.*

29. Ira G. Clark, *Then Came the Railroads*, 62.

30. W. F. Cady, acting commissioner of Indian affairs, to Hazen, February 14, 1870, Letters Sent, Land and Civilization, NA, RG 75, Microcopy 21, Roll No. 94; Parker to Hazen, February 26, 1870, *ibid.*

31. Berlin B. Chapman, "Establishment of the Wichita Reservation," *Chronicles of Oklahoma*, Vol. XI (December, 1933), 1052–53; Muriel Wright, *A Guide to the Indian Tribes of Oklahoma*, 260.

32. Cady to Hazen, August 9, 1870, Letters Sent, NA, RG 75, Microcopy 21, Roll No. 96; Cox to Hazen, August 8, 1870, Letters Received, Southern Superintendency, NA, RG 75, Microcopy 234, Roll No. 839.

33. President of the United States (by Horace Porter) to E. D. Townsend (no date), Records of the War Department, AGO, Letters Received, NA, RG 94.

34. Parker to Hazen, January 10, 1870, Letters Sent, Finance and Miscellaneous, NA, RG 75, Microcopy 21, Roll No. 93; Hazen to editor of *The Nation*, December 10, 1873, *The Nation*, Vol. XVIII (January 15, 1874), 40.

Chapter VII
Casting Stones at the Establishment

1. Regular Army Organization Returns, Sixth Regiment U.S. Infantry, January, 1871, Records of the War Department, AGO, NA, RG 94.

2. Grant Foreman, *Fort Gibson*, 43.

3. Regular Army Organization Returns, Sixth Regiment U.S. Infantry, September, 1871, AGO, NA, RG 94; Foreman, *Fort Gibson*, 37.

4. W. B. Hazen to James Garfield, July 23, 1871, Garfield Papers.

5. Garfield to Hazen, October 28, 1870.

6. Hazen to Garfield, July 23, 1871.

7. *Ibid.*

8. *Ibid.*, January 18, 1872.

9. *Ibid.*, February 4, 1872.

10. Copy of letter of R. H. Pratt to Hazen, November 25, 1871, enclosure in *ibid*. This letter was actually written sometime after November 25.

11. Garfield to Hazen, February 13, 1872, Garfield Papers.

12. *Ibid.*, February 16, 1872.

13. Transcript of the Stanley-Hazen Trial, OJAG, NA, RG 153.

14. *New York Tribune*, February 16, 1872.

15. Hazen to Hiester Clymer, March 15, 1876, *New York Tribune*, March 30, 1876.

16. Hazen to Garfield, February 23, 1872, Garfield Papers.

17. Copy of a letter of R. H. Pratt to Hazen, November 25, 1871, enclosure in *ibid*.

18. Hazen to Garfield, February 23, 1872, Garfield Papers.

19. *Ibid.*, March 2, 1872.

20. *Ibid.*, August 2, 1877; Stanley-Hazen Trial, OJAG, NA, RG 153.

21. 42 Cong., 3 sess., *House Report No. 74*, 177–80.

22. Garfield to John Coburn, April 8, 1876, Garfield Papers; Stanley-Hazen Trial, OJAG, NA, RG 153.

23. Copy of circular issued by the Department of War, March 25, 1872, Garfield Papers; *New York Tribune*, March 27, 1872.

24. Stanley-Hazen Trial, OJAG, NA, RG 153; Hazen to Hiester Clymer, March 15, 1876, *New York Tribune*, March 30, 1876.

25. Regular Army Organization Returns, Sixth Regiment U.S. Infantry, April, 1872, AGO, NA, RG 94; *New York Times*, March 4, 1876; Hazen to Garfield, May 5, 1872, Garfield Papers.

26. *Ibid.*; copy of a certificate on health of William B. Hazen, May 8, 1872, AGO, NA, RG 94.

27. Regular Army Organization Returns, Sixth Regiment U.S. Infantry, June, 1872, AGO, NA, RG 94.

28. Hazen to the Assistant Adjutant General, Department of Dakota, July 5, 1872, AGO, Letters Received, Department of Dakota, NA, RG 94.

29. Endorsement of Lieutenant General Sheridan, July 26, 1872, on Hazen to the Assistant Adjutant General, Department of Dakota, July 5, 1872, AGO, Letters Received, Department of Dakota, NA, RG 94.

30. *New York Tribune*, July 3, 1877.

31. Brevet Major General W. B. Hazen, *The School and the Army in Germany and France*, 222–23.

32. *Ibid.*, 227–29.

33. *Ibid.*, 230, 242–43.

34. *Ibid.*, 231–32.

35. *Ibid.*, 235.

36. *Ibid.*, 236.

37. *Ibid.*, 238, 240–41.

38. *Ibid.*, 245.

39. Garfield to Hazen, October 21, 1872, Garfield Papers.

40. *The Nation*, Vol. XVI (January 9, 1873), 29–30.

41. *Army and Navy Journal*, July 20, 1872.

42. *Ibid.*

43. Hazen to Garfield, September 24, 1880, Garfield Papers.

Chapter VIII
The Arid Lands Controversy

* Portions of this chapter appeared as "Deceit About the Garden: Hazen, Custer and the Arid Lands Controversy," *North Dakota Quarterly*, Vol. 38, No. 3 (Summer, 1970), 5–21.

1. An endorsement by P. H. Sheridan, October 31, 1873, on W. B. Hazen to Headquarters, Department of Dakota, November 23, 1872, Records of the War Department, AGO, Letters Received, Department of Dakota, NA, RG 94.

2. Regular Army Organization Returns, Sixth Regiment U.S. Infantry, Fort Buford, Dakota Territory, June, 1873, AGO, NA, RG 94.

3. Jay Cooke and Company, *The Northern Pacific Railroad; its Route, Resources, Progress and Business* (Philadelphia ?, 1871 ?), 48.

4. W. B. Hazen to James A. Garfield, May 5, 1872, Garfield Papers.

5. C. Henry Smith, *The Coming of the Russian Mennonites* (Berne, 1927), 72–83. Few Russian Mennonites settled on Northern Pacific land in present-day North Dakota, in part because the government did not grant the railroad's request for the withdrawal of public lands. However, thousands migrated to other Plains states in the 1870's. Many located in Kansas, where in 1874 they introduced a highly successful variety of hard red winter wheat that transformed Kansas into a major wheat producing state.

6. *New York Tribune*, February 7, 1874.

7. *Ibid.*

8. John Osborne Sargent, "Major General Hazen Reviewed."

9. *Ibid.*, 16–17, 24–25, 31.

10. *Minneapolis Tribune*, April 17, 1874.

11. *Ibid.*

12. *Ibid.*

13. *Ibid.*

14. *Ibid.*, April 21, 1874.

15. Cited in W. B. Hazen, *Our Barren Lands*, 13.

16. Cited in *Army and Navy Journal*, June 13, 1874.

17. Hazen to Garfield, May 20, 1874, Garfield Papers.

18. *Ibid.*

19. *Ibid.*

20. *Ibid.*

21. Garfield to Hazen, May 25, 1874, Garfield Papers.

22. Frank W. Blackmar, "The History of the Desert," *Kansas Historical Collections*, Vol. IX (1905–1906), 107–108.

23. W. B. Hazen, "The Great Middle Region of the United States, and its Limited Space of Arable Land," *North American Review*, Vol. CXX (January, 1875), 1–2.

24. *Ibid.*, 15–19.

25. *Ibid.*, 22.

26. *Ibid.*, 23; Hazen to Garfield, [June ?] 3, 1874, Garfield Papers.

27. Hazen, "The Great Middle Region of the United States, and its Limited Space of Arable Land," *North American Review*, Vol. CXX (January, 1875), 25.

28. *Ibid.*, 25–26.

29. *Ibid.*, 26.

30. *Ibid.*, 26–29, 32.

31. *Ibid.*, 29–30, 33.

32. *Ibid.*, 33–34.

33. Hazen, *Our Barren Lands*.

34. *Ibid.*, 30.

35. *Ibid.*

36. *Ibid.*, 33, 41, 49.

37. *Ibid.*, 13, 51–53.

38. *Army and Navy Journal*, May 8, 1875.

39. George A. Custer, *My Life on the Plains*, 291.

40. *Army and Navy Journal*, May 30, 1874.

41. W. B. Hazen, "Some Corrections of 'My Life on the Plains,'" *Chronicles of Oklahoma*, Vol. III (December, 1925), 393–94.

42. *Ibid.*, 384.

43. *Ibid.*, 394.

44. F. V. Hayden, *U. S. Geological and Geographical Survey of the Territories*, Vols. I–XII; John Wesley Powell, *Report on the Lands of the Arid Region of the United States*; G. M. Wheeler, *U. S. Geological Surveys West of the 100th Meridian*, Vols. I–VII.

Chapter IX
Belknap Brought to Bay

1. W. B. Hazen to Hiester Clymer, March 15, 1876, in *New York Tribune*, March 30, 1876.

2. Allan Nevins, *Hamilton Fish, the Inner History of the Grant Administration*, II, 804–805.

3. Hazen to Garfield, November 8, 1874, Garfield Papers.

4. Hazen to Clymer, March 15, 1876, in *New York Tribune*, March 30, 1876.

5. *Congressional Record*, 44 Cong., 1 sess., *Proceedings of the Senate, Trial of William W. Belknap*, 1876, iii (hereafter cited as *Trial of William Belknap*).

6. Full evidence on the facts of the Fort Sill scandal was presented throughout the Belknap trial and is found in the *Trial of William Belknap*.

7. Nevins, *Hamilton Fish*, II, 805; Harry J. Brown and Frederick D. Williams, eds., *The Diary of James A. Garfield*, Vol. III (East Lansing, 1973), 243.

8. *New York Times*, March 4, 1876.

9. Hazen to Clymer, March 15, 1876, in *New York Tribune*, March 30, 1876.

10. John Coburn to editor, *Cincinnati Commercial*, March 30, 1876, in *New York Times*, April 5, 1876.

11. *Ibid.*

12. *New York Tribune*, April 6, 1876.

13. Underlined for emphasis by the present author.

14. Garfield to Coburn, April 8, 1876, Garfield Papers.

15. Hazen, as might have been expected, refused to be "gagged" by the departmental order. For example, on January 19, 1875, he wrote Representative Garfield urging him "to support legislation favorable to the line." His letter was prefaced with the precautionary statement that it "must be strictly confidential, for it will be in violation of the Secretary of War's orders, which prohibits officers communicating with Congress upon military subjects." Hazen to Garfield, January 19, 1875, Garfield Papers.

16. 44 Cong., 1 sess., *House Report No. 799*, VIII, 163.

17. *Ibid.*, 164.

18. *Trial of William Belknap*, 230–31.

19. *Ibid.*, 229.

20. *Ibid.*, 230.

21. *Ibid.*, 231–34.

22. *Ibid.*, 234–35.

23. *Ibid.*, 243–44.

24. *Ibid.*, 245.

25. *Ibid.*

26. *New York Tribune*, July 12, 1876.

27. *Ibid.*, July 14, 1876.
28. *Trial of William Belknap*, 342–57.

Chapter X
Vindication and Farewell to the Barren Lands

1. James A. Garfield to W. B. Hazen, March 8, 1875, Garfield Papers.
2. Cited in *Army and Navy Journal*, July 14, 1877.
3. Charges and specifications preferred against W. B. Hazen, Colonel Sixth U.S. Infantry, Brevet Major General, July 6, 1877, enclosure in D. S. Stanley to the Adjutant General, Washington, D.C., July 6, 1877, AGO, NA, RG 94.
4. President Rutherford B. Hayes to the Office of the Adjutant General, August 1, 1877, endorsement on Hazen to the Secretary of War, July 31, 1877, AGO, NA, RG 94.
5. Hazen to Garfield, August 2, 1877, Garfield Papers.
6. Hazen's report on the mission is found in Hazen to Secretary of State William M. Ewarts, October 16, 1877, AGO, NA, RG 94.
7. *New York Tribune*, May 2, 1879; Hazen to Garfield, December 16, 1877, Garfield Papers; *New York Times*, March 14, 1879; David S. Stanley to William T. Sherman, March 18, 1879, AGO, NA, RG 94.
8. Sherman to the Secretary of War, March 19, 1879, in an endorsement on Stanley to Sherman, March 18, 1879, AGO, NA, RG 94; Sherman to G. W. McCrary, March 11, 1879, AGO, NA, RG 94.
9. W. M. Dunn to the Secretary of War, March 21, 1879, in an endorsement on Stanley to Sherman, March 18, 1879, AGO, NA, RG 94.
10. Hazen to Garfield, March 20, 1879, Garfield Papers.
11. *New York Tribune*, May 2, 1879.
12. General Court-Martial, Order No. 35, Headquarters of the Army, Washington, D.C., June 18, 1879, AGO, NA, RG 94.
13. *New York Tribune*, May 2, 1879.
14. Unless otherwise indicated the following discussion on the Stanley court-martial trial is based on facts found in the Transcript of the Stanley-Hazen Trial, Records of the War Department, OJAG (Army), General Courts-Martial, 1812–1938, NA, RG 153.
15. Hazen to Garfield, August 2, 1877, and April 19, 1879, Garfield Papers.
16. *New York Tribune*, May 5, 1879.

17. General Court-Martial, Order No. 35, Headquarters of the Army, Washington, D.C., June 18, 1879, AGO, NA, RG 94.

18. Cited in Hazen to the President, March 10, 1880, Copy, AGO, NA, RG 94.

19. *New York Tribune,* June 18, 1879.

20. Sherman to William A. Ramsey, February 21, 1881, AGO, NA, RG 94.

21. *Ibid.*

22. Hazen to Garfield, July 28, 1880, Garfield Papers.

23. *Ibid.,* November 5, 1880.

24. *Ibid.,* September 24, 1880; *ibid.,* October 28, 1880.

25. *Ibid.,* November 3, 1880.

26. *Ibid.,* November 5, 1880.

27. *New York Tribune,* December 17, 1880.

28. Hazen to Garfield, December 25, 1880, Garfield Papers.

Chapter XI
Hazen in the West: An Appraisal

1. Mildred McLean Hazen to Commissioner of Pensions, February 17, 1887, Pension File, AGO, NA, RG 94.

2. See 43 Cong., 1 sess., *House Report No. 612,* 53.

3. John Wesley Powell, *Report on the Lands of the Arid Region of the United States.*

4. T. J. Mackey, *The Hazen Court-Martial,* 359.

5. *New York Tribune,* December 17, 1880.

Bibliography

I. MANUSCRIPT MATERIALS

a. *National Archives, Washington, D.C.*
Department of the Interior: Records of the Office of Indian Affairs, Record Group 75.
Creek-Special Series A, Box 4, File No. 83595–1903.
Letters Received by the Office of Indian Affairs, 1824–81, MSS, Central Superintendency, Kiowa Agency, Microcopy 234, Roll Nos. 375–76.
Letters Received by the Office of Indian Affairs, 1824–81, MSS, Central Superintendency, Wichita Agency, Microcopy 234, Roll No. 929.
Letters Received by the Office of Indian Affairs, 1824–81, MSS, Southern Superintendency, Microcopy No. 234, Roll Nos. 838–39.
Letters Received by the Office of Indian Affairs, 1824–81, MSS, Creek Agency, Microcopy No. 234, Roll No. 232.
Letters Sent by the Office of Indian Affairs, 1824–81, MSS, Microcopy 21, Roll Nos. 93–94, 96.
Records of the Oregon Superintendency of Indian Affairs, 1848–73, MSS, Letters Received, Microcopy 2, Roll No. 14.
Records of the Oregon Superintendency of Indian Affairs, 1848–73, MSS, Letters Sent, Microcopy 2, Roll No. 6.
Records of the War Department.
Adjutant General's Office, Record Group 94.
 Letterbook, Department of the Pacific.
 Letterbook, Headquarters, Northern District, Department of the Pacific.
 Letters Received by the Adjutant General's Office.

Military Academy Merit Rolls, 1855.
Outline Index, Military Forts and Stations, Reservation Division.
Post Returns.
> Fort Buford, Dakota Territory, 1872–80.
> Fort Lane, Oregon Territory, 1855–56.
> Fort Reading, California, 1855.
> Grand Ronde Coast Reservation, 1856.
> Fort Yamhill, 1856–57.

Regular Army Organization Returns.
> Eighth Regiment United States Infantry, 1856–61.
> Fourth Regiment United States Infantry, 1855–57.
> Sixth Regiment United States Infantry, 1869–80.

The Register of Cadet Applicants, 1850–1851.

Office of the Judge Advocate General (Army), Record Group 153.
> Transcript of the Stanley-Hazen Trial, General Courts-Martial, 1812–1938.

United States Army Commands, Record Group 98.
> Department of Dakota, Letters Received.
> Department of the Pacific, Letters Received.
> Division of the Missouri, Letters Sent.

b. *Library of Congress, Washington, D.C.*
James A. Garfield Papers.
Philip H. Sheridan Papers.

c. *Oklahoma Historical Society, Indian Archives, Oklahoma City, Oklahoma*
International Council File.
Wichita Files—Farmers.

d. *Division of Manuscripts, Bizzell Library, University of Oklahoma, Norman, Oklahoma*
Sherman-Sheridan Papers, Typescript.

II. DOCUMENTS OF THE UNITED STATES GOVERNMENT

a. *Congressional*
Annual Report of the Secretary of War, 1868.
Commissioner of Indian Affairs. *Annual Reports for the Years 1856–57, 1867–71.*
Congressional Record, 44 Cong., 1 sess., *Proceedings of the Senate, Trial of William W. Belknap.*

34 Cong., 1 sess., *House Exec. Doc. No. 93.*
35 Cong., 1 sess., *House Exec. Doc. No. 2.*
35 Cong., 2 sess., *House Exec. Doc. No. 2.*
35 Cong., 2 sess., *House Exec. Doc. No. 47.*
35 Cong., 2 sess., *House Exec. Doc. No. 93.*
39 Cong., 2 sess., *House Exec. Doc. No. 45.*
41 Cong., 2 sess., *House Exec. Doc. No. 217.*
42 Cong., 3 sess., *House Report No. 74.*
43 Cong., 1 sess., *House Report No. 612.*
44 Cong., 1 sess., *House Report No. 799,* VIII.
45 Cong., 2 sess., *House Misc. Doc. No. 38.*
33 Cong., 1 sess., *Senate Exec. Doc. No. 1,* II.
34 Cong., 3 sess., *Senate Exec. Doc. No. 5.*
35 Cong., 2 sess., *Senate Exec. Doc. No. 1,* II.
40 Cong., 1 sess., *Senate Exec. Doc. No. 13.*
50 Cong., 1 sess., *Senate Exec. Doc. No. 33.*
55 Cong., 1 sess., *Senate Doc. No. 67.*
55 Cong., 1 sess., *Senate Doc. No. 68.*
57 Cong., 1 sess., *Senate Doc. No. 420.*
57 Cong., 2 sess., *Senate Doc. No. 3088.*
76 Cong., 1 sess., *Senate Report No. 110.*

b. *General Government Documents*

Hayden, F. V. *U. S. Geological and Geographical Survey of the Territories.* 12 vols. Washington, Government Printing Office, 1867–83.

Heitman, Francis B. *Historical Register and Dictionary of the United States Army from 1789 to 1903.* 2 vols. Washington, Government Printing Office, 1903.

Kappler, Charles J. *Indian Affairs, Laws and Treaties.* 4 vols. Washington, Government Printing Office, 1903–27.

Powell, John Wesley. *Report on the Lands of the Arid Region of the United States.* Washington, Government Printing Office, 1878.

Royce, C. C., comp. "Indian Land Cessions in the United States." Bureau of American Ethnology, *Eighteenth Annual Report,* II. Washington, Government Printing Office, 1899.

United States Court of Claims. Vol. XIX (1884).

United States Statutes at Large. Vol. XV.

United States War Department. *The War of the Rebellion: A Compilation of the Official Records of the Union and Confederate Armies,*

4 series. 128 vols. Washington, Government Printing Office, 1880–1901.

Wheeler, G. M. *U. S. Geological Surveys West of the 100th Meridian.* 7 vols. Washington, Government Printing Office, 1875–89.

III. NEWSPAPERS AND MAGAZINES

Army and Navy Journal.
Cincinnati Enquirer.
Dallas Herald (Texas).
Minneapolis Tribune.
New York Times.
New York Tribune.
The Nation.
Washington Post.

IV. PUBLISHED PRIMARY SOURCES

a. *Articles and Pamphlets*

George, M. C. "Address Delivered at Dedication of Grand Ronde Military Block House at Dayton City Park, Oregon, August 23, 1912," *Oregon Historical Quarterly,* Vol. XV (March, 1914).

Hazen, W. B. *Our Barren Lands. The Interior of the United States West of the 100th Meridian, and East of the Sierra Nevadas.* Cincinnati, Robert Clarke and Company, 1875.

———. "Some Corrections of 'Life on the Plains,' " *Chronicles of Oklahoma,* Vol. III (December, 1925).

———. "The Great Middle Region of the United States, and its Limited Space of Arable Land," *North American Review,* Vol. CXX (January, 1875).

Lockley, Fred, ed. "Reminiscences of Mrs. Frank Collins, Nee Martha Gilliam," *Oregon Historical Quarterly,* Vol. XVII (1916).

Sargent, John Osborne. *Major General Hazen Reviewed.* New York, G. P. Putnam's Sons, 1874.

b. *Books*

Brown, Harry J., and Frederick D. Williams, eds. *The Diary of James A. Garfield.* 3 vols. East Lansing, Michigan State University Press, 1967–73.

Cox, Jacob D. *Military Reminiscences of the Civil War.* 2 vols. New York, C. Scribner's Sons, 1900.

Crook, General George. *His Autobiography.* Ed. by Martin F. Schmitt. Norman, University of Oklahoma Press, 1946.

Custer, George A. *Wild Life on the Plains and Horrors of Indian Warfare.* St. Louis, Royal, 1911.

Frazer, Robert W., ed. *Mansfield on the Conditions of the Western Forts 1853–54.* Norman, University of Oklahoma Press, 1963.

Gammel, H. R. N., comp. *The Laws of Texas: 1822–1897.* 10 vols. Austin, Gammel Book Co., 1898.

Glisan, Rodney. *Journal of Army Life.* San Francisco, A. L. Bancroft, 1874.

Hazen, W. B. *A Narrative of Military Service.* Boston, Ticknor and Sons, 1885.

Johnson, Robert Underwood, and Clarence C. Buel, eds. *Battles and Leaders of the Civil War.* 4 vols. New York, Century, 1887–88.

Keim, DeBenneville R. *Sheridan's Troopers on the Borders: A Winter Campaign on the Plains.* Philadelphia, D. McKay, 1885.

Mackey, T. J. *The Hazen Court-Martial.* New York, D. Van Nostrand, 1885.

Marcy, R. B. *Thirty Years of Army Life on the Border.* New York, Harper and Brothers, 1866.

Nichols, George Ward. *The Story of the Great March from the Diary of a Staff Officer.* New York, Harper and Brothers, 1865.

Sheridan, Philip H. *Personal Memoirs of P. H. Sheridan, General, United States Army.* 2 vols. New York, C. L. Webster, 1888.

Sherman, William T. *Memoirs, Written by Himself.* 2 vols. New York, C. L. Webster, 1890.

The Northern Pacific Railroad; its Route, Resources, Progress and Business. Issued by Jay Cooke and Company, [Philadelphia ?, 1871 ?].

Winfrey, Dorman H., ed. *Texas Indian Papers, 1846–1859.* 3 vols. Austin, Texas State Library, 1960.

V. SECONDARY SOURCES

a. *Articles*

Blackmar, Frank W. "The History of the Desert," Kansas State Historical Society, *Collections*, Vol. IX (1905–1906).

Chapman, Berlin B. "Establishment of the Wichita Reservation," *Chronicles of Oklahoma*, Vol. XI (December, 1933).

Clark, Robert Carlton. "Military History of Oregon, 1849–1859," *Oregon Historical Quarterly*, Vol. XXXVI (March, 1935).

Coan, C. F. "The Adoption of the Reservation Policy in Pacific Northwest, 1853–1855," *Oregon Historical Quarterly*, Vol. XXIII (March, 1922).

Colwig, William M. "Indian Wars of Southern Oregon," *Oregon Historical Quarterly*, Vol. IV (1903).

Crimmins, Colonel M. L. "Colonel Robert E. Lee's Report on Indian Combats in Texas," *Southwestern Historical Quarterly*, Vol. XXXIX (July, 1935).

———. "Eighth U. S. Infantry in Texas Before Civil War," *Frontier Times*, Vol. X (January, 1933).

———. "The First Line of Army Posts Established in West Texas in 1849," *West Texas Historical Association Year Book*, Vol. XIX (1943).

Foreman, Carolyn T. "General William Babcock Hazen," *Chronicles of Oklahoma*, Vol. XX (December, 1942).

Holden, W. C. "Frontier Defense, 1846–1860," *West Texas Historical Association Year Book*, Vol. VI (June, 1930).

Hoop, Oscar Winslow. "History of Fort Hoskins, 1856–1865," *Oregon Historical Quarterly*, Vol. XXX (March, 1929).

Innis, Ben H., Jr. " 'I Have the Honor . . .,' Some Letters of General W. B. Hazen from Fort Buford," *North Dakota History*, Vol. 41 (Winter, 1974).

Koch, Lena Clara. "The Federal Indian Policy in Texas, 1845–1846," *Southwestern Historical Quarterly*, Vol. XXVIII (April, 1925).

Murray, Robert A. "The Hazen Inspections of 1866," *Montana: The Magazine of Western History*, Vol. XVIII (January, 1968).

Olson, James C. "The 'Lasting Peace' of Fort Laramie," *The American West*, Vol. II (Winter, 1965).

Reeve, Frank D. "The Apache Indians in Texas," *Southwestern Historical Quarterly*, Vol. L (October, 1946).

Sargent, Alice Applegate. "A Sketch of the Rogue River Valley and Southern Oregon History," *Oregon Historical Quarterly*, Vol. XXII (March, 1921).

Secrist, Philip L. "Scenes of Awful Carnage," *Civil War Times Illustrated*, Vol. X, No. 3 (June, 1971).

Shirk, George H. "Campaigning with Sheridan: A Farrier's Diary," *Chronicles of Oklahoma*, Vol. XXXVII (Spring, 1959).

Tucker, Glen. "The Battles for Chattanooga!" *Civil War Times Illustrated*, Vol. X, No. 5 (August, 1971).

Utley, Robert M. "A Chained Dog: The Indian-Fighting Army," *American West*, Vol. X (July, 1973).

b. *Books*

Athearn, Robert G. *Sherman and the Settlement of the West.* Norman, University of Oklahoma Press, 1956.

Bancroft, Hubert Howe. *History of Oregon.* 2 vols. San Francisco, History Company, 1882–83.

Beckham, Stephen Dow. *Requiem for a People: The Rogue Indians and the Frontiersmen.* Norman, University of Oklahoma Press, 1971.

Bender, A. B. *The March of Empire.* Lawrence, University of Kansas Press, 1952.

Berthrong, Donald J. *The Southern Cheyennes.* Norman, University of Oklahoma Press, 1963.

Billington, Ray Allen. *Westward Expansion.* New York, Macmillan, 1950.

Boatner, Mark M., III. *The Civil War Dictionary.* New York, David McKay, 1959.

Brill, Charles J. *Conquest of the Southern Plains.* Oklahoma City, Golden Saga, 1938.

Brown, Dee. *Fort Phil Kearny.* New York, G. P. Putnam's Sons, 1962.

Carpenter, John A. *Sword and Olive Branch.* Pittsburgh, University of Pittsburgh Press, 1962.

Clark, Ira G. *Then Came the Railroads.* Norman, University of Oklahoma Press, 1958.

Dunn, Jacob P. *Massacres of the Mountains.* New York, Harper, 1886.

Fatout, Paul. *Ambrose Bierce: The Devil's Lexicographer.* Norman, University of Oklahoma Press, 1951.

Fiske, John. *The Mississippi Valley in the Civil War.* Boston, Houghton-Mifflin, 1901.

Fitch, John. *Annals of the Army of the Cumberland.* Philadelphia, J. B. Lippincott, 1864.

Foreman, Grant. *Fort Gibson.* Norman, University of Oklahoma Press, 1936.

Fuller, George W. *A History of the Pacific Northwest.* New York, A. A. Knopf, 1931.

Hazen, Tracy E. *The Hazen Family in America*. Ed. by Donald L. Jacobus. Thomaston, Connecticut, Robert Hazen, 1947.

Hazen, W. B. *The School and the Army in Germany and France*. New York, Harper and Brothers, 1872.

Hebard, Grace R., and E. A. Brininstool. *The Bozeman Trail*. 2 vols. Cleveland, A. H. Clark, 1922.

Hoig, Stan. *The Sand Creek Massacre*. Norman, University of Oklahoma Press, 1961.

Hollon, W. Eugene. *Beyond the Cross Timbers*. Norman, University of Oklahoma Press, 1955.

Hughes, W. J. *Rebellious Ranger Rip Ford and the Old Southwest*. Norman, University of Oklahoma Press, 1964.

Hyde, George E. *Red Cloud's Folk: A History of the Oglala Sioux Indians*. Norman, University of Oklahoma Press, 1937.

Lang, H. O. *History of the Willamette Valley*. Portland, Himes and Lang, 1885.

Leckie, William H. *The Military Conquest of the Southern Plains*. Norman, University of Oklahoma Press, 1963.

Livermore, T. L. *Numbers and Losses in the Civil War in America, 1861–1865*. New York and Boston, Houghton-Mifflin, 1901.

Lossing, Benson J. *The Pictorial Field Book of the Civil War*. 3 vols. Hartford, T. Belknap, 1874.

Manypenny, George W. *Our Indian Wards*. Cincinnati, R. Clarke, 1880.

Nevins, Allan. *Hamilton Fish, the Inner History of the Grant Administration*. 2 vols. New York, Frederick Ungar, 1957.

Nye, W. S. *Carbine and Lance*. Norman, University of Oklahoma Press, 1943.

Oberholtzer, Ellis P. *A History of the United States Since the Civil War*. 5 vols. New York, Macmillan, 1917–37.

O'Conner, Richard. *Sheridan the Inevitable*. Indianapolis, Bobbs-Merrill, 1953.

Olson, James C. *Red Cloud and the Sioux Problem*. Lincoln, University of Nebraska Press, 1965.

Paris, Comte de. *History of the Civil War in America*. 4 vols. Ed. by Henry Coppee. Philadelphia, John C. Winston, 1907.

Paxson, Frederick L. *The Last American Frontier*. New York, Macmillan, 1914.

Prucha, Francis Paul. *A Guide to the Military Posts of the United States, 1789–1895*. Madison, State Historical Society of Wisconsin, 1964.

Richardson, Rupert Norval. *The Comanche Barrier to South Plains Settlement.* Glendale, Arthur H. Clark, 1933.

Rister, Carl Coke. *The Southwestern Frontier, 1865–1881.* Cleveland, Arthur H. Clark, 1928.

Smith, C. Henry. *The Coming of the Russian Mennonites.* Berne, Indiana, Mennonite Book Concern, 1927.

Stewart, Edgar I. *Custer's Luck.* Norman, University of Oklahoma Press, 1955.

———, ed. *Penny an Acre Empire in the West.* Norman, University of Oklahoma Press, 1968.

Tucker, W. H. *History of Hartford, Vermont.* Burlington, Vermont, The Free Press Association, 1889.

Utley, Robert M. *Frontier Regulars: The United States Army and the Indian, 1866–1891.* New York, The Macmillan Company, 1973.

Victor, Frances. *The Early Indian Wars of Oregon.* Salem, Oregon, F. C. Baker, 1894.

Webb, Walter Prescott. *The Texas Rangers.* Boston, Houghton-Mifflin, 1935.

Whittaker, Frederick. *A Complete Life of Gen. George A. Custer.* New York, Sheldon and Company, 1876.

Wright, Muriel. *A Guide to the Indian Tribes of Oklahoma.* Norman, University of Oklahoma Press, 1951.

Index